Cultural Identities
in Canadian Literature

Identités culturelles
dans la littérature canadienne

Sous la direction de
Bénédicte Mauguière,
Editor

PETER LANG
New York • Washington, D.C./Baltimore • Boston
Bern • Frankfurt am Main • Berlin • Vienna • Paris

Library of Congress Cataloging-in-Publication Data

Cultural identities in Canadian literature = Identités culturelles
dans la littérature canadienne / Bénédicte Mauguière, editor.
p. cm.
Includes bibliographical references (p.).
1. Canadian literature—History and criticism. 2. French-Canadian literature—
History and criticism. 3. Pluralism (Social sciences) in literature. 4. Literature
and anthropology—Canada. 5. Multiculturalism in literature. 6. Group identity
in literature. 7. Language and culture—Canada. 8. Ethnic groups in literature.
9. Culture in literature. I. Mauguière, Bénédicte. II. Title: Identités
culturelles dans la littérature canadienne.
PR9185.2.C85 810.9'971—dc21 97-10690
ISBN 0-8204-3389-6

Die Deutsche Bibliothek-CIP-Einheitsaufnahme

Cultural identities in Canadian literature = Identités culturelles
dans la littérature Canadienne / Bénédicte Mauguière, ed.
–New York; Washington, D.C./Baltimore; Boston; Bern;
Frankfurt am Main; Berlin; Vienna; Paris: Lang.
ISBN 0-8204-3389-6

Cover design by Nona Reuter.

The paper in this book meets the guidelines for permanence and durability
of the Committee on Production Guidelines for Book Longevity
of the Council of Library Resources.

© 1998 Peter Lang Publishing, Inc., New York

Printed in the United States of America.

Acknowledgments

I would like to thank the Academic Relations office of the Canadian Embassy and Dr. David Barry, Dean of the College of Liberal Arts at the University of Southwestern Louisiana, for their support. I am also grateful to Isabel Fernandez for the preparation of the manuscript.

Table des Matières

Introduction

The essays assembled in this collection, the diverse cultural backgrounds of the contributors as well as the authors (Europe, Africa, Asia, Russia, Acadia, Québec, Haiti. . .) allow us to better understand the influence of these different cultures on Canadian literature. Accordingly, the objective of this collection is not to identify a long-sought "Canadian identity," but rather to demonstrate that many "identities" constitute present-day Canada and to blaze a trail towards unexplored regions of one's imagination.

Jars Balan focuses on the cultural development of the Ukranian community in Canada in his study of the recent emergence of Canado-Ukranian plays in the Plains, whereas Seamus Ceallaigh presents the difficulties associated with the integration of the Gaelic community from an historical perspective.

Karin Beeler examines the questions of alterity and ethnicity in the characters of Margaret Laurence and shows through a post-colonial perspective the subversion of traditional binary categories in *The Stone Angel, A Jest of God* and *The Diviners*.

The approach of George Elliott Clarke, Africadian poet, combines in an original manner his African origins with his Acadian context.

Roseanna Dufault focuses on the work of Québécois dramatist Marie Laberge from a feminist-existentialist perspective.

Paul Hjartarson analyses the theme of personal identity and masculinity in the immigrant text *The Russian Album*, by Russian-born author Michael Ignatieff.

Marie-Claire Huot provides a comparative study of *Le clan du sorgho rouge* by Mo Yan, whose culture is radically different while at the same time paradoxically close to that of Franco-Ontarian Maurice Henrie, therefore providing the opportunity to understand the universality of literature through a set of decidedly stringent particulars.

Earl Ingersoll analyses *The Handmaid's Tale* as an auto-subversive text and offers new insight on Margaret Atwood, a major writer in Canadian literature.

The themes of personal identity and cultural belonging are at the heart of the novel by Québécois writer Hélène Ouvrard, with *L'herbe et le varech* representing the opposition with which each minority is familiar: attachment and mobility.

In his study of Elise Turcotte's *Le bruit des choses vivantes*, Pierre Nepveu redefines traditional ideas of belonging, considering the dominant role played by the media in our age.

Multiculturalism is often associated with the Tower of Babel, and Valerie Raoul shows how Francine Noël revisits this myth in *Babel, prise deux ou Nous avons tous découvert l'Amérique*, an allusion to Todorov's study, in order to validate cultural pluralism and to depict through this perspective the Québécois as immigrants.

Henri Servin shows how "Passions dévorantes et satisfactions alimentaires" plays a part in the Québécois vision of French culture in Marie-Claire Blais's *Une liaison parisienne*.

In his study of the "carnavalesque," Eugenia Sojka shows how it can shed light on the roles of language and identity in the texts of Lola Lemire Tostevin and Gail Scott through a post-colonial perspective.

Philip Spensely shares his ideas on the esthetics and bilingualism of "Franglais" theater, as well as its political content.

Michael Thérien introduces a text by Haitian-born Dany Laferrière with the goal of demonstrating (with a hint of irony) the poetry of the immigrant situation as seen by the author.

This collection which studies the cultural identities and "migrant writings" in Canada would be incomplete without a mention of the Anglo-saxon Protestant culture, which is studied by Elisabeth Thompson through several Ontarian novels.

A comparative study by Christl Verduyn of immigrant writings in English Canada and Québec closes this collection with a "mise en abyme" of differences and an affirmation of the cultural diversity of Canadian writings.

Bénédicte Mauguière

Introduction

Les textes réunis dans ce recueil ainsi que la diversité des collaborateurs et des écrivains qui proviennent de divers horizons culturels (Europe, Afrique, Asie, Russie, Acadie, Québec, Haïti...) nous permettent de mieux apprécier la richesse de ces apports pour les littératures du Canada. Dans cette perspective, l'objectif de ce recueil d'essais n'est pas de répondre à l'éternelle question de l'existence d'une identité canadienne mais plutôt d'affirmer les multiples identités qui composent le Canada actuel et de contribuer ainsi à poser les jalons de nouvelles cartographies de l'imaginaire.

Jars Balan fait le point sur le développement culturel de la communauté ukrainienne du Canada dans son étude de l'émergence des pièces Canado-ukraniennes dans les Plaines et Seamus Ceallaigh expose les difficultés d'intégration des communautés gaéliques dans une perspective historique.

Karin Beeler traite des questions d'altérité et d'ethnicité chez les personnages de Margaret Laurence et montre la subversion des catégories binaires traditionelles dans *The Stone Angel, A Jest of God* et *The Diviners* dans une perspective post-coloniale.

La démarche de George Elliott Clarke, poète Africadien, lie de façon originale ses origines africaines avec le contexte acadien.

Roseanna Dufault aborde l'œuvre de la dramaturge québécoise Marie Laberge dans la perspective d'un existentialisme féministe.

Paul Hjartarson analyse le thème de l'identité personnelle et de la masculinité dans le texte immigrant *The Russian Album* de l'écrivain d'origine russe Michael Ignatieff.

Marie-Claire Huot fait une étude comparée du *Clan du sorgho rouge* de Mo Yan, originaire d'une culture radicalement différente et en même temps paradoxalement proche du celle de l'auteur Franco-Ontarien, Maurice Henrie, nous permettant ainsi d'appréhender l'universalité de la littérature à travers le particularisme à priori le plus étroit.

Earl Ingersoll analyse *The Handmaid's Tale* comme texte auto-subversif et offre un éclairage nouveau sur Margaret Atwood, cette figure majeure de la littérature canadienne.

Les thèmes de l'identité personelle et de l'appartenance culturelle sont au centre du roman de l'écrivaine québécoise Hélène Ouvrard, l'herbe et le varech représentant les deux oppositions propres à toute minorité: l'attachement et la mobilité.

A travers le roman *Le bruit des choses vivantes* d'Elise Turcotte. Pierre Nepveu redéfinit les notions traditionelles d'appartenance en cette fin de siècle dominée par les médias.

Le multiculturalisme est parfois associé à la Tour de Babel, Valérie Raoul montre comment Francine Noël revisite ce mythe dans *Babel, prise deux ou Nous avons tous découvert l'Amérique,* une allusion à l'étude de Todorov sur la question de l'autre, afin de mettre en valeur le pluralisme culturel et d'envisager dans cette perspective les Québécois comme des immigrants.

Henri Servin montre comment passions dévorantes et satisfactions alimentaires font partie de la vision québécoise de la culture française dans *Une liaison parisienne* de Marie-Claire Blais.

Eugenia Sojka montre comment le carnavalesque éclaire les questions de langue et d'identité dans les textes de Lola Lemire Tostevin et Gail Scott considérés comme textes post-coloniaux.

Philip Spensley nous fait partager sa réflexion sur les questions d'esthétique et de bilinguisme dans le théâtre "franglais" et son contenu politique.

Michel Thérien introduit un texte récent de l'écrivain d'origine haïtienne, Dany Laferrière, afin de montrer non sans ironie, la poésie de la condition immigrante telle que vue par l'auteur.

Ce recueil sur les identités culturelles et les écritures immigrantes au Canada serait incomplet sans la culture anglo-saxonne protestante qu'Elisabeth Thompson étudie ici à travers les romans ontariens.

Une étude comparée par Christl Verduyn des écritures immigrantes au Canada anglais et au Québec clôt ce recueil dans une sorte de mise en abyme de la différence et une affirmation de la diversité culturelle des écritures au Canada.

Bénédicte Mauguière

Old World Forms, New World Settings: The Emergence of Ukrainian-Canadian Plays on North American Themes

Although Ukrainian-language theatre has enjoyed a long, rich, and remarkably vital history in Canada, it has been only superficially investigated by scholars. Hence, this extremely important phenomenon in the cultural and literary life of Ukrainians in the New World is known mainly through impressionistic accounts and the memoiristic writings of a handful of participants. Given the lack of much primary research it is difficult to draw any authoritative conclusions about the evolution of immigrant drama, or to even make preliminary generalizations on the basis of the available data. This discussion will therefore focus on one small aspect of the Ukrainian-language stage, namely the emergence of an indigeneously written theatrical literature, particularly plays that were set in Canada.

The first dramatic work written by an immigrant playwright appears to have been *Ukiinyky* (The Murderers), by the pioneer community activist and Protestant churchman, John Bodrug (1874-1952). According to the preface in the inaugural Canadian edition of this work, published sometime in the teen years of this century, the impetus for the play came from a New Jersey carpenter named Mykhailo Melnyk, a supporter of the Presbyterian-backed Independent Church, and a theatre enthusiast.[1] In 1909, he submitted a "mishmash" of a playscript to the Reformationist Ukrainian newspaper, *Soiuz* (Union) which Bodrug was editing in America, having temporarily fled Winnipeg in the wake of a bitter power struggle within radical religious circles. Hurt and embittered by his defeat, he had accepted a pastoral position with a breakaway Greek Catholic congregation in Newark.[2] There, he obligingly took his parishioners' jumbled story-line as his inspiration, but thoroughly reworked the material into a cohesive plot, initially printing it in his newspaper under Melnyk's name (in generous deference to the latter's "co-authorship"), and then issuing it in book form under the *Soiuz* imprint. Consequently, the origins of Canadian-made Ukrainian drama can be traced to the United States, there being a great deal of such cross-border movement and interaction throughout the entire history of Ukrainian theatre in North America.[3]

Ubiinyky was a five-act melodrama set in the Podillia region of Western Ukraine around the turn of the twentieth century. The sensationalistic story of the rivalry of two young bachelors for the hand of a peasant girl named Mariika; it was typical of much of the theatrical fare presented in Ukrainian villages at this time, as well as in ethnic community halls throughout the emigration. The introduction to the original Canadian edition of this play reveals that following its Newark premiere "it was performed by many theatrical circles in the United States and Canada"—prompting the Rus'ka Knyharnia press in Winnipeg to obtain permission for a reprint. Five productions of *Ubiinyky* are known to have taken place in Manitoba and Alberta between 1910 and 1914, there being a noticeable increase in the number of performances starting in January 1915. The sudden flurry of activity suggests that the Canadian edition was likely issued in the middle of the decade, especially as many of the performances recorded between 1915 and 1917 took place in such peripheral "Ukrainian" towns as Fort Frances, Ontario, and Berkut, Manitoba, or in secondary centres like Ottawa and Portage La Prairie.

Regardless, *Ubiinyky* proved to be a long-running hit with Ukrainian-Canadian audiences. Over the span of the next four decades it was staged in immigrant enclaves, large and small, from Quebec to British Columbia, including many isolated rural communities and company towns on the frontier. From its apparent debut in Winnipeg on 2 April 1910, to its last known staging in Vancouver on 4 April 1954, the play received no fewer than forty-six separate productions, and fifty-two documented performances. Although these figures are based on incomplete research, they do provide an indication of the widespread and enduring appeal of this trail-blazing work in the indigeneous repertoire of the Ukranian-Canadian.[4]

Since it is natural for authors to turn to familiar subjects and locales in their early literary endeavours, it is not surprising that the majority of the plays written by Ukrainian Canadian dramatists in the pioneer era (1891-1923), clung to Old Country or "traditional" themes and settings.[5] Examples of both types can be found in the 1918 book, *Kanadiis'kyi Kobzar* (The Canadian Minstrel), by Joseph Yasenchuk (1893-1970). Besides a patriotic play called *Slava Ukrainy* (The Glory of Ukraine), which extolls Ukraine's glorious past and new-found freedom, a one act Christmas pageant, set in Biblical times and called *Vyflyiems'ka nich* (A Night in Bethlehem), is included in this collection.[6]

Seasonal plays such as the latter also helped to launch the career of the most prolific dramatist produced by the pioneer immigration,

Semen Kowbel (1871-1906). His first theatre piece was a scripted and politicized reworking of the ritual Easter celebration of spring and the Resurrection known as *Hailky* . A note on one of the surviving typescripts in Kowbel's papers reveals that *Haivky* was "written under the influence of the declaration of the Ukrainian Republic in 1918," and "presented on the stage in Winnipeg for the first time on Easter Day 1919".[7] However, Ukraine lost its sovereignty by the end of the same year, and the manuscript was quickly dated and never published, notwithstanding a 1920 advertisement offering the text and libretto from the author for the sum of three dollars.

Equally topical was an unusual Nativity play which Kowbel wrote again, in response to Ukraine's fleeting independence, but it proved to be more adaptable to changing times and therefore enjoyed a much longer stage life. Called *Rizdviana alliegoriia 'Novyi Vertep'* [A Christmas Allegory, 'The New Crib'], extant typescripts from 1938-1940 date this political parable as having been composed in 1918 and produced in Winnipeg over several Christmas seasons beginning in 1921. Expanded, updated, and renamed "Novyi vertep" [The New Crib] in a later variant, it was subsequently remounted in Winnipeg in 1939, when it was also staged in Trzic, Slovenia (then Yugoslavia).[8]

Far more ambitious and much more successful was Kowbel's *Divochi mrii* (Girlish Dreams), a five-act tragicomedy written in Winnipeg in 1918, but set in a Ukrainian village. A cautionary tale about " . . . young girls, who dream of unattainable happiness beyond their station, and frequently because of this plunge into misfortune from which there is no return," it probably became the author's most popular stagework because of its timeless romantic theme.[9] In addition to being widely produced from 1920 onwards in Canada and the United States, *Divochi mrii* had the rare distinction of being "exported" back to the homeland, where it entered the repertoire of the Tobilevych touring ensemble of Western Ukraine.[10]

Another major play written by Kowbel around this time was *Liakho-Tatary* [Polack-Tatarss], a dramatic portrayal of Ukrainian resistance to the Polish invasion of eastern Galicia in November 1918. Presented for the first time by Winnipeg's Boian Drama Circle in April 1920, this four-act agitational piece was never published, but was produced from the manuscript in various Canadian centres in the course of the next fourteen years.[11] The author of twenty-five works for the stage, as well as a radio play broadcast on the CBC, only a handful of the titles in Kowbel's extensive output had Canadian themes or settings. Among these dramas were two satires depicting communist Ukrainian Canadians visiting the "paradise" of the Soviet Union, and a 1940 fantasy, *Parubochi mrii* (A Young Man's Dreams), that featured Indian characters and a plot developed around a native legend.[12] All of these Canadian-oriented titles appear to date from the interwar years, the fate of Ukraine being the abiding concern in most of Kowbel's plays.

A second pioneer playwright who contributed several Old World titles to the New World stage was Vasyl Kazanivsky (fl, 1911-1950), whose adaptation of an 1878 novel called *Mykola Dzheria* debuted in Winnipeg on 16 October 1915. Retitled *Pimsta za kryvdu* (Revenging a Wrong), the stage version of this literary classic had received no fewer than eleven different productions by 1928, two years before it became available in a second printing.[13] An equally early endeavour by the same author was a village comedy called *Chort ne zhinka* (Not a Woman, But a Devil), dated in the published text as having been written in 1924, but already presented in the Manitoba capital by December 1916.[14] It went on to have at least eleven documented performances, including three in 1925 by a group touring the Sudbury area, and one in Sydney, Nova Scotia, in May 1931.

Kazanivsky further wrote a stage version of a contemporary Ukrainian prose masterpiece, the 1909 Olha Kobylianska novel, *V Nediliu rano zillia kopala* (On Sunday Morning She Gathered Herbs). It seems to have been mounted in Winnipeg as far back as 1919, after which the next known productions took place at the beginning of the 1960s. The only play in Kazanivsky's dramatic œuvre that was actually set in Canada—a moralistic comedy about the evils of drinking entitled *Adamovi sl 'ozy abo Piana korova* ("Adam's Tears" or The Drunk Cow)—was issued in the mid-twenties and was his last theatrical offering. Although he remained active in theatre and the performing arts for many years, his muse apparently fell silent following this fourth play.[15]

Among other pioneer playwrights who preferred looking back to the home country for creative inspiration was a rather mysterious figure named P. Kivshenko (dates unknown). His four-act *Bezbatchenko* (The Illegitimate Son), set among Cossack descendants in the Kuban region of the Caucasus, premiered in Winnipeg on 18 November 1916. Although it was subsequently put on no fewer than eleven times in twenty-four years by Ukrainian amateur ensembles in nine Canadian communities, for some reason the play was not followed by any other works by the same author.[16]

A similar situation exists with *Mizh burlyvymy fyliamy* (Amid Turbulent Waves), credited to Vasyl Babienko (dates unknown), one of the directors of Winnipeg's Maria Zankovetska ensemble.[17] His solitary title, which depicted revolutionary events in a village in Ukraine, had three known productions between 1918 and 1922, but afterwards seems to have disappeared entirely from the Ukrainian-Canadian repertoire.[18] An early play for children with an even more puzzling performance history is the two-act *Kozats'ki dity* (Cossack Children), by "K.M.", since only one production has so far been established for it, in Winnipeg on 22 December 1916. Yet this story, drawn from Tatar times, attributable to Michael Kumka (1893-194?), was eventually issued in chapbook form in 1935—suggesting that it was probably presented on other occasions in the nineteen-year gap between its debut and its publication.[19]

It is perhaps fitting that the first Ukrainian-language play written by an immigrant author and featuring a mostly Canadian setting, actually straddled two continents in the telling of its all-too-common tale. Entitled *V Starim i novim kraiu* (In the Old and the New Country), the initial scenes unfolded in front of a tavern in Western Ukraine, after which the action shifted to a boarding-house in Canada.[20]

The premiere of this ground-breaking drama was staged at the Town Hall in Vegreville, Alberta, on the evening of Monday, 28 February 1910, thereby predating the Canadian premiere of Bodrug's *Ubiinyky* by more than a month. The event was significant for a variety of reasons: it marked the birth of a truly indigenous Ukrainian-language theatre in Canada, while also introducing, for the first time, New World subject matter to the fledgling community stage. The achievement it represented is even more remarkable when one considers that the earliest known performance of a Ukrainian-language play in Canada had taken place merely a decade earlier, and that amateur drama groups became active on a regular basis in the large immigrant centres only after 1909. Indeed, *V starim i novim kraiu* was the inaugural theatrical entertainment put on by Ukrainians in Vegreville, which later went on to develop a lively theatre scene from the mid-teens through the 1920s.

Fortunately, five days before the play was put on, an article appeared in the *Vegreville Observer* which both advertised the performance and provided a synopsis of *In the Old and the New Country.*

The play opens with the departure of two young men for the New

World, one of whom is already married, the other being a young bachelor who has promised to return with a fortune to his intended bride. But the married immigrant, Andrew, subsequently gives in to temptation, and in Canada falls in love with and proposes to his wife's cousin, Mary. Meanwhile, the virtuous young bachelor, Nykola, has most commendably devoted himself "to teaching his countrymen to read and write; also handing out moral lessons."

A humorous scene then occurs when Andrew's wife arrives unexpectedly and catches him embracing Mary. As reported by the *Vegreville Observer*, the betrayed spouse gets so angry that "Andrew is badly scared and begs for forgiveness, which is duly accorded." The newspaper account goes on to add in an unusual aside: "Any husband who has been caught by his wife in the same way as Andrew, will be sure to appreciate the 'comical' part of it." The faithful Nykola, in the meantime, has received a letter from his beloved girl telling him how she "is longing for his return."

There is a secondary plot in the play involving a Jewish tavern keeper, Moshko, who follows the immigrants to Canada and cheats some of them out of their money. He is subsequently caught by the police, and what is left of his ill-gotten gain is then returned to the rightful owners. This anti-semitic caricature was clearly a reflection of the Old Country stereotypes and prejudices brought over by the immigrants. Interestingly, the *Vegreville Observer* reporter did not see anything derogatory in the negative portrayal of Moshko, or the blatantly racist lecture that apparently concluded the play.

V starim i novim kraiu had a strongly moralistic tone, as it was written in the tradition of didactic stage literature produced by Galician priests in the nineteenth century specifically for peasant audiences. The objective of such works was to caution viewers about potential moral pitfalls, and to warn them about the wages of sin. Thus, in one scene an unemployed immigrant is scolded by his wife for spending all of his time with other Ruthenian (i.e. Ukrainian) labourers drinking in a boarding-house. The message of these depictions was not intended to be subtle, and all of the characters were presented without any ambiguities so that spectators would have no trouble distinguishing between good and evil.

Twenty-three performers took part in the staging of this four-act play, which was directed by the prominent pioneer community leader, Peter Svarich. In the review of the performance that appeared in the *Vegreville Observer* on 2 March 1910, it was noted that the Town Hall was filled to capacity, and that the amateur ensemble, the Young Ruthenian Club, probably made money on the venture. Concerning the quality of the play, the non-Ukrainian reporter was rather tactful, commenting that "As a dramatic effort it may be open to doubt whether the play ranks up to *Hamlet* or *Julius Caesar* or *Richelieu*. But by dint of following closely the programmes provided one could get a fair idea of what the actors were driving at."

The successful evening was then described as ending loyally and "royally with the rendition of God Save the King."

Curiously, no mention is made of the author of the work, even though he was a teacher in the nearby community of Royal Park. Named Zygmund Bychynsky (1880-1947), he had originally immigrated to the United States in 1904, before moving to Winnipeg three years later. There, he continued the theological studies that he had begun at a Presbyterian seminary in Pittsburgh, while at the same time getting involved in the leading circles of the pioneer Ukrainian community in Canada. Besides becoming an active Liberal, Bychynsky also joined the Independent Greek Church—a formation that had been established with Presbyterian support for the purpose of ultimately converting Ukrainian immigrants to Protestantism.

In 1908, Bychynsky became the editor of the oldest Ukrainian newspaper published in Canada, *Kanadiis'kyi farmer* (Canadian Farmer).[21] The following year, he took up ministerial duties with an Independent Greek Church parish in Edmonton. But apparently the assignment failed to work out, as later the same year Peter Svarich recruited him to teach at Kolomea school, near Mundare, in the heart of the burgeoning Ukrainian bloc settlement of East Central Alberta. Besides teaching, and tutoring people privately, Bychynsky also participated in Ukrainian affairs on a provincial level. Although it is not known exactly when he wrote *V starim i novim kraiu*, the long winter months that he spent living on a farm east of Edmonton certainly would have been conducive to such a project.[22]

A highly educated man, with an equally sophisticated wife, Bychynsky was out of place in the tiny rural settlement of Royal Park. His Protestant convictions further aroused the suspicions of some of the local inhabitants, who started a vicious rumour campaign suggesting that he was a Freemason selling souls to the devil, and that he was setting up a secret society to terrorize and strangle people at night. Because of the fear and ridicule stirred up by this gossip-mongering, the Bychynskys were forced to leave Alberta under a cloud in the spring of

1910.

Although *V starim i novim kraiu* was later published, the printed version is extremely rare and was unavailable for this discussion. It is known, however, that the play was subsequently staged in Primula, Alberta, east of Elk Point, some time in March 1917, and probably received additional productions in different parts of Canada. Bychynsky is further said to have written three or four other produced plays, but more research is required to establish their texts and performance histories.[23]

If Zygmund Bychynsky's *In the Old and the New Country* can be viewed symbolically as a kind of literary stepping-stone between Europe and North America, then Jacob Maydanyk's *Manigrula* can be taken as evidence that the pioneer wave immigrants were physically and psychologically "landed." Written shortly after Bychynsky's play had its Vegreville premiere, it was initially published in 1911 in the Winnipeg newspaper, *Kanadiis'kyi farmer* (Canadian Farmer), then issued as a thirty-two page Rus'ka Knyharnia title in 1915. The earliest documented performance of Maydanyk's one-act farce was in West Fort William, Ontario, on 12 July 1915, but as it seems rather odd that a play written by a Winnipeger should have debuted in northern Ontario, this production may not have been the first.[24]

The title of the work is a humorous mangling of the word "immigrant" which was current in the slang of the newcomers of the pioneer generation.[25] It was an appropriate choice for a name, as the speech of the uneducated characters in the play is a colourful *joual* of German- and Polish-influenced Western Ukrainian dialect, with a smattering of Anglicisms thrown in to give the work the stamp of New World authenticity. Judging from the fact that the play was presented in sixteen different communities between 1915 and 1922, and that it was issued in a second (unrevised) edition in 1926, *Manigrula* obviously struck a responsive chord with Ukrainian-Canadian audiences. Certainly, a listing of the early productions reads like a virtual map of Ukrainian settlements in Canada: Vegreville, Hampton (Saskatchewan), Sifton (Manitoba), Venlaw (Manitoba), Regina, Komarno (Manitoba), Bellevue (Alberta), Oakburn (Manitoba), Coniston (Ontario), Berkut (Manitoba), Lanuke (Alberta), Toronto, Whitkow (Saskatchewan), Slawa (Alberta), East Kildonan, and Transcona (Winnipeg).

As might be expected from a farce, there is not much of a plot to *Manigrula*, and little in the way of literary polish. Basically, it presents an uncouth group of boarding-house inhabitants—mostly single, unemployed males—drinking, singing, and playing cards as they engage in put-downs of each other in highly colloquial Ukrainian. At one point in their partying, the ten-year-old son of the boarding-house owners is sent out to buy a bottle of brandy, undoubtedly to underscore the degeneracy of the slothful celebrants. The play concludes when a fight erupts between a virtuous resident, the landlord, and a particularly rowdy bachelor—resulting in police intervention and setting up the final lecture which makes explicit the moral of this story. Although written, and one suspects generally enjoyed, as simply a low-brow comedy, *Manigrula* clearly had lofty motives in depicting the outrageous behaviour of those newcomers who were blackening the reputation of the Ukrainian community in British-Canadian society. About all that is really notable about the play, besides its rich language, is the fact that it featured a *kolomyika*, or traditional folk song, about the immigrant experience in Canada, and had a brief but surprisingly sympathetic appearance by a Jewish moneylender. The latter is shown to be remarkably patient with his delinquent clients, whereas the unemployed Ukrainian borrowers are roundly chastised for being lazy and irresponsible.

Manigrula was the only play written by Jacob Maydanyk, who is chiefly known as a prose satirist and as the creator of an enormously popular comic strip about the misadventures of a Falstaff-like immigrant called Shteef Tabachniuk (literally, Steve Tobacco). Significantly, in *Manigrula* there is a character obviously based on the cartoon figure, but he is given the name Stheef Perih, or Steve Dumpling. Jacob Maydanyk was involved in various pioneer publishing ventures, besides working as a teacher and a church painter after emigrating to Canada. For much of his long life he ran a religious supply store in Winnipeg, where film-maker Halya Kuchmij was able to make an interesting documentary about him shortly before his death in 1981.[26]

After Semen Kowbel, the most dedicated and ambitious playwright to emerge among first wave Ukrainian immigrants was Dmytro Hunkewich (1893-1953), the author of at least eighteen theatrical titles, thirteen of which were published in separate editions. Hunkewich debuted as a dramatist on 4 December 1920 with a five-act play called *V halytski nevoli* (In Galician Captivity), which was set in rural Western Ukraine in the early part of the twentieth century and climaxed with a peasant uprising against Polish rule around 1916. Although a number of references are made in the third act to the possibility of emigrating to Canada or "Hameryka" ("America"), this social-political drama was firmly rooted in the specific problems and psychology of Ukrainian village life.[27]

Another play written by Hunkewich in the pioneer era which kept to the familiar terrain of the Old Country was an historical drama about Polish-Ukrainian conflict in the sixteenth century titled *Rai i peklo na zemli* (Heaven and Hell on Earth). This story about the struggle of serfs and Zaporozhian Cossacks against the brutal excesses of Polish landowners in Right Bank Ukraine was presented in Winnipeg's Prosvita Society hall on 7 January 1922 by a cast of more than thirty actors of all ages. However, all that is known about the piece comes from a leaflet advertising this performance, as the unpublished manuscript seems to have been lost to posterity.[28]

Of greater significance was the staging of Hunkewich's first Ukrainian play on a Canadian theme, *Zhertvy temnoty* (Victims of Ignorance), on 12 February 1921, by the Ivan Kotliarevsky Drama Circle of Winnipeg.[29] A portrayal of the disastrous consequences of a male immigrant's New World bigamy and plunge into moral turpitude, the tragedy consumes an ever-widening circle of victims and culminates with the death of both the protagonist and of his opportunistic second wife. Printed in Lviv for distribution on both sides of the Atlantic, the following afterword by the author summarizes the admonitory message of this play:

Releasing into the wide world this small book, I want to say a few words to my Esteemed Readers, specifically about what prompted me to write this drama. Many of our people, leaving behind in the old country a wife and small children, go to Canada with the objective of making money there and quickly returning to the homeland. Nevertheless, having arrived in Canada they stumble into a bad crowd, where they soon forget their familial responsibilities, forget about their wife and their children, take to drinking, and from there fall victims of their ignorance. Therefore, let this booklet be a warning to those who will come to Canada, to earn money and go back to the homeland. At the same time let this be a warning to those girls, who often get married frivolously and after that tearfully bemoan their unhappy fate.

This drama is based on true facts, and I am releasng it in print to show what kind of woefull consequences follow in the tracks—of a boozing and immoral life in Canada. (44)

Although similar in terms of its subject matter to Zygmund Bychynsky's *V starim i novim kraiu*, the Hunkewich drama gives a much darker treatment to what was obviously an all-too-common problem among Ukrainian settlers in Canada.

Nine different productions have so far been established for *Zhertvy temnoty* in the decade after its premiere, the last known performance taking place in Lethbridge, Alberta, on 7 February 1931. What was important about the work, however, was that Hunkewich followed it with a string of other plays which consciously utilized New World subject matter, making him the most "Canadian" of the playwrights active in the pioneer and interwar eras. This shift in orientation started with a 1924 children's drama, *Rozhdestvens'ka nich* (Night of the Nativity) set in Canada and written specifically to address a lack of appropriate material for young immigrant audiences. As Hunkewich explained in his foreword: "In Canada one can sense a great shortage of children's plays. European publications aren't suitable for Canadian conditions and therefore few of them have attained the success that they deserve. Their content and action are uninteresting and incomprehensible to Ukrainian children born in Canada . . . ."[30]

Other New World pieces by Hunkewich then appeared in quick succession, starting in 1924 with *Sered hradu kul'* (Amid a Hail of Bullets), featuring a contemporary story that began in Winnipeg and ended on the battlefields of Western Ukraine.[31] The following year, a romantic political drama set in a "large American city" and called *Krovavi perly* (Bloody Pearls) made a successful debut in the Manitoba capital, subsequently receiving at least twenty-one Canadian productions spread out over five decades in towns and cities in five provinces.[32] Similarly popular was a five-act comedy, *Kliub sufrazhystok* (The Suffragette's Club), which took a light-handed approach to the modern women's movement, even though the author was essentially sympathetic and supportive of the feminist cause.[33] The play is also noteworthy because the lead character is a drifter and a con artist from Kentucky—suggesting that Hunkewich had by that time assimilated all of the stereotypes about American hucksters preying on trusting and innocent Canadians.

The last dramatist to appear on the Ukrainian-Canadian theatrical scene before the arrival of the interwar immigrants was an aspiring young writer named Michael Petrowsky (1897-1982), whose parents had migrated overseas when he was a boy of thirteen.

Interestingly, his first published play is on a theme remarkably similar to Bychynsky's *V starim i novim kraiu* and Hunkewich's *Zhertvy temnoty*. Entitled *Kanadyis'kyi zhenykh* (The Canadian Bridegroom), this four-act social drama depicts the struggles of an immigrant family that had recently moved to the city from the countryside and was having difficulty keeping up payments on the house. The conservative father attempts to remedy the situation by compelling his sixteen-year-old daughter to marry a rather shiftless older immigrant who appears to have lots of money, but instead turns out to be a bigamist, a card-shark, and a thug. When exposed, the prospective bridegroom murders his accuser and seriously wounds his would-be father-in-law before being apprehended by the police. However, the tale ends happily when a virtuous student, who has protested the forced marriage all along, declares his affections and receives the blessings of the chastened parents.[34]

The author of eleven plays, numerous short stories, and a novel about immigrant life, it is possible that Petrowsky contributed other works to the repertoire of the Ukrainian-language theatre in Canada during the first phase of its development. However, additional research is required to establish the details concerning premiere productions and to clarify the confusion surrounding several unpublished titles—two of which may been have staged prior to 1924, and attributable to Petrowsky.

In looking at the emergence of an indigenous Ukrainian Canadian stage literature, a couple of observations can be made on the basis of the preceding discussion. First, it seems quite surprising that immigrant playwrights should appear so quickly after the establishment of a Ukrainian amateur theatre in Canada. Although pioneer community halls were overwhelmingly devoted to presenting stageworks imported from the Old Country, it is rather striking that so many authors would take up the challenge of writing dramas when Ukrainian cultural life in the emigration was still in its relative infancy. Of course, the number of Canadian playwrights greatly increased, as did their productivity, during the "golden age" of the Ukrainian-language theatre in the 1920s and 1930s, but clearly the way had been paved for this interwar flowering by the time that the second wave of Ukrainian settlers had reached North American shores.

Second, it is obvious that pioneer Ukrainian Canadian dramatists were somewhat cautious in their appropriation of New World themes and settings. Notwithstanding the handful of works set in Canada, most early attempts at writing for the immigrant stage looked back to the Old Country for inspiration and for subject matter. This generally continued to be true for the next two decades, when the greatest number of Ukrainian plays with a Canadian content were written. However, further investigation is required on the Ukrainian-language repertoire as a whole if meaningful insights are to be obtained about the evolution of an indigeneous theatrical literature.

Jars Balan

NOTES

1. Ivan Bodrug, *Ubiinyky. Mel'odrama v piaty diiakh a odynaitsiaty vidslonakh* [The Murderers. A Melodrama in Five Acts and Eleven Partitions]. [Second Edition.] Winnipeg: Rus'ka Knyharnia, n.d. The work was subsequently republished in Winnipeg in an undated and slightly revised Ukrains'ka Knyharnia edition, indicating its continuing popularity in Canada. A second play is also attributed to John Bodrug: a comedy written under the pseudonym of Ivan Yrshcheny. Entitled *Svatannia v Skachevani, Komediia na chotyry dii* [Matchmaking in Skachewan [sic], A Comedy in Four Acts], it was published in Toronto in 1926, but as yet it has not been established that it was ever actually performed. Among Bodrug's other notable literary achievements were his Ukrainian translation of John Bunyan's *Pilgrim's Progress* (1910) and a collection of stories that he wrote about Carpathian highwaymen entitled *Khudan* (1937).

2. Interestingly, Zygmund Bychynsky, the author of *V starim i novim kraiu* (written around the same time as *Ubiinyky*), was the apparent victor of the conflict that drove Bodrug to the United States. See John Bodrug, *Independent Orthodox Church. Memoirs Pertaining to the History of a Ukrainian Canadian Church in the Years 1903 to 1913*. Translated by Edward Bodrug and Lydia Biddle. Toronto: Ukrainian Canadian Research Foundation, 1982, pp. 96-101.

3. The newspaper and the *Soiuz* edition of "a few hundred copies", which Bodrug mentions in his Canadian preface, could not be located for this discussion. Nor has it been possible to establish a date for the Newark premiere of the play. However, the *Ukrains'kyi holos* (Ukrainian Voice) review of the first performance of *Ubiinyky* identifies it as having been written by Mykhailo Melnyk, and so one of the American texts must have served as the script for the debut and for

other early performances in Canada. To date, there has been almost no research done on pioneer-era Ukrainian-language theatre in the United States, prohibiting a comparative analysis of theatrical activity in North America as a whole.

4. Statistics on the performance histories of the plays examined in this paper are largely derived from unpublished research done by Orest Martynowych for his book *Ukrainians in Canada: The Formative Period, 1891-1924*. Edmonton: Canadian Institute of Ukrainian Studies Press, 1991; and from the chronicle in Kravchuk, Petro, *Nasha stsena* [Our Stage]. Toronto: Kobzar, 1981, pp. 424-487. This information has been supplemented with additional data obtained from sources which they did not investigate.

5. The time frame used is that established by Orest Martynowych for the pioneer era of Ukrainian-Canadian history, namely from 1891 to the end of 1923.

6. *Vyflyiems'ka nich. V odnii dii* [A Night in Bethlehem: In One Act], in Yasenchuk, Iosyf, *Kanadyis'kyi Kobzar*. Edmonton: Ukrainska Knyharnia, 1918, pp. 56-63. Performances of a play by this name took place in 1912 (1), 1913 (1), 1914 (4), 1915 (1), 1916 (1), and 1918 (1), but it is likely that most, if not all, of these were presentations of the dramatic "oratorio" *Vyfleiems'ka nich* [sic] by the Galician author and librettist, I.V. Lutsyk (1858-1909). There is also an unpublished work called *Vyflyiems'ka nich* by Semen Kowhel, who emigrated to Canada in 1909, but his typescript seems to be from a much later date.

7. Whereas one variant of the script is titled "Haivky", a second version (which is only slightly different) is identified more fully as "Hailky. Na stari motyvy, na novi lad—dlia budushykh pokolin" [Hailky: On Old Motifs and on the New Order—for Future Generations]. Both spellings of the ritual are used in Ukrainian.

8. Both of the above playscripts are found in the Kowbel papers, held by his daughter, Mrs. O. Karmanin, in Toronto.

9. Kovbel, Semen, *Divochii mrii. Tragi-komediia v 6-okh vidminakh. Zi spivamy i tantsiamy* [Girlish Dreams: A Tragi-Comedy in 6 Scene-Changes. With songs and dances]. Winnipeg: Pani Dr. A. Yonker, [1920].

10. Thirteen different productions of *Divochi mrii* have been documented to date, five of which took place in rural or frontier settlements ranging from Cappon, Alberta (1925), to Kirkland Lake Ontario (1935). It was undoubtedly performed many more times than the available record shows. Although Kowbel claimed that the play

was staged from the manuscript as early as 1919, he probably had in mind the 3 January 1920 premiere production by Winnipeg's Boian drama circle.

11. In the Kowbel papers there are three versions of this play under the following titles: "Konfidenty! Tatare 20 viku abo Nove Lykholitie" [Informers! Tatars of the 20th century or The New Chaos], with a handwritten second title, "Liakho-Tatary"; "Vidvichna iazva narodu. Drama v chotyrokh diiakh, z chasiv vidrodzhennia ukrains'koi derzhavy" [The Eternal Plague of a People: A Drama in Four Acts, From the Time of the Rebirth of the Ukrainian State]; and "Vidvichna iazva narodu. Liakho-Tatary. Drama u 4—vidslonakh". The second two typescripts (the first is handwritten) are mistakenly dated October 1920; the last version also contains this inaccurate note in the author's hand: "The drama was produced for the first time in Winnipeg in the year 1921. Subsequently, it was produced in other locations in the west and east, at which time reviews appeared in periodicals and I sent the manuscript upon request."An advertisement for the playscript in the back of *Divochi mrii* (1920) announced that the play would be published later and requested that proceeds from its production be sent to the Ukrainian Red Cross.

12. One Canadian play which may have been written before 1923 is an undated thirteen-page typescript entitled "Uneznanyi svit. Drama iz chasiv prybutiia pershykh poselentsiv v Kanadu z ukrains'kykh zemel" [Into the Unknown World: A Drama from the Time of the Arrival of the First Settlers in Canada from Ukrainian Lands].

13. V. H. Kazanivsky, Pimsta za kryvdu. *Mykola Dzheria. Drama v piat'okh diiakh a shesty vidslonakh, zi spivamy i tantsiamy* [Revenging a Wrong, "Mykola Dzheria." A Drama in Five Acts and Six Parts, with singing and dancing]. Winnipeg: Ukrains'kyi Holos, 1917. A note at the conclusion of the text indicates that the work was completed by the author in June 1915. The second edition was corrected in March 1928 and published in 1930.

14. Kazanivskyi, V., *Chort ne zhinka. Zhart na 1 diiu* [Not a Woman, But a Devil. A Comedy in One Act]. Lviv: Rusalka, 1929. This work had previously been printed in *Veselyi kalendar*, 1925.

15. Kazanivsky, V., "*Adamovi sl'ozy*" *abo Piana korova. Zhart na 1 diiu. Z zhyttia nashykh pereselentsiv v Kanadi* ["Adam's Tears" or The Drunk Cow. A Comedy in 1 Act. From the Life of Our Settlers in Canada]. Lviv-Detroit: Rusalka; 1926.

16. Kivshenko, P., *Bezbatchenko. Drama na 4 dii* [The

Illegitimate Son. A Drama in 4 Acts]. Winnipeg: Ukrains'kyi Bazaar 1927. It is certainly possible that P. Kivshenko was a pseudonym.

17. There is a V. Babienko listed among the directors working with Winnipeg's Mariia Zankovetska ensemble circa 1920, and among the presidium members of the Ukrainian Red Cross, established in 1919.

18. Babienko, V.V., *Mizh burlyvymy fyliamy. Drama na 4 dii i 5 odmin* [Amid Turbulent Waves. A Drama in 4 Acts and 5 Set Changes]. Winnipeg: N.p., 1918.

19. K. M., *Kozats'ki dity. Obrazok z tatars'kykh chasiv v 2-okh diiakh* [Cossack Children. A Mini-Portrait from Tatar Times in 2 Acts]. Winnipeg: Ukrains'kyi holos, 1935. I have assigned the work to Mykhailo Kumka because he was the author of *Monol'ogy i diial'ogy dlia ditei i molodi* [Monologues and Dialogues for Children and Young People], published around the same time, and because he also was the compiler of several school-oriented anthologies of verse for recitation. The latter series of six volumes represented the largest collection of Ukrainian literature ever assembled in Canada, ranging from Old Country classics to the poems of many New World authors, including works by Kumka himself.

20. Bychynsky, Zygmund, *V starim i novim kraiu. Drama v chotyriokh diiakh. Obraz iz suchasnoho zhyttia.* [In the Old and the New Country]. N.p.: Vydavnytstvo A. Bonchevs'koho (No. 27-8), n.d. This information comes from Michael Marunchak's *The Ukrainian Canadians. A History.* As a search of all of the major Ukrainian play collections in libraries across Canada did not yield a single copy of this text, it has not been possible to verify the bibliographic data or examine first-hand the contents of the work.

21. In this capacity, he assisted in the preparation of two collections of *kolomyika* verses—Teodor Fedyk's *Songs about Canada and Austria*, and Dmytro Rarahovsky's *Workers' Songs*—that marked the birth of published Ukrainian poetry in Canada. The former book went on to appear in six separate editions, selling an impressive 50,000 copies in its nineteen-year publishing history. Bychynsky's various other literary endeavours in the pioneer era have led one historian to describe him as Canada's first Ukrainian critic. His writing career actually pre-dates his emigration, since he had had two short stories published in a prestigious Western Ukrainian journal prior to his departure for the United States.

22. The Bychynskys were billeted with Svarich's sister and brother-in-law, Anna and Fedor Kostash, the paternal grandparents of

the contemporary Alberta author, Myrna Kostash.

23. Bychynsky's son, Wilfred, recalls seeing several other plays by his father but cannot remember specific details about them.

Upon leaving Alberta, Bychynsky returned for several years to the United States, then resided in Winnipeg throughout most of the 1920s. In Manitoba, he served as the editor of the Protestant newspaper, *Ranok* (Dawn) besides being active in a number of Ukrainian secular organizations. From 1928 to 1930 he worked as an evangelist in Western Ukraine, after which he permanently settled in the United States, where he had a falling out with the American Presbyterian Church. Leaving the ministry, he spent the last years of his life in Ann Arbor, employed as a librarian at the University of Michigan.

From the time Zygmund Byshynsky composed his first stories as a student at the University of Lviv, to the end of his days in America, he was committed to writing and literature. In addition to translating Lew Wallace's *Ben Hur* in 1924, he was the author of four published Ukrainian-language books on Protestant themes: *The History and Essence of Protestantism* (1911); *Jan Hus* (1916, 1932, 1955); *Martin Luther* (1925); and *The History of the Prophets* (1927), the latter being a collaborative effort with the Canadian medical missionary, Dr. Alexander Jardine Hunter.

Bychynsky also deserves credit for writing the first Ukrainian account of Canada's past and her peoples. Entitled *Istoriia Kanady* (History of Canada), this encyclopedic 222-page book featured an introduction by the well-known Canadian author, Ralph Connor, and a twelve-page chapter on Ukrainians in Canada, including a section on their literary achievements.

Last, but certainly not least, while he was at the University of Michigan, Bychynsky completed a full-length novel about Ukrainian life in Canadian which had a number of autobiographical elements. Although set in a fictional rural colony in Saskatchewan, the work obviously drew on Bychynsky's own memories of his unhappy experience in East Central Alberta. Entitled *Kliuch zhuravliv* (A Flight of Cranes), the manuscript was recently recommended for publication on the strength of its literary qualities and its historic interest.

24. Maidanyk, Iakiv, *Manigrula. Komediia v odnii dii zi spivamy i tantsiamy* [Mangrula: A Comedy in One Act with Songs and Dances]. Winnipeg: Rus'ka Knyharnia, 1915. Especially strange is the fact that the first recorded Winnipeg presentation—according to the available

information—was the fifteenth performance of the play and took place only at the late date of 13 May 1922.

25. The fracturing of the word proceeded from "imigrant" to "manigrant" and "manigrula".

26. Entitled *Laughter in My Soul*, this half-hour movie is available through the National Film Board of Canada.

27. Hunkevych, Dmytro, *V halyts'kii nevoli. Drama v 5 diiakh, zi spivamy i tantsiamy. Predstavliaie zhytie halyts'kykh Ukraintsiv pid hnetom Pol'shchi v XX stolitu* [In Galician captivity: A Drama in Five Acts with Songs and Dances. Depicts the Life of Galician Ukrainians Under the Yoke of Poland in the XXth Century]. Winnipeg: Ukrains'ka Knyharnia, 1921. The New World references are on pp. 50-51, 54-56, and 60-61. To date, the only other performance established for this play was in Kirkland Lake, Ontario, in January 1937.

28. The leaflet, which lists cast members and provides other useful information, is found on reel one of the Hunkewich papers at the Archives of Ontario.

29. Hunkevych, Dmytro, *Zhertvy temnoty. Drama na 5 dii zi spivamy i tantsiamy. Z zhyttia ukrains 'kykh pereselentsiv v Kanadi* [Victims of Ignorance: A Drama in Five Acts with Songs and Dances. From the Life of Ukrainian Settlers in Canada]. Lviv-Winnipeg: Rusalka Publishers, 1923. This published version identifies the work as having been 'written in A.D. 1923," either mistakenly or possibly because the author extensively rewrote the script that was set for the 1921 production. According to Semen Kowbel, a second edition of *Zhertvy temnoty* was published in 1926.

30. Hunkevych, Dmytro, *Rozhdestvens'ka nich. Stsenichna kartyna na dvi dii dlia ukrains'kykh ditei v Kanadi i Amerytsi* [The Night of the Nativity: A Stage Depiction in Two Acts for Ukrainian children in Canada and America]. Winnipeg: "Mars", 1924, p. 3.

31. Hunkevych, Dmytro, *Sered hradu kul', abo Neustrashyma heroina. Tragediia v 4-okh diiakh, v 5 vidslonakh zi spivamy* [Amid a Hail of Bullets, or The Dauntless Heroine. A Tragedy in 4 Acts and 5 Curtain Separations with Songs]. Winnipeg: Ukrainska Knyharnia, n.d.

32. Hunkevych, Dmytro, *Krovavi perly. Rohitnycha drama na 5 dii* [Bloody Pearls: A Workers' Drama in 5 Acts]. Lviv-Detroit-Fort William: Rusalka, 1926-7. The last documented staging was in Edmonton on 20 March 1966. This work was also performed in the United States and in Western Ukraine.

33. Hunkevych, Dmytro, *Kliub sufrazhystok. Komediia v 5-ty diiakh z amerykans'koho zhyttia* [The Suffragette's Club: A Comedy in 5 Acts from American Life]. Lviv-Winnipeg: Rozvaha, 1925. Two other editions appeared of this play, which received no fewer than fifteen North American performances and was also mounted in Ukraine. In another of his stageworks, written to encourage enrollment in Ukrainian Saturday schools, Hunkewich promoted awareness of the founder of the women's movement in nineteenth-century Ukraine, Nataliia Kobrynska (1851-1920).

34. Petrivs'kyi, Mykhailo, *Kanadyis'kyi zhenykh. Drama v 4-kh diiakh z zhytia [sic] ukrains'kykh poselentsiv v Kanadi* [The Canadian Bridegroom: A Drama in 4 Acts from the Life of Ukrainian Settlers in Canada]. Winnipeg: Ukrains'ka Knyharnia, 1922.

Ethnic Dominance and Difference: The Post-Colonial Condition in Margaret Laurence's *The Stone Angel, A Jest of God,* and *The Diviners*

Studies in post-colonial literatures often identify a variety of dialectical relationships in post-colonial texts, including tensions between colonizer and colonized, centre and margin, or place and displacement. However, certain critics have pointed out that approaches to such texts based exclusively on binary or Manichean oppositions of "irreconcilable antagonism" (Prasad 74) are reductivist. In *The Empire Writes Back*, Ashcroft, Griffiths, and Tiffin present Wole Soyinka's firm belief that "the historical fact of colonialism inevitably leads to a hybridization of culture" (*Empire* 129). An examination of three Manawaka novels by Canadian author Margaret Laurence reveals the existence of certain dialectical tensions between imperial centre(s) and colonized subject(s). Such relationships are generally based on the principles of dominance and inferiority. Yet at the same time, these texts reflect a slippage in an oppositional strategy of representation through the elements of difference, and hybridity. This article will examine some occurrences of dominance, difference and hybridity, particularly as they are reflected in the ethnic or cultural affiliation of characters in *A Stone Angel, A Jest of God,* and *The Diviners*.[1] Within the Canadian settings of these stories, ethnic background can function as a confirmation of an individual's or a community's sense of its dominant and/or different status. Yet ethnicity[2] may also become synonymous with a fear of Otherness or with an inability to validate the existence of the Other. In the course of all three novels, but especially in *The Diviners*, Laurence attempts to subvert binary/Manichean oppositions between ethnic groups by affirming the existence of a multicultural society and the hybridization of cultures. She thus uses ethnic identity to advocate meaningful co-existence in a post-colonial Canadian world of experience, despite the differences presented by individual linguistic and cultural affiliation.

Margaret Laurence addresses the post-colonial condition in her essay "Ivory Tower or Grassroots?: The Novelist as Socio-Political Being." She calls Canadians Third World writers because "they have had to find [their] own voices and write out of what is truly [theirs] in the face of an overwhelming cultural imperialism" (17). Linda

Hutcheon, however, has taken exception to the link between Canada's postcolonial experience and those of Third World countries. In "Circling the Downspout of Empire" Hutcheon argues that treating Canada as a postcolonial country requires some specification and even explanation" (171). She states that there are marked differences between post-colonial Third World literatures and Canada's of a settler colony, emphasizing that the term "postcolonial" is applied more accurately to the cultures of the Native people in Canada: "theirs should be considered the resisting, post-colonial voice of Canada" (172).[3] I use the term "postcolonial" to embrace a variety of phenomena in Laurence's three Manawaka novels, including the Britain (old world)/Canada (new world) relationship as well as the tension between imperial centres created within the Canadian framework and the subsequent colonization of Native people and other ethnic groups. Post-colonial strategies will also be noted in the presence of hybridity and in the subversion of forms of authority such as written texts, "acceptable" forms of religion or social practice by alternative communicative, ethnic, spiritual, or sexual forces.

The Stone Angel represents Laurence's first imaginative represent-ation of the fictional world of Manawaka. Laurence has said that the chief character, Hagar Shipley, belongs to the generation of her grandparents (Fabre, 203). Thus, Hagar's historical time and values are less distant from an entrenched colonial mindset than those of Rachel Cameron and Morag Gunn, the female protagonists in *A Jest of God* and *The Diviners*. In *The Stone Angel* as in the later Manawaka texts, Laurence describes the influence of a Scots-Presbyterian background on her chief character. Hagar maintains a pride in her cultural heritage, which is manifested in the Currie name and the plaid pin that bears the motto "Gainsay Who Dare" (124), the cry of her Scottish ancestors. Throughout *The Stone Angel*, she clings to this past and imagines her legendary fore*fathers* with their "genteel" manners, an ideal which she ascribes to in her own pretentious and ultimately unsuccessful way.[4] The "imperial centre" that she creates out of the land of her Scottish ancestors causes her to value this world of experience over Canada in a typically colonial fashion: "How bitterly I regretted that he'd left and had sired us here, the bald-headed prairie stretching out west of us with nothing to speak of except couchgrass or clans of chittering gophers . . . ." (15). Her disapproval of a Canadian, postcolonial experience extends to her suspicion of John Shipley's relationship with an ethnic Other or the Métis character, Lazarus Tonnerre:

Once when I was out picking saskatoons near the trestle bridge, I saw him with the Tonnerre boys. They were French half-breeds, the sons of Jules, who'd once been Matt's friend, and I wouldn't have trusted any of them as far as I could spit. They lived all in a swarm in a shack somewhere—John always said their house was passably clean, but I gravely doubted it. They were tall boys with strange accents and hard laughter. (127)

Here Hagar echoes her father's distrust of the Métis, as she relegates the Tonnerre clan to the margins of society. Her contempt for the ethnic Other is further demonstrated in her reference to herself as "Hagar *Currie* serving a bunch of breeds and ne'er-do'wells and Galicians" (italics mine, 114) while she is married to Bram Shipley. In this scene, she asserts her Scottish, ethnic dominance or the power of hegemony; given this pride in her heritage, it is not surprising that she regrets her son John's trading of the Currie pin. However, even though John's exchange of the heirloom for Lazarus Tonnerre's knife represents a genuine loss for Hagar, the exchange also shakes Hagar's colonial attitudes and signals the emergence of a postcolonial world where cultural interaction, not ethnic superiority, is foregrounded (177).

Although a large part of *The Stone Angel* involves Hagar's affirmation of her Scottish background and a fear of ethnic difference, Laurence does permit her character to transcend her old fears of cultural Otherness in several important scenes. During her time in the hospital, Hagar meets a young Chinese girl by the name of Sandra Wong and thinks of her as a "granddaughter of one of the small foot-bound women whom Mr. Oatley smuggled in, when Oriental wives were frowned upon, in the hazardous hold of his false-bottomed boats" (286). Yet this fear of the Other is soon offset by the thought that she might owe her house to the passage money of this Chinese girl's grandmother (287). The ensuing episode depicts Hagar's selfless act of bringing a bedpan to the Chinese girl in distress. This act of mercy and the peals of laughter she and Sandra Wong share over the nurse's reprimand of Hagar represent a real breakthrough for her as she abandons her earlier suspicions of ethnic difference.

Hagar's fears of the ethnic Other abate during prolonged contact with the community of women in the hospital. One of the patients, Mrs. Reilly, has a "clear and musical" voice with a "marked Irish accent" which Hagar contrasts with the woman's mountain of flesh (259). Another occupant of the ward is a German woman by the name of Mrs.

Dobereiner whose fragments of German songs are represented in the text. These voices and those of the other occupants initially frighten Hagar, but as she spends more time in the hospital, she can identify them, and she eventually joins the chorus of utterances when she screams out Bram's name in one scene. Thus her early rejection of the foreign (including Bram, her dark-skinned husband who resembled a "bearded Indian" (45), is overturned through her awareness of feminine, ethnic and linguistic diversity.

Like Hagar, Rachel Cameron[5] in *A Jest of God* lays claim to a Scots-Presbyterian background; it is a heritage which her mother and father share. However, the Scots are not the only ethnic group in Manawaka. According to Rachel:

Half the town is Scots descent, and the other half is Ukrainian. Oil, as they say, and water. Both came for the same reasons; because they had nothing where they were before. That was a long way away and a long time ago. The Ukrainians knew how to be the better grain farmers, but the Scots knew how to be almightier than anyone but God. She was brought up that way, and my father, too, and I—but by the time it reached me, the backbone had been splintered considerably. She doesn't know that, though, and never will. Probably I wouldn't even want her to know. (81)

Here Rachel identifies the two prominent communities in her town: the Scottish and the Ukrainian. Her reference to her splintered backbone of ethnic identity is a metaphor for her challenge to an old world centre and symbolizes her desire to gain access to the other major ethnic community, that of the Ukrainians. Unlike *The Stone Angel*, which portrays Hagar's father Jason Currie as the dominant, imperial centre in the text, the inflexible authority figure in *A Jest of God* is Rachel's mother. It is Mrs. Cameron who maintains the "holier than thou" attitude.[6] Despite her constant resistance to her mother's views, Rachel is aware of her own shifting perspective in her understanding of her Ukrainian lover Nick. By dating Nick, she clearly defies her mother's earlier warning not to play "with those Galician youngsters" (78), yet at the same time she admits that like her mother she also uses the term "Galician or Bohunk" to designate a Ukrainian (78). In other words, she is complicit in her mother's marginalization of the ethnic Other. As her relationship with Nick progresses, she alternates between the image of the familiar and the different. For example, she can choose to acknowledge Nick as her male lover, or she can choose to distance herself from him by viewing his "hidden Caucasian face, one of the hawkish and long-ago riders of the Steppes" (106). In his article "Fictions of Ethnicity in Prairie Writing," E.D. Blodgett argues that Nick's abandonment of Rachel appears to reinforce the questionable morality of ethnic "otherness" because the term "ethnic" has had historical moral overtones.[7] However, despite the fact that the relationship and communication with Nick, the ethnic other, is far from ideal, he and Rachel learn about one another's respective communities through their exchange of family histories. Furthermore, Rachel's movement away from the "imperial centre" of her mother's influence paradoxically allows her to develop her own maternal instincts. The "jest of God," or the tumour which she mistakes in her confusion for a growing fetus, ironically leads to her increased sense of confidence and independence. It is also worth noting that it is a certain Doctor Raven who performs the medical examination on Rachel. Since Raven is one of the many names for the Indian mythological figure, Trickster,[8] it is possible that Laurence may be making use of yet another ethnic force to introduce a spirit of confusion into Rachel's life, a confusion which disrupts the rigid categories, centres, and attitudes formerly championed by Rachel and her mother.

Rachel's fear of the religious practices and glossalalia which occur during the Tabernacle services her friend Calla attends reveal a further manifestation of her fear of "Otherness". For example, she ascribes Greek ethnicity to her friend as she pictures her rising "keen like the Grecian women wild on the hills" (38). Calla's Otherness also intersects with Nick's since she "has that Slavic squareness and strong heavy bones" (4). It would appear that in this text, Laurence is highlighting ethnic identity to comment on unfamiliar experiences in general. Calla's difference also extends to her sexual orientation as a lesbian and to her religious affiliation. However, throughout the novel, Rachel harbours not only a distrust of ethnic, sexual, and religious differences, but also an awareness of the strangeness of her own voice and actions. Rachel thus constructs a paradigm of self and other for her own character. One of her most horrifying realizations in the text occurs in the scene where she speaks in tongues during a Tabernacle service. This encounter with the "strange" confusion of religion represents a confrontation with the self; the experience echoes the dismantling of hegemonic and secure structures which Rachel accomplishes through her interface with ethnic difference.

The Diviners is more extensive in its emphasis on colonial and post-colonial conditions than either *The Stone Angel* or *A Jest of God*. The last of Laurence's Manawaka books, it concentrates on two major ethnic groups, the Scots and the Métis. While *The Diviners* supports Linda Hutcheon's concern with the colonized status of the native, other structures of colonialism are also evident in the text which reflect the complexity of relationships based on ethnic dominance, difference, and hybridity in the novel. An early example of the link between ethnicity and dominance occurs during Morag's childhood, when young Morag remembers her fondness for "The Maple Leaf Forever," a song which praises the heroic actions of General Wolfe. She dwells on the significance of the emblems listed in the song and their ethnic parallels:

Thistle is Scots, like her and Christie (others, of course, too, including some stuck-up kids, but *her*, definitely, and they better not forget it). Shamrock is Irish like the Connors and Reillys and them. Rose is English, like Prin, once of a good family. Suddenly she looks over to see if Skinner Tonnerre is singing. He has the best voice in the class, and he knows lots of cowboy songs, and dirty songs, and he sometimes sings them after school, walking down the street.
He is not singing now.
He comes from nowhere. He isn't anybody. (70)

Here Morag draws upon the solidarity of European heritage to enforce her own sense of Scottish identity, and excludes the young Métis boy Skinner in a typically colonial fashion. She defines herself according to culture and place, while defining Jules as a displaced *persona non grata*. In this instance, she appears to reflect Hutcheon's reference to the colonial discourse and the subjecting of the aboriginal population by the white descendants of settlers in Canada. Her fear of Lazarus Tonnerre, Jules's father, is also reminiscent of Hagar's fear of the ethnic Other or Métis (140). However, Laurence does not permit this hierarchy to remain intact. Prior to this passage, she presents the distorted rendition of "The Maple Leaf Forever" as sung by the children of Manawaka, thereby undermining the authority of the imperial voice: "In days of yore/ From Britain's shore/ Wolfe the donkless hero CAME (titters; but what means *Donkless*?)[9] (69). This textual disruption occurs in this novel with greater variety and scope than in either *The Stone Angel* or *A Jest of God*. In *The Canadian Postmodern*, Linda Hutcheon discusses the paradox of the postmodern novel in its privileging of oral narratives despite references to the written medium; Laurence "sets up the oral Scottish narratives and Métis songs against Morag's writing—and, implicitly, her own" (51). This post-modern tendency to work between oral and written forms of expression is also what post-colonial critics have identified as an important facet of post-colonial literature.[10] Laurence portrays Christie and Jules primarily as purveyors of the oral tradition, but Morag and her daughter Pique combine both oral and written forms of expression to advance their past and identities.[11] The similarities between Christie's family and the Tonnerre clan are further emphasized through their marginal status in the community. The receptacle of Scottish lore is a garbage collector who can communicate with Jules Tonnerre without criticizing the latter's lack of social decorum (75). Jules in turn conveys his approval of Christie: "He's quite a guy, that Christie" (134). Class similarities therefore seem to facilitate the interaction between members of different ethnic groups, despite a history of conflict. Laurence identifies both Christie's ancestors and those of Jules as people dispossessed of their lands ("Ivory Tower" 25).[12] In the course of *The Diviners*, however, both individuals practice forms of cultural recovery; Christie refashions history, and Jules, who had been silenced by the colonial discourse of "The Maple Leaf Forever," recovers his native voice and those of his people through the specificity of his songs.

Christie and his tales represent, for Morag, the essence of her Celtic past and a tie to the old world. Yet when the mature Morag visits Scotland, presumably to find her true identity, she comes to the conclusion that the myths are her reality (390), not the geographical regions of Britain. According to Morag, her land is Canada, "Christie's real country" (391). This realization substantiates the notion that Christie's storytelling, his manipulation of fact and history, act as a post-colonial alternative to the authority of an imperial word. Her eventual recognition of the validity of the post-colonial imagination represents a radical departure from her childhood conviction that her own poetry was inferior to the English works her teacher had read in class (81). Her resistance to Susanna Moodie and Catherine Parr Traill functions as a similar rejection of the authorities of colonialism (57; 96; 170).

Morag's marriage to Brooke, the *English* professor of English, is perhaps the most graphic illustration of the British/Canadian, colonizer/colonized paradigm in the novel. Although her husband

Brooke was born in India, he was educated in Britain, and has quite a different attitude towards his homeland (India) than Morag's feeling for home (Canada). Morag believes that this is caused by the fact that his ancestors hail from elsewhere (England 244-245). His reluctance to criticize the British Raj is symptomatic of his inability to abandon imperialistic tendencies; these are further reflected in his paternalistic relationship with Morag (he calls her "child") and in his unwillingness to take her writing seriously—an extension of the Britain as centre/Canada as colony mentality.[13] The relationship between Morag and Jules, on the other hand, serves as a significant departure from this kind of binary opposition. The Scottish factor in *The Diviners* is interwined with images of Métis identity and culture. As we mentioned earlier, hybridity has been acknowledged as an important consequence of a postcolonial culture; Pique, the daughter of Morag and Jules (Skinner) Tonnerre, represents the most concrete manifestation of this idea. However, evidence of hybridity and cultural exchange is also found in Jules's service with the Queen's Own Cameron Highlanders. Jules Tonnerre, once the ostracized Other, wears a kilt as one of his uniforms, a symbol of Morag's heritage; the intersection of two cultures occurs as well in the exchange of the Currie plaid pin and Lazarus Tonnerre's knife (described for the first time in *The Stone Angel*). Thus it would appear that the more rigid notions of ethnic dominance articulated through Hagar's early attitudes are further undermined in the final scenes of *The Diviners*, where hybridity and diversity offset antagonistic binary oppositions between superior/inferior, white/native categories of experience. Although Jules's Otherness is still apparent in certain instances—he speaks English as a "foreign tongue" (244)—it exists within a framework of pluralism instead of a strict colonial hierarchy.

W.H. New summarizes Margaret Laurence's approach to diversity in her fiction as follows:

It is clear, too, that through the multicultural world of Manawaka, Laurence traces an historical shift from a generation of "discriminators" (whether Irish, Scots, Protestant, or merely middleclass to the subsequent generations of women (writers, teachers, housewives) who have rejected the old definitions of themselves and who find their dignity and freedom after they extend themselves to contact others (other women, men, city people, Métis, Catholics, Jews: characters like the Kazliks, Tonnerres, Ella Gerson, Sandra Wong). If they sometimes look first for a new rigidity, a new insulation against strangeness, they soon abandon that aim in order to embrace a new sense of their own potential; it is a progress—that is, an ongoing, active, perhaps chaotic, but not static—self and society they seek to articulate: not a world where the I controls the Other, or where the Other and I fade into one, but where the multiplicity invokes a constant renewal of self-recognition.[14] (134)

Laurence's depiction of ethnicity in *The Stone Angel, A Jest of God* and *The Diviners* reflects her recognition of the changing dimensions of language, culture, and sexuality in a post-colonial world. Although it would be difficult to deny that certain dialectical tensions between ethnic groups continue to exist in these works, her conception of the post-colonial condition in Canada stresses ethnic diversity and mutual appreciation instead of the politics of exclusion. She has described Canadians as individuals besieged by "A whole history of imperialism, of being defined in others' terms, not our own" ("Ivory Tower" 23) and she seeks to dismantle this legacy of cultural hegemony by affirming cross-cultural interaction within Canadian society. Her Canada is a hybrid world of discovery and recovery, a world where cultural difference and exchange are promoted, enabling the disenfranchised to speak and to reach others.

University of Calgary   **Karin E. Beeler**

NOTES

1. Although *The Fire Dwellers* and the collection of stories, *A Bird in the House*, also form part of Laurence's Manawaka series, I have chosen to limit my discussion to these three novels because of time constraints, and because they contain a sustained development of the dynamic relationship between ethnic diversity and post-colonialism.

2. Definitions of "ethnic" groups vary; however, for the purposes of this paper the following definition seems to apply to the examples of Scottish, Ukrainian, German, Métis, and Chinese cultures cited in Laurence's novels: "an involuntary group of people who share the same culture or . . . descendants of such people who identify themselves and/or are identified by others as belonging to the same involuntary group" (24). *Ethnicity and Ethnic Relations in Canada: A Book of Readings.* Eds. Jay E. Goldstein and Rita M. Bienvenue. Toronto:

Butterworths, 1980.

3. It is interesting that Canadian native writer and critic, Thomas King, resists the term "postcolonial" as it is applied to contemporary native literature: "Yet I cannot let post-colonial stand—particularly as a term—for, at its heart, it is an act of imagination and an act of imperialism that demands that I imagine myself as something I did not choose to be, as something I would not choose to become" (16). "Godzilla vs. Post-Colonial," *World Literature Written in English* 30, ii (1990) 10-16.

4. In "Ivory Tower or Grassroots," Laurence comments on "the tendency of women to accept male definition of ourselves" (24). Hagar's perpetuation of Jason Currie's proud and inflexible nature seems to embody this phenomenon.

5. Rachel Cameron's sister Stacey, the protagonist of *The Fire Dwellers*, breaks away from the domineering nature of her mother's home by moving to Vancouver. The fragmented narrative structure of this novel reinforces the character's disruptive existence and demonstrates a more radical reaction to the cultural and psychological hegemony of the parental environment.

6. Kenneth James Hughes argues in "Politics and *A Jest of God* that Mrs. Cameron represents the imperial power of the mother country, while Rachel symbolizes Canada trying to shed its colonial past. *Journal of Canadian Studies* 13, iii (Fall 1978) 50.

7. "The term carries with it centuries of suspicion and opprobrium. Athough both Plato and Xenophon employed the noun *to* [the] *ethnos* to mean caste or tribe, it acquired its moral sense in the New Testament where the plural was used to translate the Hebrew *goyim*: to be ethnic was to be heathen, foreign, that is, anything not Jewish or Christian." (86) *Configurations: Essays in the Canadian Literatures.* Downsview: ECW Press, 1982.

8. "The trickster is one of the most widespread mythological figures in North America. On the Pacific coast in British Columbia he is known as Raven; on the plains he is Old Man; among the Ojibway he is called Nanbozho; among the Micmacs of Nova Scotia he is called Glooscap; the Cree and Saulteaux call him Wisakedjak; among the Tagish he is known as Crow. Across the country he is also known as Mink, coyote, Bluejay, and Badger. . . . In his trickster role he behaves in a most anti-social manner, systematically violating all accepted human values, and relies on cunning deceptions and mean tricks to reach his goals, which are usually food, or the possession of women." (16) Penny

Petrone, *Native Literature in Canada: From the Oral Tradition to the Present*. Toronto: Oxford University Press, 1990.

9. Earle Birney's subtitle for his poem "Can.Lit." reads "(or *them able leave her ever*)." This word play on "The Maple Leaf Forever" illustrates the postcolonial writer's attempt to undermine the authority of the colonial expression or written word. *An Anthology of Canadian Literature in English*. Revised and Abridged Edition. Eds. Brown et al. Toronto: Oxford University Press, 1990, 296.

10. In *The Empire Writes Back*, the authors describe an interesting process of oral and written expression in postcolonial texts: "although oral culture is by no means the universal model of postcolonial societies, the invasion of the ordered, cyclic, and 'paradigmatic' oral world by the unpredictable and 'syntagmatic' world of the written word stands as a useful model for the beginnings of postcolonial discourse. The seizing of the means of communication and the liberation of post-colonial writing by the appropriation of the written word become crucial features of the process of self-assertion and of the ability to reconstruct the world as an unfolding historical process" (82). Although I question the assignment of "unpredictable" to the written realm and "ordered" to the oral world of experience in the above commentary, I believe that Laurence shows how the appropriation of the written medium can advance the identity of postcolonial subjects (Christie, Morag, and Jules) in the text.

11. When Pique sings one of her songs to Morag, her mother asks for a copy of the words, which she in turn hands to Jules, who keeps the written text (446). The interrelationship between oral and written forms of expression is reaffirmed in this process of exchange.

12. "In a good deal of my fiction, and especially in *The Diviners*, the theme of dispossession is an important one. It is shown in Christie's tales of the Highland Scots, turned off their lands during the Clearances, and in the recurrence throughout my Canadian fiction of the Tonnerre family, descendents of the Métis, who were once the prairie horselords and who gradually were dispossessed of the lands which they and their Indian brothers had lived on . . . Ivory Tower."

13. London is identified as "a centre of writing" (331) during Morag's visit to England.

14. New draws on James N. Porter's sense of the "discriminator" as an individual within a defined organization of social practices. (James N. Porter, "On Multiculturalism as a Limit of Canadian Life," in Hédi Bouraoui, ed., *The Canadian Alternative*, ECW Press, 1980, 76.)

WORKS CITED

Adam, Ian and Helen Tiffin, eds. *Past the Last Post: Theorizing Post-Colonialism and Post-Modernism.* Calgary: University of Calgary Press, 1990, 167-189.

Ashcroft, Bill and Gareth Griffiths, Helen Tiffin, eds. *The Empire Writes Back: Theory and Practice in Post-Colonial Literatures.* London, New York: Routledge, 1989.

Birney, Earle. "Can.Lit." *An Anthology of Canadian Literature in English.* Revised and Abridged Edition. Brown et al. eds. Toronto: Oxford University Press, 1990, 296.

Blodgett, E.D. *Configurations: Essays in the Canadian Literatures.* Downsview: ECW Press, 1982.

Fabre, Michel. "From *The Stone Angel* to *The Diviners*: An Interview with Margaret Laurence." *A Place to Stand On: Essays by and about Margaret Laurence.* George Woodcock, ed. Edmonton: NeWest Press, 1983, 193-209.

Goldstein, Jay E. and Rita M. Bienvenue, eds. *Ethnicity and Ethnic Relations in Canada: A Book of Readings.* Toronto: Butterworths, 1980.

Hughes, Kenneth James. "Politics and *A Jest of God." Journal of Canadian Studies* 13, iii (Fall 1978), 40-54.

Hutcheon, Linda. "'Circling the Downspout of Empire.'" *Past the Last Post: Theorizing Post-Colonialism and Post-Modernism.* Ian Adam and Helen Tiffin, eds. Calgary: University of Calgary Press, 1990, 167-189.

————. *The Canadian Postmodern: A Study of Contemporary English-Canadian Fiction.* Toronto, New York, Oxford: Oxford University Press, 1988.

King, Thomas. "Godzilla vs. Post-Colonial", *World Literature Written in English* 30, ii (1990), 10-16.

Laurence, Margaret. *The Stone Angel*. Toronto: New Canadian Library, 1968.

———. *A Jest of God*. Toronto: McClelland and Stewart/Seal, 1977.

———. *The Fire-Dwellers*. Toronto: New Canadian Library, 1973.

———. *The Diviners*. Toronto: New Canadian Library, 1974.

———. "Ivory Tower or Grassroots?: The Novelist as Socio-Political Being." *A Political Art: Essays in Honour of George Woodcock*. Ed. William H. New. Vancouver: University of British Columbia Press, 1970, 15-25.

New, W.H. "The Other and I: Laurence's African Stories." *A Place to Stand On: Essays by and about Margaret Laurence*. Ed. George Woodcock. Edmonton: NeWest Press, 1983. 113-134.

Petrone, Penny. *Native Literature in Canada: From the Oral Tradition to the Present*. Toronto: Oxford University Press, 1990.

Prasad, Madhava, "The 'other' worldliness of postcolonial discourse: a critique," *Critical Quarterly* 34, iii (Autumn 1992), 74-89.

Soyinka, Wole. "Neo-Tarzanism: the poetics of pseudo-tradition." *Transition* no. 48 (1975).

The Gaelic Middle Passage to Canada

In his description of a Cape Breton fishing village, Alistair MacLeod offers a concise history of Gaels coming to Canada.

The houses and their people, like those of the neighbouring towns and villages, were the result of Ireland's discontent and Scotland's Highland Clearances and America's War of Independence. Impulsive emotional Catholic Celts who could not bear to live with England and shrewd determined Protestant Puritans who, in the years after 1776, could not bear to live without. (108)

This history inscribes itself into the characters of these Gaels, which in turn alter the psychological landscape of Canada. The "discontent" of Ireland and the "Clearances" of Scotland resulted from centuries of invasion, alienation, forced removal, and famine that brought to Canada emigrants determined to make a prosperous and egalitarian New World. Highland Scots, both Protestant and Catholic, suffered double exile. Having fled the Hanoverian monarchs after the battle at Culloden in 1746, Highlanders settled the American colonies, particularly North Carolina, where in 1776 their ironic loyalty to this Hanoverian monarchy forced them into exile once again. In moving to those colonies which remained loyal to the Hanoverians and which later became Canada, these Gaelic-speaking Loyalist exiles figured as a very early factor in the forming of a Canadian identity separate from the identity of Canada's southern neighbor.

In trying to find a Canadian literature distinct from American and British traditions, many scholars have rediscovered Canadian literature as a rich aggregate of many voices and languages. This redefinition provokes us to reinterpret literary history through a vision that not only credits marginalized literary traditions, but acknowledges the existence of cultural identities supposedly erased by past colonial policies. Attempting such a revision, Canadian scholarship should not begrudge the leadership of Caribbean postcolonial writers who provide the metaphor of Middle Passage. Traditional scholarship recognizes formal cultural entity only through institutions such as languages, churches, schools, libraries, and publications. However, many groups came to the New World robbed of their primary languages, penalized for religious difference, prohibited from education, and very often denied access to literacy. The Middle Passage metaphor seeks to identify distinct culture by using qualifiers unrecognized by colonial thinking.

Partly fusing the Christian baptism myth of death and rebirth with African concepts of extended life and extended community, the Middle Passage metaphor records both cultural destruction and regeneration. The metaphor contains the horror of Africans crowded in the dark, shifting holds of slave ships bound for the New World. Since slave merchants made it a practice to mix the language groups of their cargo, African exiles could not speak with each other, and because of these language barriers, the exiles had little chance to communicate some comprehension of their experience. This breakdown of context and community created a very literal collapse of reality. However, the Middle Passage metaphor moves beyond this Katabasis and Dromena of experience to celebrate the energy and ingenuity with which African-Caribbeans re-invented contextual links and reassembled a distinct New World culture. The African-Caribbean culture continues to gain vitality in spite of past colonial policies and in resistance to present colonizing powers. The Middle Passage metaphor implies that cultures have relentless energies that ceaselessly change. Colonial policies may deflect or alter such energy, but they cannot arrest it entirely. If necessary, the cultural energy will flow into alien and even hostile languages and religions to translate these modes of expression back into a cultural self-possession.

Donald MacKay, in *Flight from Famine: the Coming of the Irish to Canada*, points out that on the eve of Confederation the Irish accounted for a quarter of the population of Canada (14). In the nineteenth century, Highland Scots established numerous Gaelic speaking communities from Glengarry County, Ontario, to Codroy Valley, Newfoundland. These Scots and Irish dramatically helped in lending a Canadian identity not only to Prince Edward Island, Newfoundland, New Brunswick, Nova Scotia, and Cape Breton, but to the Western provinces and the northern territories. As the material pressures of the nineteenth and twentieth century forced Gaelic-Canadians to enter non-Gaelic educational and economic systems, we might well wonder what happened to the Gaelic cultural energy and imagination. If we redefine the Gaelic-Canadian identity through the Middle Passage metaphor, we may discover that the Gaelic identity has not declined but continues to grow and evolve to significantly distinguish and enrich Canada.

Like Africans, Gaels first came to the New World in the mid-seventeenth century in the holds of slave ships. Chiefly because of Cromwell's invasions into Scotland and Ireland, 50,000 Gaelic-speaking slaves were sent to Jamaica, Barbados, Virginia, Carolina, and Maryland. Many were sent as political prisoners, or prisoners of war, but as Cromwell's forces took possession of Irish lands they arrested all Gaels unable to prove financial independence. John Prendergast recognizes in Cromwell's four-year program to relocate unemployed Gaels, patterns of colonial exploitation and rationalization all too familiar to students of African-American slavery:

They (the administrators) had agents actively employed through Ireland, seizing women, orphans, and the destitute, to be transported to Barbadoes and the English Plantations in America. It was a measure beneficial they said to Ireland, which was thus relieved of a population that might trouble the Planters; it was a benefit to the people removed, who might thus be made English and Christians; and a great benefit to the West India sugar planters, who desired the men and boys for their bondmen, and the women and Irish girls in a country where they had only Maroon women and Negresses to solace them. (89)

Prendergast imagines that the liberties and authority of these agents to capture and ship any unemployed Gael must have created scenes in Ireland "every part like the slave hunts of Africa" (90).

Although Donald MacKay reports that in the early eighteenth century Scotland saw a "brisk, ill-concealed trade" of young kidnapped Scottish boys to be sold to American plantations (*Scotland Farewell* xv), the eighteenth century, overall, saw a gradual end to the Gaelic slave trade. Instead this century witnessed the failed attempts of Gaels to regain their independence in both Scotland and Ireland. With each suppressed rising, the Colonial power entrenched itself more deeply. Colonial policies of land reform encouraged a steady flow of emigration in the late eighteenth century. In the nineteenth century such policies led if not directly, at least indirectly, to severe poverty and widespread famine, which in turn unleashed a massive migration of Gaels to Canada and the United States.

Many of the late eighteenth-century emigrants came in community groups. Occasionally, a clan chieftain would relocate the entire clan. Charles Dunn mentions that in 1772 John MacDonald, laird of Glenaladale sold his Scottish estates, bought a vast tract of Prince Edward Island, and paid for 250 farmers of his clan to emigrate with him (13). Margaret MacDonnell, in *The Emigrant Experience: Songs of Highland Emigrants in North America*, records the songs of poets who came with Lord Selkirk in his clan-emigration of 1803 to Point Prim, Prince Edward Island.

However, with the dawn of the nineteenth century, emigrants came from a more desperate Old World situation. Often fleeing starvation at home, impoverished emigrants took passage in dangerously over-crowded, disease-infested holds. R.A. MacLean, in "The Scots-Hector's Cargo", says "The conditions on the emigrant ships carrying many of the Scots were sometimes more revolting than those used in the slave trade" (114). Donald MacKay records that despite the Passenger Act of 1803, "often more people were crammed into a ship than would have been allowed in a slave ship from Africa" (*Scotland Farewell* 101).

E. Catherine Press, in "The Irish—the Urban Ethnic", reports that in 1840, because of the epidemics starting on emigrant ships, a "Colonial Lands and Emigration Commission had been formed to curb the abuses of the emigrant trade" (103). However, this commission was overwhelmed when in 1846 the large-scale failure of the potato crops unleashed a tidal wave of Irish emigration. Imported from Virginia, the potato proved to be a nutritious staple that Gaelic peasants could easily grow on the poorest farmland, which was exactly the type of farmland most Gaels possessed following Cromwell's land re-distribution. *Phytophtora infestans*, the fungus that first made its appearance in Irish potato fields in 1845, killed the potato leaves and turned the potato into a black putrid mass of slime. The parasite had no effect on other crops, and shiploads of oats, wheat, barley, beef, pork and butter continued to leave the Irish ports. In 1846, *Phytophtora infestans* struck the potato fields of Ireland and Scotland in full force. It was with immense reluctance that the colonial government interfered with the natural progess of the resulting famine.

According to MacKay:
Between 800,000 and a million people—no one can be sure—died in those five terrifying years of "famine fever" and starvation. Another million fled across the Atlantic, 300,000 to British North America, where they arrived less like emigrants than like refugees from terrible disaster. Of these, up to 20,000 died in the worst year of all, 1847, on the ships, in the quarantine stations of Grosse Isle, Quebec, and Partridge Island, New Brunswick, or out in the towns and roads of Quebec and Ontario. (*Flight from Famine* 14)

With its very real horror of mass starvation, and its psychological disorientation of having to flee a land producing an abundance of food, no other Gaelic experience comes quite so close to sharing the meaning and power of the African-Caribbean Middle Passage.

In 1655 when England needed settlers for a newly captured Jamaica, Oliver Cromwell asked his son Lord Henry Cromwell for a thousand Irish girls to be sent to serve new planters as maids and concubines. Young Henry responded that:

There would be no difficulty, only that force must be used in taking them, and he suggested the addition of from 1,500 to 2,000 boys of from twelve to fourteen years of age. "We could well spare them," he adds, "and they might be of use to you; and who knows but it might be a means to make them English—I mean, Christians?" (Prendergast 92)

The transplantation with its strong encouragement to lose linguistic, religious, and cultural identity and to become "English and Christian", to the colonial mind, would ultimately benefit the Irish slave.

Although some of the justification of sending some of the Irish to New World slavery was to Anglicize and Protestantize them, the colonial powers often resisted attempts to do the same to the Irish firmly bound to work domestic plantations. In discussing the attempts of Robert Boyle to introduce a Gaelic Bible that might educate Catholics and encourage them to convert to Protestantism, Gilbert Foster notes that the Protestant planters resisted.

Explicitly they did NOT wish Boyle and his associates to do either of two things: first, to transform their Gaelic-speaking tenantry directly into English-speaking Protestants . . . in which case they would legally be obliged to afford the native Irish formal social equality and treat them as free fellow-citizens with effective rights in the field of politics . . . second, to see their tenantry more gradually transformed into articulate, literate Gaelic-speaking Roman Catholics with a conscious knowledge of their own rights. (26)

The seventeenth-century Gaelic slaves coming to the Caribbean endeavoured over generations to shed their "otherness". Because they had light skin and because their light-skinned masters began to fear being such a minority on islands steadily filling with African slaves, the Caribbean-Gaels won the privilege to abandon their native language, religion, and identity and be absorbed by the colonial culture, an option distinctly withheld from dark-skinned Africans.

While the emigrants coming to Canada did not suffer a complete breakdown of cultural identity through slavery, they did not to so great an extent gain colonial privileges afforded to light skin. The Old World "otherness" of the Gaels came into the Canadian colonial mentality fully intact. No other colonial Canadian expresses this "otherness" more vividly than Susanna Moodie on her 1832 landing at Grosse Isle, Quebec:

A crowd of many hundred Irish emigrants had been landed during the present and former day; and all this motley crew—men, women, and children, who were not confined by sickness to the sheds (which greatly resembled cattle-pens)—were employed in washing clothes, or spreading them out on the rocks and bushes to dry . . . . The confusion of Babel was among them. All talkers and no hearers—each shouting and yelling in his or her uncouth dialèct, and all accompanying their vociferations with violent and extraordinary gestures, quite incomprehensible to the uninitiated. We were literally stunned by the strife of tongues. I shrank, with feelings almost akin to fear, from the hard-featured, sun-burnt harpies, as they elbowed rudely past me.

I had heard and read much of savages, and have since seen, during my long residence in the bush, somewhat of uncivilised life; but the Indian is one of Nature's gentlemen—he never says or does a rude or vulgar thing. The vicious uneducated barbarians, who form the surplus of overpopulous European countries, are far behind the wild man in delicacy of feeling or natural courtesy. The people who covered the island appeared perfectly destitute of shame, or even of a sense of common decency. Many were almost naked, still more but partially clothed. We turned in disgust from the revolting scene. (20-21)

Even as Susanna Moodie suffered trauma in a new country filled with stoic, noble native savages and uncouth, filthy imported savages, a certain romantic infatuation of the Highland Celt took hold of the colonial imagination, creating a nature-sensitive, emotional hero not so far removed from Susanna Moodie's construction of the Indian as "Nature's gentleman". In 1760 James Macpherson published epic poetry of his invention taken by the higher literary communities of Europe to be actual translations of ancient Gaelic Ossian tales. As Malcolm Chapman points out, "Macpherson's Ossian was largely inauthentic with respect to any genuine Gaelic verse tradition, but it was the very voice of authority for the developing sentiments of Romanticism in Europe" (42). Macpherson's Ossian, Ernest Renan's feminine and irrational Celt, and Sir Walter Scott's Highland soldier-hero all fused together to create not only an identity for a literary Celt, but an identity imposed upon, and even, for good or bad, accepted by Gaels. As Dan MacInnes says, Romanticism "re-invented" the Gael.

As the people were stripped of their land, the minutiae of their folkish lives were earnestly chronicled, their mountains charted, fauna and flora assidously recorded. It was all so Victorian a task to re-define the Gael. ("Cut Flower" 22)

Colonial powers love to invent romantic characterizations of their conquered foes and to sentimentalize these. Alistair MacLeod, in the short story "The Boat," demonstrates that such Romantic mis-constructions of the Gael as "impulsive and emotional Catholic Celts" and "shrewd determined Protestant Puritans" (108) have crossed over into the Gaelic-Canadian's defintion of self.

Conventionally, we define the Gaels as people who speak Gaelic, but, because the Gaelic language seems headed for extinction in North America, such a definition proscribes the extinction of a cultural identity. The Middle Passage suggests that cultures can maintain identity even when conforming to the outward architecture of a colonial society. By analogy we may assume that Gaels can translate elements of their language into English. Colonial powers normally impose one dialect as a standard language and dismiss all other dialects as inferior forms of the standard. When subject peoples transform the colonizing language, the colonial powers dismiss this dialectic variation as a "degeneracy". However, poets and writers in particular recognize that even an imposed language contains an immense capacity for flexibility. A "degenerate" dialect may in fact discard colonial cultural fixes and invent translations of the subject culture. For this reason many writers see "dialect" as "language".

Literature, a level of language more subtle than dialect, suffers much the same colonial privileging as does dialect. In her introduction to *The Collected Poems of Alexander McLachlan*, E. Margaret Fulton half-apologizes for the quality of the poems: "Considering that these lines were probably penned during the period when McLachlan, axe in hand, was hacking down trees and clearing land in Perth County, the wonder is that they are as good as they are" (xiii). This statement attempts to navigate around attitudes that only well-educated and leisured people can create material sufficiently dense and erudite to be considered literature. Apparently people caught up in a struggle for livelihood and shaping their artistic expression in a form relatively accessible to the readers of their community can produce only ditties and stories belonging either to folklore or to pop culture.

The nineteenth-century Gaelic-Canadian did not share the belief that the poet and writer should, armed with education and leisure, invent new modes of thought and vision often unapproachable by most of society. The Gaelic poet was an interactive component of society, not an inventor, but a voice speaking the emotions and visions of all people in the community. The works of Alexander McLachlan, written in English even though McLachlan was uneducated by formal English standards, differ little in purpose from the Gaelic work of Nova Scotia's John MacLean. Bard MacLean may have been the only Canadian poet trained in the classic bardic tradition of Scotland's clan institutions. Both poets sought to be recorders of their communities' experiences and the seers who help renew their communities' vision of self and context.

This attitude continues to exist in Gaelic-identified English-speaking writers of modern Canada. Joyce Carol Oates says of Cape Breton fiction writer, Alistair MacLeod:

> If I were to name a single underlying motive for MacLeod's fiction, I would say that it is the urge to memorialize, the urge to sanctify. This is a sense both primitive and "modernist" that if one sets down the right words in the right, talismanic order, the purely finite and local is transcended and the voiceless is given a voice. Ballads that link the living with their Scottish ancestors are sung by wholly unself-conscious men and women. ("Afterword" 159)

Treasuring remnants of the Gaelic language, clinging to nineteenth-century romanticisms, and constantly divided by involvement with a new twentieth-century colonial culture, the Gaelic-Canadian navigates yet another Middle Passage into the twenty-first century. Of this passage Dan MacInnes says:

> Our dependence intensifies as we become marginal players in a national economy which in turn is adjusting to fluctuations in the American economy. As industry dies in Cape Breton, its indigenous

culture has been increasingly overtaken by the insidious persistence of American based popular culture. In all this some of us persist stubbornly in preferring a Celtic identity. ("Gaelic/Celtic Identity" 26)

In "The Road to Ranklin's Point", Alistair MacLeod's young, dying Cape Bretoner seeks an understanding and acceptance of death from his Gaelic grandmother. Alone on the night of this Grandmother's death the character explores his fear:

My twenty-six years are not enough and I would want to go farther and farther back through previous generations so that I might have more of what now seems so little. I would go back through the superstitions and the herbal remedies and the fatalistic war cries and the haunting violins and the cancer cures of cobwebs. Back through the knowledge of being and its end as understood through second sight and spectral visions and the intuitive dog and the sea bird's cry. I would go back to the priest with the magic hands. Back to the faith healer if only I had more faith. Back to anything rather than to die at the objective hands of mute, cold science. (153)

The Gaels in the New World will continue, as they have for three hundred and fifty years, to die, to stubbornly resist, and to prosper on the alien soils changing and growing as a people into generations of poets and writers yet to come.

University of New Brunswick   **Seamus Ceallaigh**

WORKS CITED

Chapman, Malcolm. *The Gaelic Vision in Scottish Culture.* Montreal: McGill-Queen's University Press, 1978.

Dunn, Charles W. *Highland Settler: A Portrait of the Scottish Gaelic in Cape Breton and Eastern Nova Scotia.* Wreck Cove, Cape Breton Island: Breton Books, 1991.

Foster, Gilbert. *Language and Poverty: the Persistence of Scottish Gaelic in Eastern Canada.* St. John's NFD: Institute of Social and Economic Research, 1988.

Fulton, E. Margaret. "Introduction". *The Poetical Works of Alexander McLachlan*. Toronto : University of Toronto Press, 1974.

MacInnes, Dan. "The Living Culture or the Cut Flower". *The Clansman*. 6:4 (August/September 1992), 7, 22.

————. "Series to Explore Gaelic/Celtic Identity". *The Clansman*. 6:3 (June/July 1992), 7, 26.

MacKay, Donald. *Flight from Famine: The Coming of the Irish to Canada*. Toronto: McClelland and Stewart, 1990.

————. *Scotland Farewell: The People of the Hector*. Toronto: McGraw-Hill Ryerson, 1980.

MacLean, R.A. "The Scots-Hector's Cargo." *Banked Fires: The Ethnics of Nova Scotia*. Edited by Douglas Campbell. Port Credit, ON: Scribblers' Press, 1978, 113-140.

MacLeod, Alistair. *The Lost Salt Gift of Blood*. Toronto: McClelland and Stewart, 1989.

Moodie, Susanna Strickland. *Roughing It in the Bush or Life in Canada*. Ed. Carl Ballstadt. Ottawa: Carleton University Press, 1988.

Oates, Joyce Carol. "Afterword." *The Lost Salt Gift of Blood*, Alistair MacLeod. Toronto: McClelland and Stewart, 1989, 157-160.

Prendergast, John Patrick. *The Cromwellian Settlement of Ireland*. Dublin: Mellifont Press, 1922.

Press, Catherine E. "The Irish—The Urban Ethnic." *Banked Fires: The Ethnics of Nova Scotia*. Edited by Douglas Campbell. Port Credit, ON: Scribblers' Press, 1978, 93-112.

Towards a Conservative Modernity: Cultural Nationalism in Contemporary Acadian and Africadian Poetry

The critique of modernity offered by conservative Canadian philosopher George Grant must be considered by those who would conserve a nationalist or regionalist poetic. If modernity (read by Grant as the cosmopolitan liberalism of international capitalism) dissolves nationalism and regional cultures, then the embracing of modern/post-modern poetics by poets who issue from such cultures is imperilled. Indeed, the poets of Acadia and of Nova Scotia's communities settled by Black Loyalists and Black Refugees (an ethnocultural archipelago which I will henceforth term "Africadia") confront modernity without even the buffer of a state to call their own (though Acadians in Nouveau-Brunswick wield some political power). Interestingly, the challenges posed by modernity to the expression—and even the very notion of the expression—of the local and the particular are foregrounded in two recent anthologies arising from the contemporary efflorescence of both Acadian and Africadian cultural nationalism and poetry. *Rêves inachevés: anthologie de poésie acadienne contemporaine* (1990), edited by Fred Cogswell and Jo-Ann Elder, and *Fire on the Water: An Anthology of Black Nova Scotian Writing* (1991-1992), edited by the author, present works produced during the current Acadian Renaissance and Black Cultural (or Africadian) Renaissance respectively. Though the Acadian confrontation with modernity has a longer literary history than its Africadian parallel, poets from both embattled minorities have attempted to conserve aspects of their particularities while simultaneously adopting and adapting an essentially liberal poetic.

The inherent difficulties of this project are foreseen in Grant's work. In *Lament for a Nation: The Defeat of Canadian Nationalism* (1965), Grant equates "progressive modernity" (63) with a homogenizing liberalism which, valuing technique more than tradition, erodes particularisms. Grant puts his case succinctly:

Modern civilisation makes all local cultures anachronistic. Where modern science has achieved its mastery, there is no place for local cultures. (LN 54)

Hence, English Canada, "a local culture", situated "next to a society [the United States] that is the heart of modernity", is fated to disappear as a nation (LN 54). In *Technology and Empire: Perspectives on North America* (1969), Grant comments on the impact of *la révolution tranquille* on the Québécois, noting that "their awakening to modernity, which seems to them an expression of independence, in fact leaves them wide open to conquest by a modernity which at its very heart is destructive of indigenous traditions" (TE 67). Grant's critique characterizes modernity as an imperialist, technologically driven, American creed. Hans Hauge suggests that, for Grant, "Americanization is another word for modernization" (65). This vision of modernity as a colonizing force, inimical to the sustained, independent existence of "local cultures", challenges not only the long-term viability of the politics of English Canada and Québec but also the regional, Maritime cultures—and poetries—of Acadia and Africadia.

If, as Grant states, "the choice between internationalism and nationalism is the same choice as that between liberalism and conservatism" (LN 86), Maritime poets have often opted for the latter and have thus incurred the concomitant obscurity and marginalization. Gwendolyn Davies makes this point in her recovery of the "Song Fishermen", a romantic, deliberately regionalist school of Nova Scotian poets of the late 1920s who rejected insurgent cosmopolitan modernism in favour of a local poetic, stressing the writing of traditional verse, including ballads and sea chanteys, and even the use of Gaelic (164). The conservative ethos of the Fishermen, whose members included Charles G.D. Roberts, Bliss Carman, and Charles Bruce, was articulated by the poet Andrew Merkel in 1929:

> . . . We are rather isolated down here in Nova Scotia. . . . The march of progress goes by us on the other side of the hill. . . . Let us not get too ambitious. Keep your eyes free from the glare of big cities and big reputations. Keep your mind free from the contemporary illusion which names every new thing a good thing, and turns its back on old things which have been proved in many thousand years of human blood and tears. (Quoted in Davies, 168)

For their fidelity to "old things", this antimodern group has been omitted—qua group—from most Canadian literary histories. Yet, the "Fishermen" did merely what regional tradition required, for, as Erik Kristiansen notes, "anti-modern attitudes are peppered throughout

Maritime literature" (26).

Given the relative discrimination that Maritime poets in general have suffered for their dissent from modernity or, perhaps, their dissenting modernity, it is somewhat disconcerting to open *Rêves* and, in his introductory essay entitled "Une poésie qui est un acte," witness Raoul Boudreau attack Eddy Boudreau, Napoléon Landry, and François-Moïse Lanteign—"les trois premiers poètes acadiens des années 50, dont la poésie ou religieuse, ou patriotique, ou les deux reste conformiste par la forme et par le fond" (*Rêves* 8). Boudreau salvages a conservative poetic vision based on *"le pays"* conceived as an ecclesiastical community:

> Cette poésie propose une vision théocentrique du monde et elle présente l'Acadie et les Acadiens comme le peuple élu de Dieu qui, par son indéfectible attachement à sa foi catholique malgré ses souffrances et ses misères, doit servir d'exemple aux peuples de la terre. Elle incite le plus souvent à la prière et à l'action de grâce, jamais à la révolte. (*Rêves* 8)

In this modern conception, religious nationalism is retrograde: it fosters a regressive poetic in both form and content. Boudreau seems to endorse a liberalism that is, as Grant noted of that of 1960's Québécois youth, "openly anti-Catholic and even existentialist or Marxist" (LN 80). Boudreau ignores Grant's caution that "the old Church with its educational privileges has been the chief instrument by which an indigenous French culture has survived in North America" (LN 81).

Instead, Boudreau lauds such epic and epochal moments of the triumph of modernity as the founding of the Université de Moncton in 1963, an act which salvaged Acadia for the age of progress: "l'Acadie sort brusquement du folklore du 19e siècle pour découvrir d'un seul coup le marxisme, la lutte des classes, les rapports de force et la contestation étudiante" (*Rêves* 9). Sue Calhoun asserts that the establishment of the university, along with the election of Louis Robichaud, the first francophone premier of New Brunswick, resulted in the "secularization" of Acadia (7).

This "secularization" or, rather, liberalization/modernization also spawned a secular nationalism to replace the religious nationalism that had fallen from grace. This nationalism was one "of refusing to accept the status quo, though it wasn't consciously thought out at the time, nor is it well articulated even today" (Calhoun 9). For Boudreau, this nationalism is defensive: the Acadian poet has "une cause urgente à défendre, une culture à sauver du naufrage et à laquelle il s'identifie, et prendre la plume, c'est avant toute chose affirmer cela" (*Rêves* 12).

In *Unfinished Dreams: Contemporary Poetry of Acadie* (1990), the English version of *Rêves*, Boudreau quotes Alain Masson on the peril which Acadian writers felt they faced (but have since learned to overcome):

The truth is that there is a cruel dissymmetry: on one side, there is New Brunswick, administrative subdivision of a cultural empire of which the capitals are New York and Hollywood; on the other side, there is a small nation whose *survival is threatened by this empire*, but who has learned how to give itself a cultural life all its own. (Quoted in *Dreams* xxi) (Author's italics)

This 1986 note of cautious success is complemented by Masson's 1974 comment, quoted by Boudreau in *Rêves*, declaring the liberty of Acadian writers from any literary heritage: "Il n'existe pas de patrimoine littéraire en Acadie; la littérature est un projet. Paradoxalement, l'écrivain acadien se trouve ainsi placé de plein-pied [sic] avec l'universalité" (15). Both comments represent the troubled triumph of secular nationalism: the Acadian writer has learned how to defend his/her identity amid what the Québec nationalist Henri Bourassa termed "cette mer immense de l'américanisme saxonisant"; and, he/she is free to invent his/her literature at will within the empire of "l'universalité". Naturally, the two positions are contradictory: Masson would bake his cake as a literary universalist— disregarding the Acadian poetic tradition, but he would sell it as an Acadian nationalist.

Masson would have at least one customer however—M. Boudreau, who would slice off the plain, nationalist icing to consume the cosmopolitan content and savour the international flavour. Indeed, Boudreau condemns the nostalgia of some contemporary Acadian poets for the secular nationalism of the early 1970s—the first phase of the Acadian Renaissance—as a kind of modern folklore: "pour beaucoup de lecteurs, à l'intérieur et à l'extérieur, l'image de l'Acadien pleurnichant est rassurante, et l'"exotisme est si rentable littérairement" (*Rêves* 16). In the post-modern present, Acadian poetry, liberated from nationalist yearning, is "En phase avec les courants mondiaux de la littérature" (*Rêves* 18). In the brave, new Acadie, "L'Acadien joue de sa francité pour résister à l'Amérique et il joue de son américanité pour résister à l'hégéomonie de la culture française" (*Rêves* 18). Boudreau continues on to note, with complete aplomb, "Certes, cela ne va pas sans risques dont l'avenir nous dira l'ampleur" (18-19). Freedom is the watchword of the day:

> Ignorant presque tout de la métrique du vers français dont ils ne se préoccupent guère, les poètes acadiens bouleversent, parfois même inconsciemment, les règles de leur art. En ce qui concerne la langue, ils se donnent la liberté d'écrire, à un moment ou l'autre, en bon français, en mauvais français, en chiac ou même en anglais. (*Rêves* 15)

With this comment, the conservative poetic tradition of Acadie seems buried for good: the Acadian poet, liberated from the past and from any need to fear assimilation, is free to write as he/she pleases— *même en anglais*!

Such de facto assimilationism would be the logical result of Masson's and Boudreau's flirtation with a variant of Quebec's then-opposition leader Robert Bourassa's 1969 programme, "American technology, French culture," which seeks to combine a liberal belief in technique with a conservative idea of culture (LN ix). Ultimately, Grant suggests, one cannot have it both ways: the conservative desire to maintain particularity must surrender before the will to technical and individual liberty.

However, Boudreau perpetuates the attempt to fuse these two notions warring within the bosom of a single poetic. Despite his liberal characterization of Acadian literature as "une contre littérature inventant un nouveau code auquel il serait vain d'appliquer des critères anciens" (*Rêves* 19), he reverts to a conservative, almost religious nationalism to assert the importance of the literature: "aucune autre n'a eu un tel impact sur le tissu même de la conscience collective d'un peuple; aucune autre n'a été chargée d'une telle responsabilité; aucune autre n'a joui d'une telle liberté dans l'élaboration d'un projet littéraire qui se confondait avec un projet d'existence" (*Rêves* 20).

Within only a few pages of castigating some poets for bemoaning a lost nationalism, Boudreau himself emerges as a nationalist. His split consciousness is an apt metaphor, as we will see, for contemporary Acadian poetry.

Africadian poets have also attempted to articulate their particularity in the face of modernity. Descended from the ranks of the 3,000 Black Loyalists who came to Nova Scotia in 1783 to escape the slavery-sanctioning, fledgling United States, they share with Acadian poets a literary tradition which has its genesis in a conservative religious nationalism. James Walker states that the Black Loyalists developed a sense of themselves as the "elect" of God:

As they regarded the more formalised white churches which had segregated them, they noticed that God did not seem to speak to those older churches in quite the same way as he did to them, the blacks. Inevitably, this produced a feeling of being close to God, of being, in fact, a chosen people, an elite group of Christians whom God regularly visited and whose role it was to preserve the truth of the moment of salvation. (78)

This religious nationalism was consolidated in 1854 with the birth of the African Baptist Association (ABA), a separate association of Africadian Baptist churches. The wish to maintain this symbol of particularity was so strong, notes Frank Boyd, that when, in 1895, a motion was discussed to dissolve the ABA and to join the white Maritime Baptist Convention, the motion was soundly defeated: "African Baptists wanted to maintain their identity through continued separatism" (Boyd v). If Acadia, a particularity defined by language (and religion), is, as the back cover blurb of *Unfinished Dreams* insists, "a country which exists in the imagination and words of its people," Africadia—a particularity defined by race and religion—is a community of believers: "For the black Nova Scotians the Promised Land became a realm of the spirit, a place where they could be themselves and find their own destiny. . . ." (Walker 396).

Like pre-modern Acadian literature, pre-modern Africadian literature reflected the Church, an institution which, writes Robin Winks, was dominated by a few families, thus creating "an aristocracy of the faith, and often [holding] the church to more than ordinarily frozen and conservative theological and social positions" (346). Interestingly, a similar conservative nationalism dominated pre-modern Acadie (Calhoun 7). Moreover, just as Acadie and its poets converted to modernity, so did Africadia and its poets. However, the advent of modernity for Africadia was marked, not by the founding of a university or the election of a premier, but by the bulldozers of "progress" destroying the Seaview African United Baptist Church and the entire community of Africville (an Africadian village on the outskirts of Nova Scotia's capital, Halifax) at the end of the 1960s in the name of integration and urban development. The failure of the ABA to protect 150-year-old Africville and its church fostered a defensive, apparently secular nationalism. Indeed, Donald Clairmont notes that "Africville has become central in the new black consciousness in Nova Scotia" (74). As a result of the Africville debacle and the establishment of new, secular organizations, modernity has come to Africadia. Literature has left the Church, the ABA, and taken to the streets. J.A. Mannette characterizes contemporary Africadian writers thus:

. . . they are part of the indigenous Black Nova Scotian middle class. They are educated; most have, or are seeking, postsecondary academic training. They took advantage of the spaces provided by a conjuncture of historical forces in the 1960s and 1970s which propelled some black people into upward mobility. . . . They tend to live in the Halifax metro area. They are self-consciously black. (4)

Africadian poets have helped in particular to create the current Black Cultural Renaissance. Along with other Africadian artists, they "delineate black initiatives and black decisions on how to live black in a white society" (Mannette 3). If art is a cry for identity, then "black artists are publicly expressing Nova Scotian blackness in a black voice" (Mannette 8).

The inscription of this identity is accompanied by an explicitly anti-modern stance which recalls the conservatism of the "Song Fishermen" without, however, mimicking the group's formalism. For instance, in "Epitaph," Africadian poet David Woods describes a black traitor as "a modern type" (Fire II 145). Hence, though Africadians share the same tongue as the "American empire," they continue to explore a dissenting modernity. This critique arises from a conservatism that persists in the culture, which is essentially African-American. According to Boyd, "there are a number of continuities between Afro-Nova Scotians and Afro-Americans, South and North, especially in their religious and social organizations: the African Baptist churches which Afro-Nova Scotians established are denominationally typical of the South, from which regions Afro-Nova Scotians derived. . . ." (Boyd xxiv). The African-American church tradition emphasizes, writes Charles P. Henry, "faith, collectivism, suffering, and authoritarianism. . . ." (62). Hence, it opposes the liberal ideal of "possessive individualism" (Henry 107).

This African-American (and Africadian) vision resembles Grant's recollection of an English-Canadian nationalism that, based upon British conservatism, "expressed itself in the use of public control in the political and economic spheres" (LN 71). In fact, "Canadians have been much more willing than Americans to use governmental control over economic life to protect the public good against private freedom" (LN 71). African-American theologian Cornel West echoes Grant when he states that "the modern world has been primarily about the power of big business, about the expansive possibilities of science and technology" (45). Finally, West's dream of a Black nationalism that would stress "[p]reservation of Black cultural integrity, acknowledgement of Black cultural distinctiveness" (47) mirrors Grant's memory of traditional, English-Canadian nationalism.

This implicit alliance between Canadian red toryism and African-American socialism validates the notion that "group identification can serve as a basis for radical as well as conservative political consciousness" (Henry 15). Group identification and a politic rooted, like that of African-America, in a "black church tradition that blends sacred and secular vision" (Henry 107), certainly animates Africadian poets.

If there is a difference between Acadian and Africadian poetry, perhaps it lies in the relative hesitancy—thus far—of the latter to repudiate religion as the opiate of the poets. But, then again, perhaps Boudreau was too hasty to proclaim the victory of a post-nationalist, post-religious poetic, while I have been too hasty to assert the triumph of a nationalist, quasi-religious poetic for Africadians. It is time to compare a few, representative poems.

Boudreau describes Acadian poet Herménégilde Chiasson as a "poète fondateur de la poésie acadienne moderne" (*Rêves* 11). Along with his fellow, nationalist poets of the early 1970s—Raymond LeBlanc and Guy Arsenault—Chiasson created work that is "à coup sûr un acte et un événement" (*Rêves* 12). "Rouge," one of his most striking poems, is a lyrical nationalist plaint:

Acadie, mon trop bel amour violé, toi que je ne prendrais jamais dans les draps blancs, les draps que tu as déchirés pour t'en faire des drapeaux blancs comme des champs de neige que tu as vendus comme tes vieux poteaux de clôtures . . . tes vieilles chimères, blancs comme une vieille robe de mariée dans un vieux coffre de cèdre. Acadie, mon trop bel amour violé qui parle à crédit pour dire des choses qu'il faut payer comptant, qui emprunte ses privilèges en croyant gagner ses droits . . . .

Arrache ta robe bleue, mets-toi des étoiles rouge sur les seins, enfonce-toi dans la mer, la mer rouge qui va s'ouvrir comme pour la fuite en Egypte; la mer nous appartient, c'est vrai, toute la mer nous appartient parce que nous ne pouvons pas la vendre, parce que personne ne peut l'acheter. (*Rêves* 50-51)

Chiasson cries for his beloved country in the tones of a betrayed lover. Though his nationalism arises from secularization, the process by which a nation sells its soul to market forces, Chiasson laments this reality. One hears in "Rouge" the moan of Grant's melancholy: "We find ourselves like fish left on the shores of a drying lake. The element necessary to our existence has passed away" (LN 4). M. Darrol Bryant casts Grant's *Lament* as a "meditation", a "religious form which is . . . reflective and reflexive" (Bryant 112). Hence, "Rouge" can also be considered, in Bryant's term, a "meditative-lament" (118). Thus, Chiasson's poem, despite its modern appearance, recapitulates a classical, religious form to lament—like Jeremiah—national immorality which endangers the existence of the nation.

Chiasson's "Eugénie Melanson" also falls into the category of a religious lament. His comparison of her with Evangéline (the heroine of Henry W. Longfellow's sentimental epic, *Evangéline* (1847), on the expulsion of the Acadians in 1755) echoes the tone of the writer of *Lamentations*:

Tu étais la plus belle, pourtant
Quand tu te déguisais en Evangéline pour pouvoir
recréer avec des Gabriels de parade les dates mémorables d'un passé
sans gloire, englouti dans les rêves et les poèmes d'antan
que tu n'avais jamais lus. (*Rêves* 47)

Chiasson concludes his long poem on an aptly bitter note:

Tu t'endormis
Tu t'endormis en rêvant
Tu t'endormis en rêvant à de nouvelles déportations. (*Rêves* 49)

Lamentations sounds a similarly caustic impression of Jerusalem:

How doth the city sit solitary, that was full of people! how is she become a widow! she that was great among the nations, and princess among the provinces, how is she become tributary. (Jer. 1:1)

Despite his best intentions perhaps, a religious, biblical rhetoric infuses the poetry of Chiasson.

In contrast, Frederick Ward seeks to cheer Africadians to assert their right to be, and in his poem, "Dialogue #3 (Old Man to the Squatter)," to actually set about to rebuild the destroyed community of Africville. He posits a positive, hopeful nationalism:

. . . You' ain't 'a 'place. Africville is us. When we go to git a job, what they ask us? Where we from. . . and if we say we from Africville, we are Africville! And we don't git no job. It ain't no place, son. It was their purpose to git rid of us and you believed they done it—could do it! You think they destroyed something. They ain't. They took away the place. But it come'd round, though. Now that culture come'd round. They don't just go out there and find anybody to talk about Africville, they run find us, show us off—them that'll still talk, cause we Africville. NOT-NOT-SHACK-ON-NO-KNOLL. That ain't the purpose . . . fer whilst your edifice is foregone destroyed, its splinters will cry out: We still here! Think on it, son. . . . Now go back . . . and put your dwelling up again. (Author's italics) (Fire II 19-20).

Nevertheless, this vision is also conservative. Like Grant, Ward seems to reject a modern liberalism that must "undermine all particularisms" (TE 69). His poem, published in 1983, anticipates the current re-visioning of the destruction and then eulogizing of Africville "as an indictment against racism, as a critique of technocratic, imposed approaches to social change, and as a celebration of community and the human spirit" (Clairmont 74).

Ward's poem is conservative—not just in content, but in form. Though it seems modernist, it arguably conserves the form of two traditional elements of African-American culture—"the Black Christian tradition of preaching and the Black musical tradition of performance" (West 136). Ward does not share Boudreau's suspicion of the folkloric, but rather integrates the particular tongue of Africadians (Black English) with standard English to create this preaching-performance. His poem conserves the African-American and Africadian sermonic tradition. Thus, the influence of the Church continues to be felt in Africadian literature despite the collision with modernity.

Another example of the persistence of an informal religiosity occurs in Africadian poet Maxine Tynes's frankly nationalist poem, "The Profile of Africa": "we wear our skin like a flag / we share our colour like a blanket (*Fire* II 74). Likewise, the aggressively modern verse of Acadian poet Dyane Léger, particularly her long poem "Lesbiennes latentes" (*Rêves* 163-169), cannot avoid traces of religious imagery and the expression of love in tones and rhythms that probably refer/defer to a sermonic tradition: "Il n'est pas intéressé à lire une description du mort et encore moins par une description de fleurs, de pleurs et de prières; il veut vivre tes émotions fortes, tes états d'âme!" (*Rêves* 167).

A particularly radical view of the African-American (and I would add Africadian) practice of literary modernism would transfigure it into a conservative and nationalist instrument. Houston A. Baker defines African-American modernism as "renaissancism," that is, "a spirit of nationalistic engagement" (91). This nationalist modernism seeks to effect a blend "of class and mass" (Baker 93), that is, to integrate the Black oral and folk tradition with modern literary practice: "Our modernity consists, finally, not in tumbling towers or bursts in the violet air, but in a sounding renaissancism where a blues (i.e. folk or popular or communal) reason may yet prevail. . . " (106). Though Baker's nationalist modernity seems innovative, Boudreau unconsciously posits a like view in his essay.

Raymond Guy LeBlanc is a poet who seems to represent a kind of Acadian "renaissancism." His "Je suis acadien" enacts the same kind of fusion of folk/vernacular (in this case, chiac) and literary elements that Ward achieves:

> Je jure en anglais tous mes goddams de bâtard
> Et souvent les fuck it me remontent à la gorge
> Avec des Jésus Christ projetés contre le windshield
> Saignant medium-rare
>] . . . [
> Je suis acadien
> Ce qui signifie
> Multiplié fourré dispersé acheté aliéné vendu révolté
> Homme déchiré vers l'avenir (*Rêves* 144-145)

Moreover, LeBlanc's seemingly secular nationalism encodes, again, a lament. And his poem revels in the folkloric, thus becoming a "blues".

In her discussion of Québec novelist Hubert Aquin's *Trou de mémoire* (1968), Sylvia Soderlind asserts that Aquin uses "a vernacular full of anglicisms and colloquialisms to emphasize the homelessness or non-territoriality of the (standard) French language in Québec" (92-93). Her belief that Aquin's *joual* performs "a phatic, territorial function" (93) can be applied to the chiac employed by LeBlanc. This point stresses the vindication of the folkloric that Baker's concept of "renaissancism" demands. Furthermore, such inscribing of the vernacular would seem to represent a conservative defence of "local culture". Hence, the interest of Baker and LeBlanc in defining a populist modernism mirrors the early efforts of the "Song Fishermen" to construct a regional poetic. Furthermore, if LeBlanc's radicalism is, like that of Aquin, "religious and aesthetic before it is political" (Soderlind 107), it hints that a nationalist poetic must always return, even if chorused by curses, to the precincts of faith.

Africadian poet George Borden sounds an irreligiosity that echoes LeBlanc. His long poem, "To My Children I Bequeath," treats Africadian history as a catalogue of oppressions and deprivations:

> To my children
> I bequeath:
> my Baptist religion—
> for which I had no choice
> but received it second-hand
> from those who ruled my life.
>]...[
> To my children
> I bequeath:
> my tar-paper mansion . . .
> my over-crowded bedroom . . .
> my hand-me-down wardrobe . . .
> my probation officer . . .
> my high-blood pressure . . .
> my hate . . .
> my anguish . . .
> my despair . . . (*Fire* I 166)

Like LeBlanc, Borden expresses a secular nationalism that shades into the blues, the spiritual of the dispossessed. The title of his book of poems, *Canaan Odyssey* (1988), suggests that, like LeBlanc in *Cri de terre* (1986), he seeks to articulate the experience of a particularity.

As it turns out, the poets of both Africadia and Acadie have pursued an essentially similar poetic. Thus, even seemingly secular

Africadian and Acadian poets write in styles that mimic Church traditions. Moreover, though Boudreau has argued for the internationalism of contemporary Acadian poetry, the poets themselves have continued to speak from a sense of their particularity. And Boudreau has had to articulate a nationalist ethos in order to insist upon the specificity of Acadian poetry. Indeed, the poets of both cultures, despite their embrace of liberal modernity, continue to espouse conservative nationalism. They attempt to nationalize modernity, to conservatize liberalism, to convert secularism, in order to make it possible for themselves to speak, to articulate their nations, to preserve some aspect of the local within the universal, the provincial within the cosmopolitan. Hence, the cryptically religious nationalism of Ward and Chiasson and the deceptively secular nationalism of Borden and LeBlanc both require an ultimately conservative poetic, despite the seemingly liberal, that is, non-traditional, forms of their poems. It might appear, then, that Grant's thesis has been disproved.

However, Grant insists upon the "impossibility of conservatism in our era" (LN 69). Because "science produces such a dynamic society, it is impossible to conserve anything for very long" (LN 67). Hence, those who seek to act conservatively, that is nationalistically, tend to "harness the nationalist spirit to technological planning" (LN 45); in poetic terms, they express their nationalism through modern technique, believing all others to be outmoded. Yet, the issue of whether Africadian and Acadian poets will be able to sustain their particularisms beyond the present will depend, ultimately, upon their abilities to conserve their respective religious and folk traditions.

University of Queen's   George Elliott Clarke

WORKS CITED

Baker, Houston A., Jr. *Modernism and the Harlem Renaissance.* Chicago and London: University of Chicago Press, 1987.

Boudreau, Raoul. Introduction. *Rêves inachevés: Anthologie de poésie acadienne contemporaine.* Eds. Fred Cogswell and Jo-Ann. Elder. Moncton: Les Éditions d'Acadie, 1990.

———. Introduction. *Unfinished Dreams: Contemporary Poetry of*

Acadie. Eds. Fred Cogswell and Jo-Ann Elder. Fredericton: Goose Lane Editions, 1990.

Bourassa, Henri. *La langue, la gardienne de la foi.* Montréal: L'Action française, 1918.

Boyd, Frank Stanley, Jr., ed. *A Brief History of the Coloured Baptists of Nova Scotia and Their First Organization as Churches, A.D. 1832.* By Peter E. McKerrow. 1895. Halifax: Afro-Nova Scotian Enterprises, 1976.

Bryant, M. Darrol. "The Barren Twilight: History and Faith in Grant's Lament." *George Grant in Process: Essays and Conversations.* Ed. Larry Schmidt. Toronto: Anansi, 1978, 110-119

Calhoun, Sue. "Acadia Rising: the MFU and the New Nationalism." *New Maritimes.* January/February, 1992: 6-13.

Clairmont, Douglas. "Moving People: Relocation and Urban Renewal." *The Spirit of Africville.* Ed. The Africville Genealogical Society. Halifax: Maritext-Formac Publishing Company Limited, 1992. 53-76.

Clarke, George Elliott, ed. *Fire on the Water: An Anthology of Black Nova Scotian Writing.* 2 vols. Lawrencetown Beach, N.S.: Pottersfield Press, 1991-1992.

Cogswell, Fred, and Jo-Ann Elder, eds. *Rêves inachevés: Anthologie de poésie acadienne contemporaine.* Moncton: Les Éditions d'Acadie, 1990.
————. *Unfinished Dreams: Contemporary Poetry of Acadie.* Fredericton: Goose Lane Editions,1990.

Davies, Gwendolyn. *Studies in Maritime Literary History, 1760-1930.* Fredericton: Acadiensis Press, 1991.

Grant, George. *Lament for a Nation:The Defeat of Canadian Nationalism. 1965.* Toronto and Montreal: McClelland and Stewart Limited, 1970.

————. *Technology and Empire: Perspectives on North America.* Toronto: House of Anansi, 1969.

Hauge, Hans. "George Grant's Critique of Frye." *Essays in Canadian Literature.*Eds. Jorn Carlsen and Bengt Streiffert. Lund, Sweden: The Nordic Association for Canadian Studies, 1987, 61-70.

Henry, Charles P. *Culture and African American Politics.* Bloomington and Indianapolis: Indiana University Press, 1990.

Hooks, Bell, and Cornel West. *Breaking Bread: Insurgent Black Intellectual Life.* Toronto: Between the Lines Press, 1991.

Kristiansen, Erik. "Time, Memory, and Rural Transformation." *New Maritimes.* March/April 1990. 22-27.

Mannette, J. A. "'Revelation, Revolution, or Both': Black Art as Cultural Politics." Lecture. *400 Years: African Canadian History.* Toronto, June 1990, 3-8.

Soderlind, Sylvia. *Margin/Alias: Language and Colonization in Canadian and Quebecois Fiction.* Toronto: University of Toronto Press, 1991.

Walker, James W. St. George *The Black Loyalists: The Search for a Promised Land in Nova Scotia and Sierra Leone 1783-1870.* Halifax: Longman & Dalhousie University Press, 1976.

Winks, Robin W. *The Blacks in Canada.* New Haven, CT: Yale University Press, 1971.

Marie Laberge's Feminist Existentialism

A successful playwright, actress, and director, Marie Laberge enjoys a firmly established reputation in contemporary women's theatre in Quebec. She has recently published two novels, *Juillet* (1989) and *Quelques Adieux* (1992). Questions and crises centering around male/female relations form the thematic basis for most of Laberge's work, which is deeply inscribed in contemporary Québécois society. As she analyzes couples representing various age groups and social classes, it becomes clear that, in her work, mutually satisfying relationships between men and women are virtually non-existent; good sexual rapports are rare and short-lived. Overall, most of Laberge's characters lead unfulfilling lives because of their intense fear of risk or loss. Caught in a conflict between socially accepted behaviour and personal truth, they suppress their feelings in favour of appearances. Failing to come to terms with their deepest emotions, they are unable to experience true intimacy in authentic human relationships. As Laberge weighs the consequences of living in fear against the risks of facing the truth, a strong existentialist element emerges in her work. She consistently develops male characters who choose to escape the stress of existence rather than to create meaning for themselves. At the same time, Laberge depicts women who, relegated to the status of "Other," have little opportunity to exercise free will. In recent works, however, notably in *Aurélie ma soeur* (1988) and in *Juillet* (1989), Laberge creates female characters who engage in authentic living. These characters embrace their own freedom and encourage the freedom of others.

In *Avec l'hiver qui s'en vient* (1981), Laberge portrays an older couple, Maurice and Cécile Gingras, who have always done what was "correcte". As they approach the end of their life, they feel isolated, misunderstood, and unloved. Maurice, who recently retired, has become an invalid; he cannot speak, nor can he care for himself. Medical examinations fail to reveal any physical explanation for his illness. His condition appears to result from a negative reaction to his "nouvelle inutilité" (82). During his more productive years, Maurice denied his personal freedom as he fulfilled the role of hard-working husband and model father. Having based his life on preconceived notions, he now resembles Simone de Beauvoir's "serious man." As she states in *The Ethics of Ambiguity*, "if it happens that a failure or old age ruins all his justifications . . . he no longer has any relief except in flight . . . this important personage is now only a 'has-been' " (51). Maurice reacts by withdrawing into himself, behaving like a baby and abdicating all responsibility for his actions. As Simone de Beauvoir describes it, "Conscious of being unable to be anything, man then decides to be nothing" (52). Meanwhile, Cécile, who must care for Maurice, complains about her lot in life. Overwhelmed by her tedious chores, Cécile exclaims, "J'ai toffé toute ma vie!" (83). Her anger against her neighbour, who declares that Cécile's desire for freedom is "pas normal," and against the young doctor who insensitively equates her own difficult menopause with her husband's transition into retirement, escalates when she learns that Maurice, who never really spoke to her, touched her, loved her, or even saw her (99), was witty and collegial at work, and was even on very friendly terms with his secretary. When Cécile demands that Maurice communicate with her, he reverts mentally to his childhood; the play concludes with both characters virtually on the brink of insanity.

Laberge illuminates the societal pressures and economic constraints that limit the freedom of choice and "instruments of escape" (Beauvoir 48) available to her characters. At the same time, she portrays them as regretting their passivity and resignation; both Maurice and Cécile wish they had taken more initiative in creating for themselves a meaningful existence. Laberge dramatizes the deplorable consequences of their timid, cowardly approach to life. Although Laberge treats both characters sympathetically (both have been victims of a deep, all-pervading sense of Catholic guilt) her emphasis is on Cécile. It is Cécile who speaks out to express her anger and her pain at the indignity of her stifled existence. Through Cécile, Laberge criticizes the double standard that kept Cécile confined in a loveless marriage while her husband flirted openly with his secretary. Laberge obviously deplores the lack of options available to women of Cécile's generation in her particular socioeconomic environment.

More examples of women who had little chance of acting upon the world may be found in other plays by Marie Laberge. In *Eva et Evelyne*, a one-act play first presented in 1979, two elderly spinsters wonder how their lives might have been different if they had been more adventurous and if they had found suitable mates. Eva, who served as postmistress in their small town while Evelyne kept house for their parents, regrets the lack of romance in their lives. She muses, "j'pense que parsonne nous a jamais touchées nous aut', parsonne nous a jamais pris dans leu bras, jamais embrassées . . ." (74). These women admit that they resigned themselves to a mundane existence because they were too timid to take a risk. As Eva declares, "La vrée histoire, c'est qu'on s'meurt de peur" (75). On the other hand, the only apparent means of escape would have been to marry. When Eva and Evelyne exchange stories about their former suitors, it becomes clear that their options were, indeed, extremely limited. In this way, Laberge addresses the question of constraints that prevent people from making authentic decisions.

In *L'Homme gris*, another one-act play published in 1986 along with *Eva et Evelyne*, Roland Fréchette, a rather pathetic individual who believes very strongly in his role and his rights, has just "rescued" his daughter from an abusive relationship. Unfortunately, his concern is not for her safety and well-being, but rather for what people might think. He asserts gallantly that he will never let her go back to a man who mistreats her; nevertheless, he hopes to keep her troubles a secret: "J'aime autant avoir la honte du divorce que d'risquer qu'un jour ça se sache" (26). Further, he scolds his daughter for causing him potential shame and embarrassment: "Si des affaires de même se savaient, as-tu pensé à la honte que ça nous ferait?" (26). Roland adheres to a system of values established outside himself. He feels justified in forcing his wife and daughter to submit to his authority and to the unconditional value he has chosen. Roland is a "tyrant" (Beauvoir 49); having abdicated his own freedom, he also suppresses that of his daughter. Driven to despair, Christine finally asserts herself. Known as "Cri-cri," she eventually does cry out in self-defense, exclaiming "Tu veux m'tuer!" (59), as she viciously attacks her drunk and emotionally abusive father.

Similarly, in *Jocelyne Trudelle trouvée morte dans ses larmes* (1983), a father refuses to face the fact that his daughter committed suicide. He claims that she drugged herself, then accidentally shot herself in the mouth while attempting to clean a gun. Although Georges Trudelle insists that he cares deeply about his daughter, it becomes clear as the play progresses that he never really loved her or her mother. Like Roland Fréchette in *L'Homme Gris*, Georges Trudelle asserts his authority on the basis of "the ethical universe recognized by him," and he "ignores the value of the subjectivity and the freedom of others" (Beauvoir 48-49). George Trudelle also expresses more concern about appearances than he does about his daughter's life. Rather than acknowledge his own very real contribution to her despair, he

maintains that she was demented: "a l'était un peu craquée, a l'a
jamais été ben normale" (60). Carole, Jocelyne's closest friend, obviously
sees through his ruse and his motivation when she remarks
sarcastically that his explanation certainly protects his own
reputation: "Ça l'a pas mal de bon sens, ça, monsieur Trudelle, j'pense
que vot'honneur va être correque, vos tchums vont jusse vous plaindre un
peu, pis vot'femme va se r'mette plus vite" (62). Meanwhile, Jocelyne
Trudelle hesitates between life and death in her hospital bed.
Ultimately, suicide, as an existential alternative, seems far more
attractive to her than the prospect of remaining in her repressive
environment.

In *Aurélie, ma soeur* (1988), Laberge presents two women of
different generations who exercise free will in the face of difficult
problems. Aurélie, the older woman, has raised La Chatte, who is both
Aurélie's sister and her niece as a result of their father's incestuous
interest in Charlotte, a sculptor who exiled herself in Italy after La
Chatte's birth. Both Aurélie and La Chatte have accepted this
complex situation with honesty and dignity. Further, when La Chatte
was still a child, Aurélie came to terms with her own marital
dissatisfaction. She blames the Catholic church, in part, for imbuing
any pleasure she might have experienced in her relationship with her
husband with a sense of guilt. She maintains that she was much
happier once she abandoned her preconceived notion of "une femme
normale" (61) and obtained a divorce. Now, she acts ethically and
creates value by devoting her life to helping disadvantaged children.
Aurélie's courage is evident when she states, "je regarde mon
impuissance en pleine face tous les soirs" (90). Meanwhile, La Chatte,
now in her early twenties, loves an "older" man who can't seem to
extricate himself from his unhappy marriage. Eventually, in
existential terms, she understands that he is a coward, "un lâche," who
will never leave his manipulative wife because he always falters
"quand y est question d'agir, de passer aux actes" (81-82). La Chatte
realizes that he has created a trap for himself: "c'est son piège à lui"
(82), and that while she still loves him, she can do nothing to
countermand his decisions: "C'est ça: moi je l'aime, pis lui, y choisit"
(86). She acknowledges his choice to remain where he is, and she
embraces her own freedom to move on with her life. Laberge affirms the
exuberance and vitality of Aurélie and La Chatte. She also notes that
men find their strength and their "franchise" hard to deal with. It is
undoubtedly significant that both women have chosen to make their

way alone.

Laberge develops another strong, independent female character in her novel, *Juillet*. Her protagonist, Catherine, longs to disengage herself from "ce couple archi-faux, archi-souffrant" that she forms with her husband, David (56). In particular, Catherine has come to realize that she disagrees entirely with her husband's system of values, "des valeurs bourgeoises, tranquilles, rigides et conservatrices" (103). While Catherine makes a rational decision to live her life freely, her husband, claiming rights and authority based on his personal sense of propriety, attempts to suppress her choice. When Catherine explains openly, calmly, and honestly that their relationship is over, David actually attacks her physically. Catherine's openness causes David to feel inadequate as a male; he feels intimidated by her strength and confidence and knowledge of herself. Meanwhile, Catherine's mother-in-law, Charlotte, worries about what her friends might think when they learn that her son's marriage has failed. She frets, "Qu'est-ce que les gens diraient?" (142-143), and she quickly intervenes to reaffirm the preconceived values she shares with her son. She shoots and kills Catherine with her father's hunting rifle. Still concerned with appearances, she calmly sets about cleaning up the mess so that her son won't be shocked and so the police won't know what happened. As Laberge elaborates her plot, she reveals the anguish many women experience as they attempt to reconcile traditional roles, still narrowly defined by patriarchal values, with the personal and professional freedom to which they are entitled.

In *Juillet*, Laberge develops the same themes and examines the same questions as she has previously done in her works for the theatre. She frequently portrays unhappily married couples, emphasizing the wife's frustration at her inability to communicate authentically with her husband. She weighs the consequences of repressing feelings and emotions against the risks of facing the truth. Invariably, Laberge favors truth; as she states in her article about her work, "écrire pour le théâtre," she urges her audience or her reader to "persister, exister, lutter," as she does herself, and to live life fully and honestly, "la tête hors de l'eau douceâtre du mensonge" (221). In her writing, Laberge attempts to "faire face à des émotions violentes et irrépressibles" (219); thus, her conclusions are usually sombre. They tend to reflect "une certaine solitude violente, irrémédiable" (221). Nevertheless, her strongest characters are women who have the courage to seek a meaningful life in authentic human relationships. They express a desire to live fully and intensely, and to love and to seek love even in the face of death.

Laberge's work reflects women's concerns in contemporary Québécois society. Further, her works reflect many of the concepts developed by Simone de Beauvoir in her approach to existentialism. Sarah Lucia Hoagland's summation that "to be authentic, we must engage in this living, embrace our finiteness, and make our choices as if what we create were eternal—with that degree of emotion, energy, and commitment" (205), effectively describes the underlying theme of Laberge's work. Throughout Laberge's numerous plays and in her recently published novels, she continues to elaborate and refine her distinctive philosophy, which could be described as a kind of feminist existentialism.

Ohio Northern University   **Roseanna Lewis Dufault**

WORKS CITED

Beauvoir, Simone de. *The Ethics of Ambiguity.* Trans. Bernard Frechtmar. New York: Citadel, 1964.

Hoagland, Sarah Lucia. *Lesbian Ethics: Toward New Value.* Palo Alto: ILS, 1988.

Laberge, Marie. *Avec l'hiver qui s'en vient.* Montréal: VLB, 1981.

———. *Aurélie, ma soeur.* Montréal: VLB, 1988.

———. "Ecrire pour le théâtre." *Etudes littéraires* 18.3 (1985): 213-222.

———. *L'Homme gris suivi de Eva et Evelyne.* Montréal: VLB, 1986.

———. *Jocelyne Trudelle trouvée morte dans ses larmes.* Montréal: VLB, 1983.

———. *Juillet.* Québec: Boréal, 1989.

————. *Quelques Adieux.* Québec: Boréal, 1992.

Identity, the State, and Masculinity: The Representation of the Male Subject in Michael Ignatieff's *The Russian Album* [1]

. . . [T]o the family tradition, trade and industry were interesting hobbies but not serious vocations. State service remained the only conceivable path. (*The Russian Album*, 92)

"My Father's Son"

Michael Ignatieff's award-winning narrative, *The Russian Album*, is ostensibly a portrait, in narrative and photographic images, of his paternal grandparents, Count Paul and Countess Natasha Ignatieff, wealthy and powerful aristocrats (Paul Ignatieff was the Minister of Education in the government of Tsar Nicholas II) who fled Russia on the eve of the Revolution and who eventually settled in Canada. *The Russian Album*, however, is as much self-portrait as portrait, for the life story of Natasha and Paul Ignatieff is embedded in Michael Ignatieff's own very personal reflections on what at the outset of the narrative he terms "the problem of personal identity"(3). "Because emigration, exile, and expatriation are now the normal conditions of existence," he argues in the opening paragraphs of *The Russian Album*:

it is almost impossible to find the right words for rootedness and belonging. Our need for home is cast in the language of loss; indeed, to have that need at all you have to be already homeless. Belonging now is retrospective rather than actual, remembered rather than experienced, imagined rather than felt. Life now moves so quickly that some of us feel that we were literally different people at previous times in our lives. If the continuity of our selves is now problematic, our connection with family ancestry is yet more in question. Our grandparents stare out at us from pages of the family album, solidly grounded in a time now finished, their lips pen, ready to speak words we cannot hear. (1)

In this passage, as throughout the introductory chapter of *The Russian Album*, Ignatieff contrasts a "now" in which homeless people form "their thoughts in a second language among strangers" (1) and a "then" in which our ancestors lived "solidly grounded" in their families, their communities, their languages, their landscapes, and their past. Feeling "the need for home," and drawn to the sepia image of his paternal grandparents in the faded photographs, Michael Ignatieff, an historian, returns their gaze, listens. *The Russian Album* is his account of what he hears. In unearthing their past, in attending to their story, he discovers his own: portrait becomes self-portrait.

Like so many second-generation immigrants, Michael Ignatieff has two very different pasts: the relatively accessible Canadian past of his "mother's family, the Grants and Parkins . . . highminded Nova Scotians who came to Toronto in the last century and made a name for themselves as writers and teachers" (8); and the elusive, mournful Russian ancestry of his father's family, a past marked by revolution, exile, and dispossession. "Between my two pasts, the Canadian and the Russian," he writes in the opening pages of *The Russian Album*:

I felt I had to choose. The exotic always exerts a stronger lure than the familiar, and I was always my father's son. I chose the vanished past, the past lost behind the revolution. I could count on my mother's inheritance; it was always there. It was my father's past that mattered to me, because it was one I had to recover, to make my own. (10)

That writing *The Russian Album* involved more than simply the lure of an exotic or a vanished past, Ignatieff acknowledged in a comment he made last year to the journalist, Sandra Martin. Looking back on the book's composition, he remarked, "At the time, thinking about my Russian grandparents and great-grandparents was a way of working through stuff with my father" (58). Michael's father, George Ignatieff, died of a heart attack in August 1989. " . . . More than two years later," Sandra Martin points out, "Michael still thinks of his father as the 'major relationship of my life'—an extraordinary admission from a middle-aged man who is not only married but the father of two children. It is nonetheless," she adds, "as true as it is telling" (44-45).

The compelling nature of that relationship and of the unnamed "stuff" Michael Ignatieff felt he had to work through is perhaps indicated by the Russian proverb he employs as an epigraph to the opening chapter of the book: 'Dwell on the past and you'll lose an eye./ Ignore the past and you'll lose both of them" (1). Like the epigraph, Ignatieff is divided in his response to his own and his father's past: on the one hand, he acknowledges the need to "recover," to "work though," to make his father's past "his own"; on the other, he declares that there is nothing compelling about that past. "Styles of inheritance," he declares:

are now individual: we are free to take or refuse our past. Children have as much right to refuse interest in these icons as they have to stick to their own opinions. Yet the more negotiable, the more invented the past becomes, the more intense its hold, the more central its invention becomes in the art of making a self. (2)

Over and against the conception of the self as product of the past, of relationships structured by ancestry, Ignatieff sets his view that "the self is constantly imagined, constructed out of what the self wishes to remember" (6-7). "To a Russian," Ignatieff reflects, "I am Michael Georgevitch, George's son, a self rooted in a family past. In the non-Russian world I live in, I am known for what I do, for how I am now, not for the past I embody" (2).

In this essay, I should like to explore the tension between Ignatieff's turning to the past and his disavowal of its power over him, the contradiction between his sense of himself as product of his past and his assertion that the self is an identity he creates; and, since gender, like race and class, is fundamental to identity, I shall focus on the representation of masculinity in *The Russian Album*. Masculinity has emerged in recent years as an important issue within gender studies. My approach in this instance is through narrative. Like Steven Cohan and Linda M. Shires, I believe that "stories structure the meanings by which a culture lives" (1). *The Russian Album* structures the meaning of gender difference through the narrative representation of male subjectivity; what is more, such gendered narratives are often shaped by and are certainly reproduced in familes. *The Russian Album*, however, is not just a masculine narrative, but an immigrant text as well. In the movement between countries, languages, and cultures, I shall argue, the male narrative is disrupted and called into question. Although this paper focuses on *The Russian Album*, it juxtaposes that account with the narrative offered by Michael's father, the Canadian diplomat, George Ignatieff, in his memoir, *The Making of a Peacemonger*. In reading Michael Ignatieff's narrative against his father's, I shall argue that *The Russian Album* is a second-generation immigrant male's struggle to rewrite the narrative of masculinity he inherits.

Given that subject position is central to my analysis of texts such as

The Russian Album, I should indicate something of my own relation to this one I was fascinated by *The Russian Album* when I first read it in 1987, but it is the very nature of fascination that we are drawn to that which we do not understand. I recognized that Michael Ignatieff and I were both the sons of immigrants, that we both had inherited from our fathers a past from which we were, at the same time, cut off, and, finally, that neither of us could speak the language of our fathers. Although many people find my ancestry exotic (my forefathers immigrated to Canada from Iceland) my paternal grandparents were neither aristocrats nor wealthy: they did not come to Canada to escape revolution; they did not, I have been told, necessarily even intend to settle. Reading and rereading *The Russian Album*, however, these similarities seemed finally much less compelling than the feeling of loss I encountered in reading Michael Ignatieff's narrative. I shared his need for the past and his denial of it. Both the need and the denial, I came to recognize, were focused on our fathers and their fathers before them, and both involved the representation of men in uniform. In my case, that representation was limited to my father who enlisted in the Royal Canadian Air Force at the outbreak of World War II and who subsequently made a career for himself in the services. I grew up on military bases in the fifties, went to school in buildings named after war heroes, played baseball in parks similarly named, and chose finally not to follow in my father's footsteps but to pursue a career in English. Like Ignatieff, I was denying a past to which I was, at the same time, drawn. I offer these observations not to explain my response but to help you understand, as I am struggling to articulate, the dynamics of my own reading.

"In Service to the Tsar"

Michael Ignatieff's grandparents died two years before he was born; for him, Count Paul and Countess Natasha Ignatieff exist, for the most part, as image and text: the images are primarily photographic, from the "family album"; the texts are the unpublished memoirs written by each of the grandparents. Although in *The Russian Album* Michael Ignatieff offers a portrait of both paternal grandparents, the focus of much of the text, I shall argue, and of my paper is on his portrayal of his grandfather, Paul Ignatieff, and on his critique of the Ignatieff male narrative. Interestingly, Michael Ignatieff dedicates *The Russian Album* to "Theo and His Grandfather," that is, to his own son, Theo, and to Theo's grandfather, Michael's own father, George Ignatieff. In focusing on the male narrative, I do not want to deny either the account of the Ignatieff women offered in *The Russian Album* or the importance of Natasha in Paul Ignatieff's life and the life of the family. Were it not for her strength and determination, the Ignatieff family might not have survived the revolution. Frequently in *The Russian Album*, Michael uses Natasha's account of events to critique her husband's. Speaking of Paul Ignatieff in the opening chapter of the book, for example, he remarks:

> I . . . found myself face to face with what I liked least about myself. My grandfather's favourite phrase was, 'Life is not a game, life is not a joke. It is only by putting on the chains of service that man is able to accomplish his destiny on earth.' When Paul talked like this, my grandmother Natasha always used to mutter, 'The Ignatieffs would make hell out of Paradise.' (13)

While *The Russian Album* celebrates Natasha's life, its focus finally is on Michael's need to rewrite the Ignatieff male narrative.

In *The Russian Album* Paul Ignatieff's life story is inextricably bound to that of all Ignatieff males. "When my Russian grandfather was nineteen and choosing a career," Michael Ignatieff writes:

> the tramlines of his past ran straight into his future: he would enter a Guards regiment like his father, grandfather and great-grandfather before him. He could then make a career in the army or return to the family estates and live as a gentleman farmer. At some point in his life he would be expected to leave the estate and serve the Tsar, as his grandfather and father had done. He would 'shoulder the chains of service.' It is in these precise senses—a destiny inherited and shouldered without questioning—that his identity is irrevocably different from my own. My identity—my belonging to the past he bequeathed me—is a matter of choosing the words I put on a page. I am glad that this is so: his is not a fate or an identity which I would wish as my own. (9)

Michael Ignatieff traces the male line of descent back not just to his paternal grandfather, Count Paul Ignatieff, but to his grandfather's grandfather, the first Paul Ignatieff who as a young man "once held his regimental colours aloft on the Champs Elysées when, having driven Napoleon from Russia, the Preobrajensky Guards rode into Paris in 1815" (41).

The life story of that first Ignatieff male establishes the paradigm for those who follow: military service in the Guards leads to recognition by the Tsar and a career in state service. In this version of events, the life story of the Ignatieff male is inseparable finally from the narrative of the nation. Above all, the Ignatieff men act decisively and on deeply held principles in critical moments of their own and their country's history. Two years prior to the publication of *The Russian Album*, Michael's father, George Ignatieff, published his own memoirs, *The Makings of a Peacemonger*. In that book he offers the following account of "the first Ignatieff." "Though both my parents could trace their ancestry back to the Middle Ages," George Ignatieff writes:

the first Ignatieff to emerge from relative obscurity was my great grandfather, Paul Nikolayevich Ignatieff. During the Decembrist uprising in 1825, when ideas spawned by the French revolution were sweeping across Europe and some Russian officers were siding with the rebels, he made sure that the company of guards which he commanded stood firm in defence of the tsar in front of the Winter Palace in St. Petersburg. (4)

In the more detailed and dramatic account offered in *The Russian Album*, the young Tsar Nicholas I watches anxiously from the balcony window of the Winter Palace for officers to come to his defence. "The first platoons to stream beneath the arches and take up position," Michael Ignatieff declares, "were commanded by Captain Paul Ignatieff" (41; emphasis mine). Consequently, "while his Decembrist friends paid for their dreams in Siberia," Michael writes:

Paul Ignatieff was showered with the Tsar's favour. Appointed aide-de-camp at twenty-eight, by his early thirties he was already commander of the Corps des Pages and in this post he remained for twenty-five years, the schoolmaster to two generations of the Russian military elite. He had former pupils in every ministry of the Winter Palace. (41-42)

"After choosing to serve the Tsar against his Decembrist friends," Michael remarks, "he found the groove of power and followed it steadily" (42).

When Paul's first son was born, Tsar Nicholas attended the

christening. The child, christened Nicholas, was educated at the Corps des Pages and then made aide-de-camp to the Tsar. According to family tradition, the actions of the second Ignatieff male are even more heroic than those of the first. Two events in particular distinguish the life of this second Ignatieff. In 1860, at the age of 27, he negotiated the Treaty of Peking, and then traversed the whole of Asia on horseback in just six weeks to defend the treaty in person before the Tsar. In 1878 he became a national hero when, once again overcoming innumerable odds, he negotiated the Treaty of San Stefano. For concluding the treaty of Peking, "which presented Russia with the rich Ussuri region, gave it access to the Sea of Japan, and enabled it to establish a naval port at Vladivostok," the Tsar awarded him the order of St. Vladimir, "one of the country's highest decorations" (*The Making* 5, 6). According to George Ignatieff, in personally presenting the medal, "The Tsar commented that the motto of the order seemed particularly fitting: 'Service, Honour and Glory' " (6). Those three words aptly summarize the Ignatieff male narrative, as it developed in the nineteenth century. Michael Ignatieff's grandfather, the second Paul Ignatieff, initially portrayed in *The Russian Album* as a sensitive and withdrawn youth who resisted the male narrative articulated by his forefathers, ultimately followed the path blazed by "the first Ignatieff": he served in the regiment of guards in which both his father and grandfather had served, gained the recognition of the Tsar, and secured honour in service to him.

"The Broken Path"

Two images in *The Russian Album* aptly represent this male narrative: they are the photographs of two Ignatieff men, the first Paul Ignatieff and his son, Nicholas, dressed in their military uniforms, their chests covered in medals and braids. Michael Ignatieff titles the first chapter of *The Russian Album* "The Broken Path," as if to underline his inability to follow in the footsteps of his forefathers. Whereas for Michael Ignatieff's grandfather "the tramlines of his past ran straight into the future," for the author of *The Russian Album* they do not: he could never enter a Guards regiment like his grandfather and his father and grandfather before him; he could never win honour and glory by "shoulder[ing] the chains of service" for the Tsar. In this line of argument, that path, that narrative, was forever broken by the revolution of 1917 and by the long years in exile. "I am glad that this is so," Michael Ignatieff declares, "his is not a fate or an identity which I would wish as my own" (9).

Another reading of the figure of the "broken path," however, is possible. Michael Ignatieff focuses *The Russian Album* on his grandparents. Although in the last chapter he recounts the fate of Paul and Natasha's five sons, he says little about his father; instead, he uses the pages ostensibly devoted to his father to recount the death of Paul and Natasha themselves. Thus, in a book in which the author is reportedly working through his relation with his father, there are very few references to George Ignatieff. The absence of Michael Ignatieff's father from the pages of *The Russian Album* can be explained in several ways. Michael Ignatieff may have been understandably reluctant to speak of his immediate family. Moreover, at the same time that Michael was writing *The Russian Album*, his father was completing *The Making of a Peacemonger*. Michael may have wished to give the events recounted in his father's memoir a wide berth.

Without dismissing the first explanations, I should like to offer a third. George Ignatieff's *The Making of a Peacemonger* is, in many ways, similar to *The Russian Album*. Like *The Russian Album*, it offers an account of the family fortunes from the first Paul Ignatieff to the author's own day. Like *The Russian Album* as well, it characterizes the male narrative as one of "Service, Honour and Glory" (8). The opening chapter of *The Making of a Peacemonger* is in fact titled "In the Service of the Tsars." In George Ignatieff's narrative, however, there is no suggestion that the path has been broken; despite the loss of country, security, and status, Michael's father, like his father and his grandfather before him, prospered: a Rhodes scholar, he married into one of this country's most distinguished families, became one of Canada's leading diplomats and gained considerable honour in public service. In *The Making of a Peacemonger* George Ignatieff sees his own life story very much in terms of the Ignatieff male narrative. For example, concerning his own early retirement from the Department of External Affairs, he writes:

Strangely enough, premature retirement was to become a recurring theme in the history of the Ignatieffs. Though the circumstances were vastly different in each case, both my father and I eventually chose to leave public service rather than remain under conditions which we considered unacceptable. (8)

In George Ignatieff's narrative, the "tramlines of the past" still run straight into the future.

"The Same Fatal Unwinding"

The son's account of the Ignatieff male narrative, then, stands in opposition to the father's. *The Russian Album*, however, constitutes less a denial of that male narrative than a reworking of it. In Michael's account, the Ignatieff male narrative is fatally flawed; the path followed by successive generations of Ignatieff men leads finally to their own undoing; it leads not to honour and glory but to dismissal and "inner wreckage" (117). Whereas the family narrative centers on the early decades in each successive Ignatieff male's life, on the rise to power, the account offered in *The Russian Album* places that narrative in the larger context of each man's entire life story and of the ultimate collapse of the state they so faithfully served. Thus, in the opening paragraphs of the chapter titled "Fathers and Sons", we see the patriarch of the Ignatieff family, the first Count Paul Ignatieff, in old age "loaded with infirmities [as well as] honours" (40). The early life stories of the two founding patriarchs, Paul and Nicholas, are embedded in a narrative of the first Paul Ignatieff's final years. And old age is not very kind to these men. In Michael's account, then, the path followed by the Ignatieff men is broken long before revolution leads to the dispossession and exile of the family.

For Nicholas Ignatieff humiliation and disgrace follow hard upon the heels of honour and glory. In "February 1878," Michael Ignatieff writes:

the treaty of San Stefano made him a national hero; in April the Tsar honoured the family; all male descendants of Paul Ignatieff were to take the title of Count. But in May, Count Nicholas found himself banished to his estates south of Kiev; in September, brooding on the front porch of the manor at Kroupodernista, he read the telegraph reports from the conference in Berlin where his treaty was dismembered and everything he had striven to achieve for fifteen years was traded away. (52)

Three years later, following the assassination of Tsar Alexander II, Nicholas Ignatieff regained his position of power only to be dismissed by Tsar Alexander III and once again "sent packing to his estates" (60). "For a man whose blood needed the oxygen of power," Michael Ignatieff writes:

banishment was like a stroke. It aged him overnight. For a decade more, he schemed and struggled to return to the centre of power. He sat in his study with his Khivan swords, Chinese silks and the portrait of William Ewart Gladstone and wrote up his memoirs of Constantinople. . . . By 1890, he knew he was finished. (60)

Disillusioned and bitter, Nicholas spends the last decades of his life reliving the glories of his youth and squandering the family fortune. In Michael Ignatieff's narrative, his great-grandfather is "destroyed by his service to the Tsar" (83). "He had lived too long," the author of *The Russian Album* writes of his great-grandfather's final days, "and it had all slipped through his fingers, and when they buried him, in the village church, there was only the family to mourn him, led by his dry-eyed son" (83).

The Russian Album is focused, however, on the second Count Paul Ignatieff, and in retelling that life story Michael Ignatieff offers his most detailed critique of the family's male narrative. From the outset of that narrative, the author of *The Russian Album* foreshadows the fate awaiting Count Paul Ignatieff later in life. Concerning Paul's marriage to Natasha, Michael Ignatieff writes:

These weeks just before their marriage were to be the only extended time they had alone together for the next twenty years. 'My husband never belonged to himself,' [Natasha wrote in her memoir with some little irony] 'always serving the state and is countrymen.' Duty, duty. He did not belong to himself. He did not belong to her. (69-70)

According to the Ignatieff male narrative, Paul's life belonged to the Tsar. "When close friends like Vladimir Nabokov disposed of their court uniforms in protest at the unpunished pogroms of Kishinev and plunged into party politics," Michael Ignatieff writes:

Paul could not follow them. Party politics was anathema to him, a betrayal of the oath of service he had given to the Tsar personally when serving in the Preobrajensky regiment during his military service. No matter that his father had been destroyed by service to the Tsar, no matter that the regime of Nicholas II was increasingly unpalatable to the liberals of his generation, Paul's life had meaning only within the terms of fidelity to his family's tradition of service. (83-84)

A decision Paul made on the eve of WWI confirms this view. Early in 1914 he was named joint heir to the Maltsev industrial empire, one of the largest in Russia. For the first time the Ignatieff family was truly wealthy. In Petersburg, it was widely expected that he would resign from public service to manage the industries he had inherited; instead, he formed a limited company and hired someone to manage it in his name. "[T]o the family tradition," Michael Ignatieff writes, "trade and industry were interesting hobbies but not serious vocations. State service remained the only conceivable path" (92). If it is true that family traditions made Count Paul Ignatieff, it is also true, the author argues, that "family traditions drew him under" (95). The narrative of the war years is the story of Paul's undoing. "By the autumn of 1915," the author of *The Russian Album* notes, "he was the last Russian liberal at the heart of the regime" (102). While as Minister of Education he began reforming the educational system, Count Paul Ignatieff was increasingly unable either to influence Cabinet decisions or to avert the "conflagration" he saw looming. When the Tsar decided to take personal command of the army, the Cabinet, including Paul Ignatieff, resigned but the Tsar would accept their resignation. "Through the year of 1916," the author writes, "Paul slowly came apart" (103). Finally, in November 1916, on the verge of nervous exhaustion, he was replaced as Minister of Education. "Paul had been a liberal constitutional monarchist," the author of *The Russian Album* observes:

his father a defender of autocracy: both had gone under at fifty, at the height of their powers, cast away by a regime they had tried to serve. They were too much alike, too much of one flesh, for Paul to escape the same fatal unwinding, the inner dissolution that had befallen his father. The coils of energy, will and motive wound tight for fifteen years began to unravel. (108)

Weeks later, in his study, Paul watches "the floodtide of the revolution surging past his window" (111). "The depression that had descended upon him following his dismissal by the Tsar," Michael Ignatieff remarks, "now turned into a complete nervous collapse, accompanied by a recurrence of violent asthmatic attacks and pains in the liver and chest" (114). While his wife, Natasha, struggles to cope with events and to plan for the family's future, Count Paul Ignatieff "continued to lie in bed gazing at his inner wreckage" (117).

"Inventing the Past"

In the line of argument I have been developing, *The Russian Album*
is a cautionary tale. "Someone once said," Michael Ignatieff observes in
the closing pages, "that devotion to the past is one of the disastrous
forms of unrequited love" (184). Certainly Paul Ignatieff's devotion to
the past is, in Michael's account, his own and his family's undoing.
Although the Ignatieffs escaped the revolution and settled in Canada,
the experience seems to have broken Paul and traumatized the family.
Paul's youngest son, George, however, appears no less devoted to the
past. In *The Making of a Peacemonger* he translates the Ignatieff male
narrative to Canada and sets his own diplomatic career in the context
of his forefathers' devotion to "state service." In 1971 that career led,
however, to his premature resignation and, seven years later, to the
humiliation of being first touted as the next Governor-General of
Canada and then passed over in favour of Ed Schreyer. According to the
journalist Sandra Martin, "Family friends and diplomatic colleagues
were so enraged that afterwards some of them could never bring
themselves to refer to Schreyer by name, uniformly dismissing him as 'a
minor political figure'" (44). Little wonder, then, that Michael
Ignatieff argues in *The Russian Album* for individual "styles of
inheritance" (2).

Michael Ignatieff's father, George; his grandfather, Paul; and his
great-grandfather, Nicholas, all wrote memoirs in the final years of
their life, once their career in state service was over. Michael
published *The Russian Album* at the age of forty, not at the end of his
career but nearer the beginning. "I never learned the language," he
confides early in that book:

> In my inability to learn Russian, I can now see the extent of my
> resistance to a past I was at the same time choosing as my own. The
> myths were never forced upon me so my resistance was directed not at
> my father or my uncles but rather at my own inner craving for these
> stories, at what seemed a weak desire on my part to build my little life
> upon the authority of their own. . . . Yet the stronger my need for them,
> the stronger too became my need to disavow them, to strike out on my
> own. To choose my past meant to define the limits of its impingement
> upon me. (12-13)

Although Michael Ignatieff asserts that the "myths were never
forced upon [him]," the suasive power of the Ignatieff male narrative is
apparent in this passage and throughout *The Russian Album*. Michael

Ignatieff attempts to limit its impingement by rewriting the family narrative. At stake is his conception of himself as a man. "My father always said," he reports at the outset of *The Russian Album*:

> that I was more Mestchersky than Ignatieff, more like his mother than his father. Since he was more Ignatieff than Mestchersky, the statement underlined how complicated the ties of filiation really were between us. Inheritance is always as much a matter of anxiety as pride. If I was a Mestchersky what could I possibly make of myself? (13)

What, indeed. To answer that question, he needs not only to rewrite the Ignatieff male myth but to imagine himself the subject of other narratives.

In the opening chapter of *The Russian Album* Michael Ignatieff confides that for a long time he was tempted to write not the history of his father's family but a novel based loosely on Paul and Natasha's lives. In Asya, published in 1991, he does indeed transform their lives into the stuff of fiction. In the closing pages of that novel, a young Canadian journalist of Russian descent, Peter Isvolsky, travels to Britain to speak with a ninety-year-old Russian, Princess Asya Galitzine, who decades earlier had been his father's lover. With him, he brings his father's diaries and the unbearable knowledge that his father committed suicide. In traveling to Great Britain and then Russia, he seeks to understand his father's life and to come to terms finally with his death. To Asya he describes his father's suicide on an Ontario highway:

'Asya, my father was hit in the middle of the road. Facing the oncoming traffic. Not on the side, by the car, as Mother always said. Right in the middle of the road. The driver of the logging truck said Father just stepped out from the side of the road and held his hands out, like this.'

With tears in his eyes, Peter opened his arms, palms outstretched in a gesture of welcome, like a man going to greet his deliverance.

Asya leaned back in her chair and covered her face with her hands.

'That's why I came. Can't you see? Fathers are where we all start from, where we get our reason for going on, for living. Do you understand what I am saying?

She nodded. 'My father died when I was eighteen. I know.'

'But he died.'

'Yes, in my arms.'

'But he died. That's the point. Mine didn't want to live. And I feel him behind me, draining the point of everything, emptying me out. . . .' (313-314)

Peter's declaration that "Fathers are where we all start from" is remarkable, for if we can be said to "start" from anyone, it is from our mothers, not our fathers. Peter's assertion does suggest, however, the importance of the father in men's lives and the need many men feel both to work through their relationship with their father and to imagine alternatives to the narratives men so often tell one another. For we are not only our father's son but our mother's as well. "If I was a Mestchersky," Michael Ignatieff asks, "what could I possibly make of myself?" More men, I suspect, need to ask their own version of that question.

University of Alberta   **Paul Hjartarson**

NOTE

This paper developed out of a graduate course in Canadian literature I taught during the 1990-1991 semester. I should like to thank the graduate students in the course for a very stimulating seminar on *The Russian Album*, particularly Linda Warley, whose presentation sparked the discussion, and Dan Coleman, whose comments are always insightful and whose own work on Canadian immigrant texts is redefining the field.

WORKS CITED

Cohan, Steven, and Linda M. Shires. *Telling Stories: A Theoretical Analysis of Narrative*. New York: Routledge, 1988.

Ignatieff, George. *The Making of a Peacemonger*: The Memoirs of George Ignatieff. Prepared in Association with Sonja Sinclair. 1985; Markham, Ontario: Penguin Books Canada, 1987.

Ignatieff, Michael. *The Russian Album*. 1987; rpt. Markham,

Ontario: Penguin Books Canada, 1988.

————. *Asya*. 1991; rpt. Toronto: Penguin Books Canada, 1992.

Martin, Sandra. "Favourite Son." *Saturday Night* (July/August 1992), 42-47, 55-61.

Déroutage du roman du terroir: Deux romans du terroir contemporains: Un texte franco-ontarien *La chambre à mourir* de Maurice Henrie et un texte chinois Han *Le clan du sorgho rouge* de Mo Yan

> "Le souvenir est le seul paradis
> dont nous ne pouvons être
> chassés."
> Jean-Luc Godard,
> *Nouvelle Vague* (1989)

L'objectif de cet article est de comparer deux textes contemporains, l'un chinois (Han), l'autre canadien (franco-ontarien) pour exposer le déroutage du roman du terroir à l'ère postmoderne, que ce soit dans une aire géographique du Premier-monde ou du Tiers-monde. J'espère pouvoir ainsi déraciner quelques vieilles conceptions, quelques préjugés persistants sur la question d'identité masculine inscrite dans le texte littéraire de la terre.

Les deux auteurs des œuvres à l'étude sont des hommes. Mo Yan, né en 1956, d'origine chinoise et vivant en Chine, a écrit un cycle intitulé *Le clan du sorgho rouge* (1986)—son premier roman—qui l'a rendu célèbre et qui a été transposé à l'écran par Zhang Yimou. Mo Yan vient de la région du Shandong où se passe l'action, le comté Gaomi qui se trouve au nord de la Chine et qui a été un des bastions de résistance durant la guerre antijaponaise. C'est une région tout à fait rurale, où l'on vit de la culture du sorgho et de l'ail. Depuis 1976, Mo Yan est rattaché à l'Armée de Libération Populaire grâce à laquelle il a pu faire des études. Maurice Henrie, né en 1936, d'origine canadienne-française, vit à Ottawa où il occupe un poste dans la haute fonction publique. *La chambre à mourir* (1988) est sa première œuvre; l'action se situe dans l'Est ontarien, où l'auteur a grandi. L'Est ontarien est une région majoritairement francophone et défavorisée. Par exemple, c'est la région du Canada où l'on retrouve le plus grand nombre d'analphabètes. La majorité des gens qui y vit encore aujourd'hui est soit sur l'assistance sociale, le chômage ou travaille en ville. Peu cultivent encore la terre.

Pour plusieurs, en particulier les femmes, le terme "roman du terroir" évoque l'ennui. Il suffit cependant d'avoir lu le merveilleux ouvrage de Patricia Smart, *Ecrire dans la maison du père* pour penser autrement et vouloir relire *Angéline de Montbrun* et *Le Survenant* avec une nouvelle perspective critique. L'ouvrage de Smart, une recherche de l'émergence de l'écriture féminine au Canada français, analyse le roman de la terre comme le bastion de l'écriture masculine. Selon elle, le roman du terroir est fondé sur et traduit un rêve de pérennité (des valeurs catholiques, patriotiques, patriarcales) qui s'écrit selon des normes réalistes et dans une narration unifiée. Le roman du terroir est une volonté d'emprise et de main-mise sur le territoire national (et simultanément sur la femme), bref un projet toujours (tragiquement) voué à l'échec. Pour Smart, la déchéance progressive du roman du terroir est en proportion directe avec l'avènement d'une écriture féminine qui, elle, est signe de modernité.

Son ouvrage conçoit le roman du terroir de façon progressive, notamment grâce à l'émergence d'écrivaines qui introduisent des failles dans cette "Maison du Père". L'évolution pour elle, c'est la fin du roman du terroir, qu'elle assigne au roman *Les grands-pères* de Victor-Lévy Beaulieu (1971) qui ne sont peut-être, à son avis, que violent et autodestructeur, voire apocalyptique parce que toujours construit sur les mêmes fondations, maintenant définitivement minées par les femmes.

Quoique la démonstration de Smart soit fort habile et judicieuse, il n'empêche qu'on hésite à accepter entre les sexes dans l'expression d'emblée sa démarcation littéraire. En effet, lorsqu'on lit des passages de son ouvrage, on pourrait remplacer tout simplement le nom de Geneviève Guèvremont, l'auteure du *Survenant* et de *Marie-Didace*, par celui de Maurice Henrie:

Chez (Guèvremont) Maurice Henrie, la portée essentielle de l'écriture se rouve dans une densité de vie qui échappe à la linéarité de la trame narrative: une atmosphère de maison chaleureuse, une attention autant à ce qui fait la qualité d'un bon repas qu'aux gestes et aux rires, aux petites envies, mesquinerires, ou générosités qui constituent la texture de la vie quotidienne. Texture qui se loge souvent dans l'espace entre les mots, comme dans cette conversation tout en ellipses (...) ou dans la merveilleuse séquence toute attentive aux silences de l'amitié entre hommes (. . .). (Smart 141)

Les citations suivantes, toujours de l'ouvrage de Smart, et portant sur l'écriture des femmes, conviennent tant à l'oeuvre de Maurice Henrie qu'à celle de Mo Yan:

Ecriture de la jouissance et du risque, sans autre message que celui du "comment vivre" (Smart 140).

C'est donc en deçà des certitudes contenues dans les codes idéologiques et les dogmes religieux qu'émerge la texture de l'écriture de Guèvremont (Henrie et Mo), dans l'imperfection même de la temporalité que ses personnages cherchent une incarnation qui subvertit la Loi. Aucun des personnages du récit n'est "porteur" de signification, car ils s'en approchent tous sans jamais y atteindre. A la différence du roman de la terre masculin, l'Un est devenu ici multiple, et il n'y a plus de Vérité à laquelle s'accrocher, sauf celle de l'interrelation des êtres et des choses, l'ouverture au changement et la richesse de l'échange. (Smart 166)

Aussi, lorsque Smart énonce une certaine définition de l'écriture féminine (à partir de l'oeuvre de Anne Hébert), on ne peut qu'en être dérouté:

Cette identification aux voix muettes écrasées par la culture—que ce soit les voix de la terre ou celle des êtres réduits au silence—semble bien être une des caractéristiques fondamentales de l'écriture féminine. (Smart 192)

Si cette affirmation est vraie, alors les deux auteurs masculins des textes à l'étude (se) sont-ils féminisés? (Se) Sont-ils aliénés même de leur sexe? En outre, s'il est vrai que, et je cite Smart, "le roman de la terre (est un) genre masculin et paternaliste par sa forme réaliste et sa vision désincarnée" (35), alors est-ce que ce que Henrie et Mo ont écrit appartient au genre du roman du terroir? Si oui, ne défont-ils pas cette "maison" de Smart qui, pourtant, en a déjà constaté la démolition?

Les deux textes à l'étude peuvent, en effet, être considérés comme des romans du terroir tout en étant résolument modernes, voire postmodernes. Le terroir, c'est selon le *Petit Robert*, "une étendue limitée de terre considérée du point de vue de ses aptitudes agricoles" ou encore "un sol apte à la culture du vin." C'est encore une "région rurale, provinciale, considérée comme influant sur ses habitants." Or, le texte de Maurice Henrie est un album de photos d'une famille de cultivateurs vivant dans l'Est ontarien dans les années 1940 à 1950; celui de Mo Yran, un scénario d'une famille de distilleurs d'alcool fait à partir de sorghos, une céréale rappelant le maïs, durant la fin des années '30. Leurs personnages sont tous des gens solidement "enracinés" dans leur terroir. En outre, dans les deux textes, on retrouve des idiotismes qui *sentent* le terroir, des coutumes d'antan, des modes de vie ruraux. Aussi *La chambre* et *Sorgho rouge* sont, par leur thème, conformes à ce qui est défini par "roman du terroir".

Mais ni *La chambre à mourir* ni *Le clan du sorgho rouge* ne se conforme à l'écriture masculine des romanciers du terroir. D'abord, on ne retrouve pas dans ces textes de capitalisation sous aucune forme. L'idée de permanence, voire de transcendance, de devoir hérité en est absente. Dans *Le clan du sorgho rouge*, la femme et son amant ont en fait usurpé le pouvoir; c'est en période de guerre (anti-japonaise) et leur fabrique d'alcool en sera ruinée. Dans *La chambre à mourir*, les voisins travaillent en ville, les tracteurs et autres machines agricoles remplacent les hommes, les femmes regardent des catalogues de mode de Montréal. C'est un monde au bord de la ruine, un monde fêlé, ici et là.

Il n'y a pas non plus de valorisation du patriotisme ni de la religion. Les "héros" de *Le clan du sorgho rouge* embusquent les Japonais non pas par patriotisme mais par vengeance, parce que ceux-ci ont volé leurs mules, les bêtes de somme et parce qu'ils ont écorché vif leur ami et serviteur. Nulle part dans ce roman n'y a-t-il mention des communistes alors que le roman type du terroir chinois pose toujours l'Armée rouge au premier plan.[1] Le roman est d'habitude relié à l'histoire officielle (comme celui d'ici, d'ailleurs). Mo Yan introduit des fissures dans le roman du terroir chinois en racontant la petite histoire de son grand-père *et* de sa grand-mère sur un mode subjectif. Voici le début du texte:

En 1939, le neuvième jour du huitième mois du calendrier lunaire, mon père, cette graine de bandit, a un peu plus de quatorze ans. Il talonne le commandant Yu Zhan'ao—celui qui par la suite va devenir le héros légendaire connu de tous—; avec l'escouade, il se dirige vers la grand-route Jiao-ping pour embusquer le convoi des Japonais (...).

C'est ainsi qu'il s'engage dans la course qui va le mener à cette pierre tombale, verte et sans inscription, dressée au milieu des sorghos rouges de mon pays natal. ...La stèle est depuis longtemps envahie par les herbes sèches et frissonnantes. Un jour, un jeune garçon est venu ici faire paître sa chèvre et tandis que tranquillement elle broutait, l'enfant, debout sur la pierre, a pissé un grand coup furieux et a entonné:—Les sorghos ont rougi.... Le Japon est ici.... Debout mes camarades!... Prêts à la canonade!

On raconte que c'était moi, ce petit berger. Je ne sais pas si c'était moi ou pas. Par le passé, j'ai éprouvé pour la contrée Gaomi du nord-est un amour extrême; par le passé j'ai éprouvé pour la contrée Gaomi du nord-est une haine extrême. Une fois grand, *après avoir conscientieusement étudié le marxisme-léninisme,* j'ai finalement compris: la contrée Gaomi du nord-est est sans conteste, de toute la terre, l'endroit le plus beau et le plus laid; le plus sublime et le plus vulgaire; le plus pur et le plus sale. (*SR* 9-11; les italiques sont les miens)

Dans le roman type du terroir canadien-français, patriotisme et religion sont les pierres d'angle de l'édifice. Or, chez Henrie, on pratique sa religion comme tout autre pratique sociale, on ne s'engage pas en politique, on vote parfois bleu parfois rouge; on protège farouchement son français par pur isolationnisme, par défi aux Anglais qui les entourent. Maurice Henrie introduit ainsi des fissures dans le roman du terroir d'ici en ne misant pas sur le patriotisme ni sur la religion, ni d'ailleurs, sur le patriarcat. Sa grand-mère occupe autant de place que son grand-père. Rien n'est hiérarchisé, rien n'est unifié. Et, surtout, rien n'y est solide:

C'était une bonne terre et qui rendait bien que le grand-père avait reçue de son père à lui. De la terre forte, aimait-il à dire, conscient du fait que ces simples mots désignaient le meilleur des sols. (...) Il n'avait pas oublié non plus ses parents qui avaient vécu sur cette terre avant lui et qui avaient laissé tant de traces encore visibles.

Mais voilà que dans cet univers tout d'une pièce il sentait comme une fêlure. Quelque chose qu'il ne parvenait pas à bien saisir, à comprendre tout à fait. Quelque chose qui menaçait le bel ordonnancement des mois et des saisons, les règles et prescriptions non écrites qu'il avait apprises très jeune et selon lesquelles il avait toujours vécu. C'était quasiment imperceptible, bien sûr, mais ça ne lui échappait pas, à lui, même s'il n'arrivait pas à nommer l'ennemi invisible et d'autant plus dangereux qu'il était, par certains côtés, plus séduisant que menaçant. Une sorte d'ennemi charmeur, au sourire large et invitant. Mais c'était quoi, à la fin, ce danger? Le grand-père ne pouvait rien répondre. Mais il savait. (*CM*, "La palissade" 159-160)

Ce qu'il sait, c'est la présence de voitures, le déménagement des voisins en ville, l'attrait des études pour son fils, l'attrait de la grande ville pour sa fille, la volonté de modernisation de sa propre femme, mais aussi cette séduction sur lui-même. Des monologues intérieurs, l'un du fils Jean-Paul ("Les mains" 55-59), l'autre de la grand-mère ("Alexandrine" 182-190) confirment cette "fêlure". Voici un extrait du monologue de la grand-mère qui compare sa vie à celle de sa sœur Alexandrine, mariée à un médecin fortuné et vivant en ville:

De son côté, et pendant vingt-cinq ou trente ans, la grand-mère n'entretient jamais, ne fût-ce qu'un seul instant, le moindre doute sur l'excellence de son choix de jeune fille et se félicita longtemps, intérieurement, d'être restée sur la terre, comme ses parents l'avaient fait avant elle et comme elle croyait qu'il était naturel, presque nécessaire, qu'elle le fasse aussi. (...)

Mais au fur et à mesure que les années passaient, on aurait dit que cette conviction, qui avait été si forte, si spontanée, si inébranlable au début de son mariage, se craquelait, s'effritait, devenait friable comme une motte de glaise blanche séchée au soleil. Si bien qu'un doute imperceptible était né à son insu, puis avait grandi sans que jamais la grand-mère ne le reconnaisse pour ce qu'il était ni n'en devienne pleinement consciente, comme si longtemps il y avait eu en elle un mécanisme d'autodéfense qui empêchait qu'une trop grande lucidité lui laisse entrevoir d'un coup, sans aucune transition, la vérité crue. Mais il était là, ce doute, accroché à son visage comme sa verrue au menton. ("Alexandrine" 187-188)

Sa "moins grande certitude" (188) ne vient pas que de sa comparaison avec Alexandrine, mais encore des effets de la ville sur ses enfants, de l'exil des voisins, bref des mêmes réalités que son mari exprime un peu différemment.

Tant chez Henrie que chez Mo Yan, le roman du terroir devient une mise en scène de l'ambiguïté des sentiments, des petites fêlures dans la vie des personnages. Ce ne sont pas des oeuvres de représentation d'une réalité qui est Une, vraie, mais des œuvres qui construisent des effets de réel, qui se construisent autour de subjectivités diverses.

Le réalisme, supposément essentiel au roman du terroir, n'est donc pas l'unique mode de représentation du genre. Avec Mo Yan et Maurice Henrie, le lecteur se retrouve dans des mondes hautement subjectifs. Les deux oeuvres ont un "je" autobiographique. Ces "je" ressassent des souvenirs d'enfance. Chez Henrie, la remémoration provient de ses fréquents séjours prolongés chez ses grands-parents, dans le rang de la Canaan alors que le "je" était enfant. Chez Mo, les souvenirs sont moins "propres" au "je" puisque celui-ci, à quelques exceptions près, présente/ invente les souvenirs de son père. Son affabulation est même ostentatoirement avouée dans les exemples suivants:

Mon père connaît bien ce sentier. Il le reverra souvent, plus tard, lorsqu'il sera obligé de travailler aux fourneaux japonais. *Mais il ne sait pas* les aventures amoureuses qui pour grand-mère se sont jouées sur ce chemin. *Je sais, moi. Il ne sait pas* que son corps satiné, d'un blanc de jade, s'est laissé aller sur cette terre d'obsidienne à l'ombre des sorghos. *Cela aussi, je le sais.* (*SR* 15)

(...) La rivière dans les lameaux de brume, rouge et verte, sévère et blanche... . Au sud, c'est l'étendue égale des sorghos, sans une ride, chaque épi dressé comme une face pourpre, et la vaste réflexion de leur corps vigoureux.—*Mon père était encore un jeune à l'époque, trop jeune pour de telles rêveries, c'est mon imagination qui s'évade.* (*SR* 49; mes italiques)

Mais il n'empêche que le "je" du *Le clan du sorgho rouge* a lui aussi une mémoire de ce qu'il présente:

En 1976, quand mon grand-père est mort, c'est mon père qui lui a fermé les yeux, de sa main gauche, celle à laquelle il manquait deux doigts. Quand grand-père est revenu des montagnes désertiques de Sapporo, en 1958, (...) le village avait organisé une grande cérémonie pour fêter son retour, même le chef du district était là. *Je n'avais que deux ans, à l'époque, mais je me souviens encore que* sous le ginkgo à l'entrée du village avaient été dressées huit grandes tables (...) Mon grand-père s'est levé avec maladresse, tournant des yeux gris-blanc il a voulu répondre: "Heu... Heu... Fusil...Fusil..." Je l'ai vu porter le bol à ses lèvres, son cou tout ridé s'était raidi, sa pomme d'Adam montait et descendait, c'est à peine s'il a bu, l'alcool a dégouliné sur son menton, sur sa poitrine. (*SR* 148-149; mes italiques)

Heureusement (pour les lecteurs), ces "je" ne souffrent pas d'amnésie (ou de manque d'imagination). On dira plutôt qu'ils ont une mémoire hypertrophiée. En effet, pour Henri, il s'agit de reculer environs quarante ans dans le passé; pour Mo Yan, de couvrir environs cinquante ans et de reculer jusqu'avant sa naissance! L'enterprise de Henri est, il est vrai, plus circonscrite dans le temps et dans un temps qui lui est personnel. Voici des extraits du dernier texte qui clôt le recueil, mais qui donne—en toute fin—un repère temporel. Le curé vient à la ferme, au beau milieu de l'après-midi:

—Toi, t'es un petit chanceux.
Nous nous regardions tous en silence, au fur et à mesure que le mystère augmentait (. . .). Il se décida enfin à nous tirer d'embarras et se

mit à expliquer que j'étais accepté comme pensionnaire de la grande ville (. . .)

Déjà, je n'écoutais plus, tout entier occupé à contenir le spasme de terreur qui me fouillait le ventre comme un soc de charrue et me déchiquetait par l'intérieur (. . .)

A partir de ce moment-là et à l'insu de tous, une idée grave comme la mort commença à germer en moi, comme si mon âme même s'arc-boutait contre ce destin de malheur. De toutes mes forces, j'allais résister à ceux qui, pour mon plus grand bien, avaient décreté mon arrachement à ces terres grises et décidé de mon exil vers la ville et dans les livres. Si je luttais avec assez de vaillance, si je m'opposais assez longtemps, peut-être qu'un jour, avant qu'il ne soit trop tard, ces terres ensorcelantes me seraient enfin rendues.

Ces terres qui m'appartiennent depuis toujours et qui m'attendent encore. ("L'arrachement" 193-194)

Hormis ce dernier texte, tous les autres de *La chambre à mourir* sont ordonnés suivant une logique autre que celle linéaire, plutôt déroutante. L'ordre semble aléatoire; c'est comme un album de photos (couleur sépia jauni, comme l'est d'ailleurs la jaquette du livre) qu'on feuillette à tout hasard. Ici et là (dans le 2e, 3e, 4e), on retrouve un "je" parmi les autres personnages, ou encore un enfant, un "il" qui est ce narrateur omniscient de son "je" de jeunesse (5e, 17e). Il n'empêche que tout le texte est perçu comme subjectif, très loin d'un narrateur omniscient, désincarné, sachant tout et disant tout. Le lecteur lit les souvenirs de quelqu'un, mais aussi les projections biaisées, à partir de détails vus, sentis, entendus par quelqu'un. Dans son deuxième recueil du terroir, *Le pont sur le temps* (1992), le "je," autobiographique, a l'âge de l'auteur et parle ainsi de lui-même:

Je ne suis pas, comme tant d'autres l'ont été et le sont encore, un marchand de souvenirs, de leurs souvenirs à eux, dont ils veulent nous entretenir et nous charmer, croyant obscurément et à tort que nous y sommes autant qu'eux attachés (. . .)

A la masse imposante de mon passé qui, à chaque instant, me défait et me refait d'une autre manière, je ne veux pas faire allusion, à moins que ce ne soit absolument nécessaire ou que cela n'arrive que rarement ou encore par accident. Si je consens à parler de moi-même, c'est en fait pour mieux parler des autres, pour mieux parler de vous. ("Le printemps sans fleurs" 126)

Ailleurs, dans *Le pont sur le temps*, ce "je" dit: "Je suis à la fois le seul acteur et le seul spectateur" (81). Il y a chez Henrie une grande retenue qui traverse tous ses textes, qui ne se limite pas qu'à l'absence de propension autobiographique et qui s'explique par la lucidité, une conscience post-moderne de ce qu'est la mémoire et l'anamnèse, l'identité/altérité, et aussi l'écriture. Il pourrait bien s'agir d'aliénation, en ce que l'on est toujours possédé et dépossédé de ce qui nous "appartient", tout en ne nous "appartenant" pas. La mémoire du terroir pour un citadin (pour Maurice Henrie, pour Mo Yan) en est sans doute le cas le plus prégnant. Son inscription, en écriture, en un roman aux formes brouillées—en mémoire—est la forme la plus vivante, la plus exaltante de la nostalgie.

Une même délectation dans l'écriture—comme l'ultime site du débordement—se retrouve chez Mo Yan. Son épilogue (non traduit en français) reprend et développe sur un mode excessif une affirmation du début du texte:

Capables de tuer pour voler, entièrement dévoués à leur patrie, ils ont été les acteurs de tragédies héroïques et nous aujourd'hui, petits enfants indignes, nous savons bien le fossé qui nous sépare d'eux. Plus je mûris et plus je sens cette décadence humaine. (*SR* 14)

Ce texte est un appel à ces âmes héroïques et malchanceuse qui errent sur la terre toute rouge sans frontières, sans limites de mon coin de pays. Je suis votre descendant indigne, je veux m'extirper le coeur noyé dans la sauce soya, le hacher en petits morceaux, le placer dans trois bols, le déposer sur la terre de sorgho. En espérant que vous apprécierez ce repas! Oui, appréciez! (*Honggaoliang* 250; ma traduction)

Dans *Le clan du sorgho rouge*, il n'y a quasiment pas de moment présent qui tienne, comme l'atteste le passage suivant:

(de la blessure de Wang Wenyi) se dégage une odeur semblable à celle de la vase de la rivière Mo—en plus frais. Une odeur plus forte que le parfum de la menthe, plus forte que l'amertume sucrée du sorgho, une odeur qui enchaîne en souvenirs pressés ce présent fugitif au passé immortel, à la vase de la rivière et à la terre noire des champs.(. . .) (*SR* 22)

Grand-mère est étendue, baignée par la tendre clarté des sorghos. (...) Les images ont ralenti leur mouvement dans sa tête. (. . .) Tous ce visages et leur poids d'émotions—haine, gratitude, cruauté ou bonté...n'ont fait qu'apparaître pour mieux disparaître. Ces trente

années d'histoire de sa vie, tout son passé à l'heure où elle est en train
d'y ajouter une dernière ligne, ne sont plus que fruits parfumés qui
tombent et s'écrasent au sol. L'avenir? A peine si elle devine quelques
halos de lumière éphémère. Il n'y a plus que le présent, ce présent
poisseux, fuyant et trop bref auquel désespérément elle s'accroche. . . .
(*SR* 134)

En fait, tout le roman est un jeu sur les temporalités. La trame
principale de *Le clan du sorgho rouge* se passe en une journée, du petit
matin jusqu'à l'après-midi, soit jusqu'à la fin de l'embuscade. Mais le
"je" ne nous présente pas cette journée dans sa linéarité. Tout est prétexte
à bifurquer: le père du "je" suit le commandant Yu, son père, vers la
rivière; l'odeur de la rivière appelle (lui rappelle) ses souvenirs de
pêche aux crabes; les crabes, le plaisir, de les manger avec sa mère; sa
mère, une fumeuse d'opium pourtant si belle, ayant gardé un teint de
pêche; et ainsi de suite. Le texte suit les remémorations la plupart du
temps olfactives du père du "je". C'est comme un film entièrement
constitué de flash-backs mais aussi comme une suite ininterrompue
d'évocations proustiennes. Ceci dit, il faut tout de suite préciser que,
dans le roman de Mo Yan, il s'agit de souvenirs souvent fort grotesques
d'un enfant de 13 ans, le père du "je", qui a l'expression crue ainsi que
l'éclat sensoriel souvent propre aux enfants. A titre d'exemple, il est
fasciné par les oreilles du serviteur ami de la famille qui, ayant désobéi
aux Japonais, est en train de se faire écorcher vif:

(le boucher) déposa (dans une assiette blanche) une oreille, puis
l'autre...
Lentement, l'assiette à la main, le soldat passa devant les ouvriers
et les villageois pour mieux leur montrer—mon père les vit—les grosses
oreilles blafardes du vieux Liu qui sautaient encore et frappaient la
porcelaine.(...)
Sans ses oreilles, à la place desquelles coulaient quelques gouttes de
sang, la tête du vieux Liu semblait extrêmement nette. (*SR* 68-69)

La fragmentation du temps va de pair dans les deux romans avec la
focalisation et donc l'amplification de certains détails. En fait, cette
manipulation temporelle fixe certains moments, certains objets et les
concrétise maximalement, empêchant l'abstraction.
Patricia Smart, à la suite de Luce Irigaray, met à découvert la
métaphore de l'oeil (mâle) qui fait sien tout ce qu'il embrasse soit en le

colmatant ensemble lui donnant ainsi une fausse unité, soit en le fétichisant et donc le réifiant, comme dans les descriptions des femmes et de la nature, ainsi pacifiées, dans le roman du terroir masculin. Or, l'empire colonisateur de l'oeil n'a pas cours dans les textes de Mo ou de Henrie car ce sens est toujours soit tellement myopique que l'ensemble est perdu, soit synesthétiquement mêlé à un autre sens (chez Mo surtout à l'olfactif; chez Henrie, surtout à l'auditif). On assiste à une forme d'hyperréalisme: les boyaux au jus vert des mules dans la rivière pleine de carcasses dans *Le clan du sorgho rouge* font contrepoint à l'odeur de la menthe, du sorgho et surtout l'odeur âcre du sang humain. Dans *La chambre à mourir*, la main broyée du grand-père est sujet de conversation alors que l'on mange de la soupe aux tomates.

Mon père revoit nos deux pauvres mulets noirs. . . . Il s'en souvient encore: longtemps après que la route a été achevée, quand le vent venait du sud-est, l'odeur infecte des cadavres est arrivée jusqu'au village. (...) Leurs ventres sous le soleil gonflaient jusqu'à exploser, découvrant des boyaux luisants qui s'ouvraient comme des fleurs et un jus vert foncé qui s'en allait au fil de l'eau (*SR* 73).

Tremblants de peur, mon père et un groupe d'enfants se précipitèrent pour regarder du haut de la berge: Yu gisait sur le dos, face tournée vers le ciel. De son visage, seule la bouche était restée intacte, son crâne avait volé en morceaux et sa cervelle dégoulinait sur ses oreilles, un de ses yeux avait été arraché de son orbite, il pendait sur le côté, comme un grain de raisin. Son corps en tombant avait éclaboussé partout et brisé la tige du frêle lotus blanc dont la fleur à présent reposait auprès de sa main. On pouvait encore sentir son parfum (*SR* 109).

Contre le silo est arrêtée aussi depuis deux jours l'ensileuse à blé d'Inde (. . .) Une petite machine qui n'a pas l'air si terrible, mais qui a tout de même tranché inexorablement, imperturbablement, méthodiquement, de son couteau à trois lames rendu invisible par sa propre vitesse, les doigts, la main, puis le poignet de l'homme qui lui fournissait le mais à ensiler. De petites tranches fines et propres qu'elle a ensuite soufflées (. . .) jusqu'à la fenêtre percée tout en haut (. . .), d'où tombent à l'intérieur le mais et les mains d'homme, comme une pluie organique jaunâtre, rougeâtre. (. . .)

Le midi, en mangeant sa soupe aux tomates, le grand-père, qui n'a pas encore parfaitement maîtrisé les mouvements de sa main gauche, échappe sur la table un peu de jus rouge et se salit le menton *"aux gars qu'il exhorte de reprendre le travail avec l'ensileuse, le grand-père dit: 'Je m'en vais vous donner un coup de main' "*. ("L'ensileuse" 26; 29)

On est plongé, écrasé, suffoqué parfois dans le concret, visible et non-visible. Chez Henrie, les silences ont "lieu", meublent vraiment la maison rurale où on ne parle qu'à demi-mot, de la mort, de ses amours, de ses désirs. Comme chez Mo, ce sont les corps qui parlent. L'exemple le plus "parlant" chez Maurice Henrie est peut-être le texte qui donne son titre à l'oeuvre, "La chambre à mourir". La grand-mère malade est gentiment conseillée par sa fille Jacqueline de s'installer dans la chambre du bas parce que c'est plus commode pour la soigner. Or, c'est dans cette chambre que les aïeux de la grand-mère sont venus mourir. Installée là par sa fille, elle examinera et entendra tout ce qui l'entoure, dans la chambre comme à l'extérieur; puis, seule, elle remontera lentement l'escalier pour aller se coucher dans sa propre chambre, en haut.

Il est curieux que le seul long monologue intérieur de *Le clan du sorgho rouge* soit également celui de la grand-mère mourante du "je". Atteinte d'une balle, elle gît par terre et ses dernières impressions sont remplies d'odeurs de sorgho, de sang, de visions de sorgho, de colombes, de souvenirs de sexe et de nourriture. De même, dans *La chambre à mourir* comme dans *Le clan du sorgho rouge*, la mère est absente.

La chambre à mourir est une écriture minimaliste, au ras des choses, où presque rien ne se passe: pas de mort humaine, pas de tragédie, pas de peine d'amour, ni de guerre ni conflit. A l'image du coin de pays d'où vient Maurice Henrie. *Le clan du sorgho rouge* est une écriture qui en est l'envers: morts violentes, torture, guerre, exil, tous amplifiés à l'excès, sans fin. A l'image de la Chine, avec ses "cinq mille ans d'histoire."

L'écriture du terroir correspond nécessairement au sol d'où il a pris sa culture: une terre à sorgho, une terre à blé d'Inde. Mais, en revanche, l'écriture n'est pas enracinée dans cette terre puisque Mo Yan et Maurice Henrie offrent de nouvelles fondations pour le roman du terroir, un déroutage du roman du terroir qui n'est plus évaluable en termes spatiaux (géographiques) mais bien en termes temporels.

Université de Montréal   **Marie Claire Huot**

NOTE

M. Duke, dans un ouvrage publié en 1985, note que la majorité des plus de 300 romans qui ont été publiés en Chine depuis 1978 ont comme thème des sujets historiques (Duke 149). X. Giafferri-Huang affirme que c'était le même cas durant les années '50 et '60: "Durant la période de reconstruction du pays, les luttes communistes d'avant 1949 représentait la majeure partie des sujets de romans (...)" (26) "Dans les années '60, la résistance contre l'occupation japonaise constitue encore une source d'inspiration importante des romanciers. (...) Les romans de la guerre anti-japonaise soulignent tous cette situation difficile. Un grand nombre d'entre eux évoquent la résistance armée des guérillas derrière la ligne de blocage des occupants, essentiellement dans les plaines et les montagnes du Nord de la Chine" (94).

OUVRAGES CITES

Giafferri-Huang, Xiaomin. *Le roman chinois depuis 1949*. Paris: PUF, 1991.

Han Shaogong. "Wenxue de gen" (Les racines de la littérature). Revue *Zuojia*. (Ecrivains). Shanghai: (1985), 4, 2-5.

Henrie, Maurice. *La chambre à mourir*. Québec: L'instant même, 1988.

————. *Le pont sur le temps*. Sudbury: Prise de parole, 1992.

Lee, Leo Oufan. "Beyond Realism: Thoughts on Modernist Experiments in Contemporary Chinese Writing", *Worlds Apart: Recent Chinese Writing and Its Audiences*, H. Goldblatt, ed., "Studies on Contemporary China". New York, London: M.E. Sharpe, 1990, pp. 64-77.

Mo Yan. "Hong gaoliang," *Hong gaoliang: bashi niandai Zhongguo dalu xiaoshuo xuan 1*, Xi Xi ed., Taipei: Hongfan, 1988, 143-250.

————. *Le clan du sorgho*, trad. par Pascale Guinot et Sylvie Gentil, Aix-en-Provence: Actes Sud, 1990.

Sacks, Oliver. *"L'homme qui prenait sa femme pour un chapeau"* et *autres récits cliniques.* Trad. Edith de la Héronnière, Paris: Seuil, 1988.

Smart, Patricia. *Ecrire dans la maison du père: L'émergence du féminin dans la tradition littéraire du Québec.* Montréal: Québec/Amérique, 1990 (nouvelle édition revue et corrigée).

Margaret Atwood's *The Handmaid's Tale* as a Self-Subverting Text

In *The Handmaid's Tale* Margaret Atwood's first-person narrator Offred ends her story with a description of stepping into the black van which has come for her. She is escorted by her lover Nick who calls her by her "real name" and tells her it's "Mayday," the apparent code word of the underground. The chapter ends:

> Whether this is my end or a new beginning I have no way of knowing: I have given myself over into the hands of strangers, because it can't be helped.
> And so I step up, into the darkness within; or else the light. (295)

We turn the page to learn whether this is her "end or a new beginning". There is more to the novel, a handful of pages remaining. But we discover that Atwood has played a clever narrative joke on her readers. The "last chapter" is not another chapter of Offred's first-person narrative at all. We are in an even more distant future—2195, perhaps exactly 200 years after the future present. Offred apparently survived her last narrated words, but is now only text, the box of her audiotapes.

It is this section of *The Handmaid's Tale,* called "Historical Notes," which problematizes the ending of Atwood's novel. As she has indicated in her interviews, her novel reads like George Orwell's *1984,* among other dystopias. For Atwood, Orwell's "Appendix"—"The Principles of Newspeak"—is an integral part of his novel, a "last chapter." Speaking of Orwell's "Principles of Newspeak" and her own "Historical Notes," she claims that Orwell "did the same thing. He has a text at the end of *1984,*" then goes on to say:

> In fact, Orwell is much more optimistic than people give him credit for . . . Most people think the book ends when Winston comes to love Big Brother. But it doesn't. It ends with a note on Newspeak, which is written in the past tense, in standard English—which means that, at the time of writing the note, Newspeak is a thing of the past. (217)

Although we might question her reasoning, Atwood evidently sees Orwell's "Appendix" and by implication her own "Historical Notes" as crediting a future in which Oceania and Gilead are no more. The time-shift into a more distant future in the "Historical Notes" section jolts the first-time reader. However, if we check the table of contents, we note that it *has* been anticipated there, since more space has been left between this section and the preceding chapter than there is between the other chapters. Unlike Orwell's novel proper, however, which ends with the ironic assertion that Winston Smith now "loved Big Brother," Atwood's novel does not end: it stops. Furthermore, since it has been told in the first person, this narrative depends on "Historical Notes," as Orwell's "Appendix" does not. Without Atwood's "Historical Notes," we have no way of knowing how Offred's narrative exists as a text. Thus, we have a narrative which cannot be a narrative unless we read what appears to be another related text, outside the narrative proper, a text whose authenticity may be even more questionable than the text it seems meant to authenticate.

Much as she may dismiss the classification "postmodernist," Atwood is clearly problematizing, if not "deconstructing"—to use a once more fashionable term—the modernist, open-ended narrative. Her manipulation of narrative desire here, seemingly offering two "endings," yet actually providing none, recalls the helpful suggestions of Peter Brooks in his book *Reading for the Plot: Design and Intention in Narrative* (1984).

Brooks argues that narrative is the scene of conflicting desires: one is the desire for the end; the other is the desire to postpone the end. It is the end which, if anything, can offer meaning. As Brooks notes, Jean-Paul Sartre recognized as a young man that it is not until a life is over that we can know what it meant; Sartre decided to live his life as though it were a biography read by posterity, or as he so succinctly put it: "I became my obituary" (Brooks 22). Thus, the reader moves through a narrative, drawn between the same oppositions as in experience. We enjoy what we read, but we long for the end since only the end can confirm meaning. As Walter Benjamin asserts, "Death is the sanction of everything the storyteller can tell" (Brooks 22). In reading, our efforts at making sense of a narrative are best seen as the "anticipation of retrospection": we wait for an end that will legitimate our looking forward to a meaning we sensed we were missing as we passed through. In one sense, the ending of a narrative precedes its beginning, for when we begin we know on one level that the narrative is already over, completed. Along the way, that desire for the end is held up, retarded, by the "middle," if you will. We long for the end, yet willingly allow its postponement because the ending *is* the death of the narrative and because it must be the *right* end for the meaning to be realized. Jumping ahead to read the last page, always a temptation, is a readerly "suicide," a short-circuiting of the desire inherent in narrative.

If one direction in which narrative desire moves the reader is a longing for the end, Atwood's *The Handmaid's Tale* problematizes that desire by offering the reader a first-person narrative that stops and "Notes" in a seemingly separate text. Neither is an "ending," in the conventional sense of the term. Offred's last words leave us in the dark about her ending: is she "saved" in the "final reel," like the heroine of countless thrillers such as *The Perils of Pauline*; or, is Nick an Orwellian betrayer of her naive faith that she is such a superior specimen of humanity that no harm could *really* come to her? Even before our readerly rush into the "Historical Notes" has taken us far enough to validate our faith that she "survived," the narrative desire peaking here in its "death" may not settle our doubts about the substantiality of this text. Offred *must* survive to "tell" her story, because, as Brooks reminds us, the completion of the action must precede the beginning of the "plot," i.e., narrating cannot begin until the action to be narrated has completed itself—unless, of course, the telling is sandwiched in between episodes of the "plot."

Whether the ending is Offred's last words or it is the ironic conclusion of the academic symposium ("Are there any questions?") we are propelled backward into the narrative "proper." Suddenly, we are forced to ask the sort of fundamental "existential" readerly question: how does this text authorize its own existence? As Offred makes clear again and again, as a handmaid, she is a "sacred vessel" to hold what Gilead will have her contain. She has no "inside," or privacy of person, no "room of her own." Unlike Winston with his dangerous fountain pen scribbling in his illusory sanctuary, Offred hasn't even a pencil. Where, then, would she hide a tape recorder?

We return, then, to the narrative "proper," from the "Historical Notes" which speculate that Offred made the tapes *after* her escape, and what we find is an eerie sense of indeterminate time. Offred offers the reader an historical "present," on the one hand, and what she continually refers to as a "reconstruction," on the other, and both are bound up with storytelling and the sense of interminable repetition. She says: "I would like to believe this is a story I'm telling . . . then I have control over the ending. Then there will be an ending, to the story, and real life will come after it." At best, it's a story that she's "telling," she indicates, "because I have nothing to write with and writing is in any case forbidden." She is compelled by this telling, even if it's going on only in her head, because a story is like a letter, and therefore there must be someone out there, even an anonymous someone, who will receive her "letter."

It is the sense of repetition and the burden of telling/repeating the action ("I'm too tired to go on with this story," she says) which Offred foregrounds here. She tells us:

> This is a reconstruction. All of it is a reconstruction now, in my head, as I lie flat on my single bed rehearsing what I should or shouldn't have done, how I should have played it. If I ever get out of here. . . .

but, of course, she is "out of" that room when she's telling the story in that illusory "present" which is already past in a future which may await us. But she proceeds:

> When I get out of here, if I'm ever able to set this down, in any form, even in the form of one voice to another, it will be a reconstruction then too, at yet another remove. It's impossible to say a thing exactly the way it was, because what you say can never be exact, you always leave something out . . .

As we approach the end of Offred's narrative, we readers begin to feel that suspenseful anxiety about the end. It is, as Peter Brooks would say, an end like death that we both dread because after it is nothingness yet also desire because it is only the end which can affirm meaning. Offred herself expresses this anxiety about the end of her telling, especially as she foregrounds her own inability to *change* this story. At the brothel Jezebel's, she encounters her pre-Gilead friend Moira whom she had cheered on when she escaped from handmaidenhood, now a sort of temple prostitute. We read:

> Here is what I'd like to tell. I'd like to tell a story about how Moira escaped, for good this time. Or if I couldn't tell that, I'd like to say she blew up Jezebel's, with fifty Commanders inside it. I'd like her to end with something daring and spectacular, some outrage, something that would befit her. But as far as I know that didn't happen. I don't know how she ended, or even if she did, because I never saw her again. (250)

Ironically, it is just such a melodramatic ending that the Harold Pinter screenplay imposed upon the ending of the film.

In a sense, Offred is preparing herself and us readers for her end. In these last pages she highlights herself as narrator, as a storyteller playing with the text of her tale, even at one point ficting three separate renditions of the first love scene with Nick, beginning the second rendition with "I made that up. It didn't happen that way. Here is what happened" (261) and the third with "It didn't happen that way either. I'm not sure how it happened; not exactly. All I can hope for is a reconstruction: the way love feels is always only approximate" (263). In the last major section, "Salvaging," Offred confesses to sins against humanism like her willingness to sacrifice Nick to save her daughter and herself as well as her participation in the mutilation of the supposed rapist:

. . . it hurts me to tell it over, over again. Once was enough: wasn't once enough for me at the time? But I keep on going with this sad and hungry and sordid, this limping and mutilated story, because after all I want you to hear it, as I will hear yours too if I ever get the chance, if I meet you or if you escape, in the future or in heaven or in prison or underground, some other place. . . . I believe you're there, I believe you into being. Because I'm telling you this story I will your existence. I tell, therefore you are. (267–268)

This last is the postmodern version of the Cartesian *cogito*: because I tell stories you exist as listener/reader and I exist as teller/writer. Existence is finally textual.

The existential being of Offred's text is further problematized by the "Historical Notes." First, as the co-editor of the text indicates in his conference presentation, what we have been reading as *The Handmaid's Tale* is a transcription and therefore a translation of a spoken text rearranged and named by its editors, "based on some guesswork." The tapes were found in Maine, suggesting that Offred managed to get that far from what appears to have been Washington, D.C. The editor proceeds to a preoccupation with the historical antecedent of Offred's Commander, and only in the closing paragraphs returns to the speculation which is obviously of most interest to us, namely, "the ultimate fate of our narrator." He asks: "Did our narrator reach the outside world safely and build a new life for herself? Or was she discovered in her attic hiding place, arrested, sent to the Colonies or to Jezebel's, or even executed?" Shifting into comforting platitudes like "the past is a great darkness," our professor ignores the potentially most interesting questions: first, why does the narrative stop, rather than end? Did Offred have to leave for the last leg of her journey to deliverance or was the sanctuary of her speaking/writing place violated by her pursuers who would've thought her a "madwoman in the attic," indeed! Did Offred simply run out of tape? Was she then unwilling to erase earlier portions of the "last" tape and thus allowed an absence of closure or ending to stand?

What, finally, Atwood's conference presenter in "Historical Notes" does not consider is the effect of the unending-ness of Offred's narrative. If her narrative has no ending, or "death," how can the reader's desire for the end and the meaning it promises be satisfied? Can *The Handmaid's Tale*, which its editors reconstruct, and by implication then Atwood's text of the same name, have "meaning" without "death"? Is Offred a sort of fly trapped in the amber of eternity, a limbo of timelessness outside death, a reminder that all the Gileads and Oceanias and Brave New Worlds are not "historical," but infinitely possible recurrences? Or, is the narrative paradigm Peter Brooks inherited from Freud inherently "male," and is Offred a promise of a future in which alternative "female" paradigms of narrative will be found, along the lines of what Teresa de Lauretis and others have sought? Is Offred's "female" narrative a variety of "écriture feminine" and we male professors, like the co-editors of *The Handmaid's Tale*, "just don't get it"?

SUNY College at Brockport   **Earl G. Ingersoll**

WORKS CITED

Atwood, Margaret. *The Handmaid's Tale.* Boston: Houghton Mifflin, 1986.

Brooks, Peter. *Reading for the Plot: Design and Intention in Narrative.* New York: Knopf, 1984.

Hancock, Geoff. "Tightrope-Walking Over Niagara Falls" in *Margaret Atwood: Conversations.* Ed. Earl G. Ingersoll. Princeton, NJ: Ontario Review Press, 1990, 191-220.

Lauretis, Teresa de. *Technologies of Gender: Essays on Theory, Film, and Fiction.* Bloomington and Indianapolis: University of Indiana Press, 1987.

Orwell, George. *1984.* New York: New American Library, 1961.

Fictions et réalités du territoire
dans *L'Herbe et le varech* d'Hélène Ouvrard

L'espace territorial est un lieu privilégié de convergence symbolique et politique dans toutes les littératures issues de sociétés de type minoritaire. Il se charge d'une signification toute particulière quand les femmes doublement minoritaires dans ces sociétés se mettent à écrire. Les correspondances symboliques s'élargissent notablement et associent alors étroitement l'image du pays à conquérir et à redéfinir à celle du corps à délivrer et à réinventer. Les symboles du corps et du pays et les relations intimes qu'ils entretiennent dans *L'Herbe et le varech* (1980) d'Hélène Ouvrard illustrent particulièrement bien la richesse et la complexité de cette thématique qui revient à l'ordre du jour dans un Québec post-référendaire. La définition qu'Hélène Ouvrard donne de l'écriture au début du roman est significative à cet égard: "Dans l'écriture, le grand jeu, c'est celui de l'affabulation. Mise en place d'éléments (amants, voyages, séparation) qui permet que d'autres informations, complètement étrangères à cette situation (pays, vie intérieure, relations humaines), circulent, soient dites. L'affabulation a ses règles, qu'il faut non seulement découvrir mais imposer" (HV 12).

Le voyage de la narratrice aux confins du pays illustre de cette façon, avec la fuite d'un amour impossible, la grande passion qui aurait dû être: celle de l'homme et celle du pays. La fuite vers "ce pays corrosif, qui sans cesse me détruit en se détruisant"(115) trouve en effet son origine dans "l'éternelle absence" de l'"Homme québécois" (39). Le cheval blanc qui apparaît dans ses rêves symbolise ainsi l'homme à aimer, le pays à faire et l'oeuvre à réaliser, qui sont tous trois étroitement liés. Ce roman illustre ainsi l'étroite interaction entre identité nationale, identité sexuelle et identité culturelle. La forme utilisée privilégie cet aspect puisqu'il ne s'agit pas d'un roman à proprement parler, mais plutôt d'un texte qui associe les genres de l'essai poétique et du journal qui permet à la narratrice de dévoiler son cheminement intérieur: "Il n'y aura ici ni histoire ni personnages. Simplement livrer les incidences visuelles, mémo-psychiques, qui sont au fond la seule raison d'être du voyage, et seront celles du livre. Et les laisser, comme dans la vie, se court-circuiter allégrement" (HV 13). Une telle mise au point laisse donc à penser qu'il peut s'agir d'un texte autobiographique (la narratrice se définit par "je", sans jamais mentionner son prénom), mais que ce dernier est issu du voyage en question (il est dit au tout début qu'elle emporte un carnet de notes "en vue d'un roman"). Le découpage de l'ouvrage en trois parties intitulées successivement: "Notes de voyage", "Notes de séjour" et "Notes de retour" confirme également ce point de vue. Cette constatation va dans le sens de la volonté de l'auteur de mélanger les genres, de les "court-circuiter" car les frontières entre le réel et l'imaginaire sont constamment repoussées. Ce voyage se veut ainsi une quête de soi à travers un pays inaccessible, un "voyage parmi des fantômes" dans "une automobile hantée": "Je suis un souvenir et je glisse dans le reflet d'un pays disparu. . ." (HV 11).

Ce parcours initiatique à travers le pays est à l'image du voyage de la création littéraire et, par la même occasion, d'un voyage aux confins de soi. L'écriture agit comme un révélateur. L'image du pays, omiprésente, souligne l'*identification du destin individuel au destin collectif* (le premier ne pouvant se réaliser qu'à l'intérieur du second): "Tout ce qui n'est pas identique à moi m'échappe. **Moi**, seule, parcourant un **moi** plus grand: le pays" (HV 10). Une double association s'impose ici. L'une d'ordre psychique, reliée à la "conscience d'une identité intérieure, intimité bien abritée d'une structure psychique commune" (Freud).[1] Cette perception est particulièrement intéressante quand on l'applique aux femmes chez qui le besoin d'identification est très fort. Le "moi plus grand" dont parle Hélène Ouvrard serait ainsi un moyen de définir son identité intérieure de façon "viable", en l'occurence, au sein d'une "supra-identité" nationale. Il s'agirait d'une véritable "stratégie de survie" dans le sens où l'entend Annis Pratt. Cette stratégie est cependant limitée dans le temps et il est clair ici que la formation de l'identité "commence là où cesse l'utilité de l'identification" (Erikson 61).

L'autre association d'ordre symbiotique évoque celle du foetus avec sa mère.[2] Pareil retour sur soi s'accompagne en effet d'une véritable mystique féminine, nostalgie de l'idée de symbiose maternelle et de matriarcat ancien, retour nécessaire aux origines, aux temps mythiques où l'être était libre: "On vient ici, [...] pour retrouver en soi l'être originel, l'être antérieur, l'être des éternels recommencements. [...] (Antérieur: à la civilisation, à la pollution, à l'éducation, à ce que la vie a fait de nous)" (HV 18).

Ce retour aux origines, à des temps immémoriaux, loin de la corruption de la civilisation, est donc la condition première de la création car "pour écrire, il faut se reprendre, soi": "Je suis la pierre du début du monde, au moment de sa fusion pour l'éternité. Entendre et saisir en ce moment unique ma voix originale (HV 11). La dimension onirique et mythique du roman n'empêche cependant pas une lecture politique de celui-ci. Ainsi, le personnage du rêveur adopté résolument par Hélène Ouvrard illustre l'affirmation faite par Arguin en littérature québécoise selon laquelle "le personnage du rêveur est l'incarnation de l'aliénation" (Arguin 53).

Incapables d'affronter le réel, les personnages se réfugient alors dans un monde imaginaire. Comme plus tard dans *la Noyante*, la narratrice s'évade dans le pays mythique à défaut de posséder le pays réel, le passage de l'un à l'autre, par la métaphore de l'accouchement, s'avère douloureux et difficile: "Car n'était-ce pas mourir à soi-même que de s'arracher à cette terre et à cette mer originelles?" (HV 27). L'évasion systématique du personnage dans le rêve attesterait de son inadaptation à l'environnement et dans le cas d'Hélène Ouvrard, de son incapacité à se définir de façon exclusive par le biais d'une identité nationale. Beaucoup de personnages du roman québécois se trouvent plongés dans un monde qu'ils n'ont pas choisi, qu'ils n'acceptent pas et dans lequel ils se croient incapables de survivre.[3] Pour les personnages féminins, la définition de l'aliénation, à savoir être "étranger à soi-même", s'applique doublement. Il faut ainsi un véritable effort de la part de la narratrice pour reconstituer le puzzle de son identité éclatée: "Il y a en moi une étrangère. Cette nuit encore j'ai saisi une des bribes de sa vie. Incohérente comme toujours. Il me faut être plus attentive. Réunir suffisamment de bribes de son existence pour arriver à les accoler les unes aux autres et savoir **qui** elle est" (HV 85). Le recours à la troisième personne pour parler de soi installe une distance qui symbolise le chemin à parcourir pour recouvrer son identité personnelle. La syntaxe hachée illustre également cette distance: "Le lent retour à soi-même. Rentrer dans sa peau. Dire: **moi**. Recommencer à laisser venir les mots" (HV 10).

Tous les éléments mythiques contenus ultérieurement dans le roman *La Noyante* sont ici présents: la quête d'une identité personnelle, l'image du pays comme entité cosmique dans laquelle le sujet désire se fondre sans y parvenir, le frère jumeau avec qui l'alliance est impossible et la rivière comme élément féminin et source d'inspiration comme le résume ce passage:

> Je suis les méandres de la rivière
> Capricieuse comme le désir, comme l'inspiration
> Comme tout ce qui se cherche un corps
> Une âme, peut-être
> Une rivière qui fouille un pays pour s'y creuser une place...

J'attends. J'espère. Qui? Quoi? (HV 19)

De multiples lectures sont ici possibles. Il est cependant essentiel de relever l'image de la rivière comme élément féminin, l'"Eau-mère" selon la narratrice, élément à la fois désiré et redouté.[4] Le roman ayant été écrit à la fin des années soixante-dix, une lecture idéologique nous permet de situer celui-ci dans un contexte référendaire. La rivière "qui fouille un pays pour s'y creuser une place..." représenterait alors la difficulté des femmes à être admises dans le projet nationaliste, en même temps que les hésitations des instances politiques en charge de ce projet (le Parti Québécois) à les y admettre.[5] La lutte des femmes pour la reconnaissance de leur corps (contraception, avortement) s'inscrirait ici dans la lutte pour la reconnaissance du corps physique ou géographique: le pays ("comme tout ce qui se cherche un corps"). L'attente du "libérateur de la nation" (constante de l'idéologie nationaliste de Lionel Groulx à nos jours) se superpose ici à l'attente de l'homme, du "jumeau", du "double", qui accepterait enfin de reconnaître la femme comme son égale et sa partenaire. La reprise en mains du pays s'effectue en effet à double sens: "Pays dont je reprends possession. Pays qui reprend possession de moi. Mes racines nouvelles s'agrippent à cette terre où mes racines anciennes avaient déjà reconnu leur lignage (HV 32)".

Tous les adjectifs utilisés pour qualifier le pays pourraient de la même façon s'appliquer à la narratrice qui se qualifie d'"étrangère" à elle-même,[6] la liste en est significative: "pays multiple"(29), "pays indéfini"(55), "pays sauvage"(78), "pays éphémère"(109), "pays corrosif"(114), "pays incertain", "pays sans bon sens"(146), "pays futur"(148), "pays insaisissable"(149), "pays utopique"(150), "pays inexplicable"(150), "pays inconnu"(153), "pays incertain"(146, 154), "pays imaginaire"(156), "pays révélé"(156), "pays mouvant"(168)...

En dépit de ces références constantes, le pays est en danger et le sujet individuel par la même occasion. La métaphore de l'île assiégée rejoint bien ici les diverses composantes de l'imaginaire québécois: "La mer assiège mon île depuis trop longtemps. Ses assises ont cédé sous elle. [...] Le pays que j'ai connu s'efface peu à peu en sa révolution tranquille et je ne sais si ses sursauts violents auront raison du mal lent qui le gruge et nous retourne en sable" (HV 114). L'image est à nouveau développée à la fin du roman dans la symbolique de la maison considérée comme le dernier refuge contre un réel menaçant. Dans l'obscurité de la maison déserte, elle dit: "j'ai recréé autour de moi les limites du monde. Refermé l'univers—oeuf, ventre, nuit—" (HV 45).[7]

Le monde extérieur est en effet trop souvent le plus fort, qu'il s'agisse du "raz de marée de l'anglicisation"(114) sur la société québécoise ou, sur un plan plus individuel, du réel sur l'imaginaire de la femme (identité individuelle et identité collective étant ici confondus): "Le combat de ma vie, c'est celui de l'intérieur contre l'extérieur, l'extérieur gagnant toujours". Les deux combats sont menés parallèlement, la lutte, continuelle, n'est jamais gagnée d'avance. Le découragement et l'échec sont également partagés: "D'où me vient [...], le sentiment que tout est raté, notre destin collectif et nos destins individuels, au confluent desquels j'avais cru que nous nous rencontrions, toi et moi? [...] Nous sommes une grande nation qui fut brisée à sa naissance. (Nous vécûmes les débuts d'un grand amour toi et moi.)" (HV 148). L'échec du référendum est ici en filigrane dans un pays qui se dérobe toujours davantage: "Je vois, de jour en jour, ce pays si difficilement connu et accepté, bâti pierre à pierre, se défaire pierre à pierre, nous échapper de partout" (HV 117). Sentiment d'impuissance total quand le pays à réaliser toujours hors d'atteinte est qualifié de "fantôme", voire d'"inexistant"(160): "Fantômes d'un homme, d'un pays, que j'ai crus miens, que j'ai aimés" (HV 101).

L'association littéraire de l'échec amoureux et de l'échec national peut s'expliquer par le fait que l'amour, selon Van Schendel, est "le point de convergence de l'existence sociale et de la littérature". Ainsi, la littérature aurait toujours chargé l'amour "d'épouser ou au contraire de tromper le moment de l'histoire qu'elle avait pour fonction latente de représenter à la conscience" (154). L'amour est ainsi un "signe" de la structure et des relations sociales, en quelque sorte un "lieu mythique" qui exprimerait "le rôle malade de la tradition" et la dépossession comme le dit van Schendel: "Il n'est pas possible de parler de l'amour, quand l'amour devient le sens intime d'une réalité dont chacun, quant à soi et collectivement, est aliéné" (HV 162). C'est dans ce sens que la narratrice dit à son amant qu'il est l'être le plus agressif qu'elle ait connu mais elle souligne en même temps que "son agressivité *a une cause antérieure* à [elle], antérieure même à [ses] relations avec les femmes, bien que ce soit sur elles qu['il] la dévers[e]" (HV 61). Expression des relations inter-personnelles, elles-mêmes liées à un inconscient collectif, l'épanouissement personnel passe de cette façon par la libération collective. Ce douloureux épanouissement du sentiment amoureux en littérature serait alors dû à ce que Van Schendel désigne comme l'"inadéquation presque absolue des désirs à la réalité" (154).

C'est cette dualité constante chez Hélène Ouvrard qui s'exprime à travers le titre *l'Herbe et le varech* qui "se départagent très exactement le monde", l'herbe symbolise la réalité et le varech, le rêve ("le varech remplace sur les terres du rêve les dures réalités de l'herbe"(16)). L'herbe fixée au sol et le varech vagabondant au gré des flots qui le portent, constituent ainsi: "deux zones antagonistes [...], deux parties inconciliables qui ne peuvent se détruire l'une l'autre" (HV 108).

Pour ces mêmes raisons, l'antagonisme entre pays fictif et pays réel ne semble pas pouvoir se résoudre. Cette dualité revêt en effet des aspects multiples et irréconciliables, comme dans *la Noyante*; il y a opposition entre la ville et la campagne (Montréal est qualifiée de "ville étrangère", de "mère insensible", de "mère impitoyable" et d'"intruse", à l'origine de "mauvais sentiments" et de "rancune". Au sein même de la ville, il y a opposition entre l'ouest anglophone, "coeur monstrueux de la ville battant le pouls d'une puissance étrangère"(107) et l'Est francophone: "Montréal, me crachant à la face le mépris de ma langue" (106). En effet, pour Hélène Ouvrard: "Le procès de notre identité se jouait dans la rue, au jour le jour"(147). La ville est ainsi rejetée parce qu'elle incarne l'aliénation et l'assimilation croissante. De façon plus générale, ce pays est le leur (aux Canadiens-français) quand ils sont entre eux (au Québec) et ne leur appartient plus dès l'ouest de la ville qui semble être un avant-poste du Canada anglais à l'ouest de la province: "A l'ouest de la rue Saint-Laurent, un autre pays se bâtissait [...], un pays menaçant où l'on nous faisait bien sentir que nous n'étions pas chez nous" (HV 107).

Un tel passage renforce le thème privilégié de l'idéologie de survivance, la menace d'extinction par asphyxie. Il y a cependant subversion, dans une perspective féministe, de ce thème traditionnellement nationaliste. Ne dit-on pas qu'il existe une rue Saint-Laurent des sexes qui départage "de la même façon, entre hommes et femmes, les mêmes extravagants pouvoirs" (107).[8] Hélène Ouvrard illustre cette dualité lorsqu'elle nous dit qu'elle était "née à l'est dans les deux cas" (107). Elle se reconnaît objet d'aliénation à la fois sociale, nationale et sexuelle.[9] A la problématique nationale, se superpose constamment la problématique sexuelle, ce qui constitue une caractéristique originale de l'écriture des femmes. La condition féminine y est d'abord perçue comme un handicap car: "On n'échappe pas à la condition féminine. Un jour ou l'autre, elle nous rattrappe . . ." (65). Mais la condition de minoritaire est tout aussi aliénante: "J'appris que l'on peut naître handicapée par un pays, comme d'autres, naissent aveugles ou pieds-bots" (HV 147). Souvent à l'insu de l'auteur, la fiction se fait ainsi, articulation littéraire des démarches théoriques entreprises au même moment par les femmes.

Une autre dualité entre pays fictif et pays réel provient du rapport conflictuel avec la France.[10] Ainsi, symboliquement, le monde du *vrai* en Amérique du Nord parle la langue du père, le français standard étant considéré comme abstrait ou trop féminin. René Lapierre dit à ce sujet que la culture populaire n'accepte pas "de préférer le langage de la mère, plus doux et plus troublant, à celui du père dont la puissance est plus facile à mimer" (10). Cette dualité rêve/réalité, concret/ abstrait, culture/pouvoir, intérieur/extérieur, engendre de nombreuses frustrations. Devant ce dilemme, ajoute Lapierre, la culture populaire au Québec "trouve au niveau d'une valorisation de ce qu'elle estime être du concret (du "vrai") l'expression de sa force en face d'une culture historiquement écrasante" (8). C'est la démarche suivie par Hélène Ouvrard quand elle abandonne son rêve d'étudier à la Sorbonne, cette "Vie de l'Esprit qui n'était pas la Vraie Vie..." (147). C'est également cette dualité qu'elle exprime à travers la description du séjour de son arrière-grand-père aux Etats-Unis dans: "Cette Amérique de la matérialité, de la facilité, de la réussite, mais au seuil de laquelle on dépose son nom, sa langue, sa foi..." (HV 151). La France apparaît comme une entité abstraite dans l'imaginaire québécois, "la généralité française" comme l'appelle François Ricard (20) ou "la France mythique" selon Jacques Godbout qui engendre inévitablement isolement, désir, exaspération, destruction de la part du Québécois, d'autant que cette confrontation s'inscrit généralement en termes négatifs. Hélène Ouvrard abonde dans ce sens quand elle parle de la France comme d'"un pays fantôme" (11): "Je ne suis pas d'ici, je ne suis pas de là" (112). Plus loin, elle oppose très nettement "intégration au Nouveau-Monde" et "**contrepoids immatériel** de son amour, de sa langue, de sa foi . . ."(151), comme dans une lutte entre deux mondes qui s'affrontent. N'est-ce pas la définition même du thème du roman *l'Herbe et le varech*, à savoir l'opposition entre rêve et réalité, ces "deux parties inconciliables qui ne peuvent se détruire l'une l'autre" (108)? C'est aussi la définition du pays insaisissable: "Pays éphémère où le rêve porte en lui-même la réalité. Où la réalité enfante le rêve" (HV 109). Même la distance "nécessaire" de la France ne résoud pas pour autant la question de l'**ici** et de son identité. Le sentiment d'échec collectif et individuel qui anéantit la narratrice est trop fort: "Je vois en sa pérégrination tout un peuple à la recherche de lui-même et je porte en moi la triple blessure de mon déracinement familial, individuel, collectif" (HV 116).

Devant l'incapacité de ce peuple à déterminer son avenir et à choisir entre deux positions irréconciliables, "ce pays à trouver et à créer" ne peut donc se révéler qu'un demi-échec. C'est en ces termes que l'on peut qualifier les deux référendums sur la souveraineté du Québec où, bien qu'à un dizaine d'années d'intervalle, aucune majorité n'a pu clairement se manifester. Le québécois semble condamné à errer sans cesse en quête d'une définition de lui-même, d'une maison, d'un pays habitable: "S'il m'en coûte tant de me décider à habiter cette maison, c'est qu'elle ne pourra jamais être la nôtre. . . [. . .] C'est toujours la même que je reconstruis à l'image d'un monde qui n'existe pas" (HV 116).

Il est intéressant de remarquer ici que cette désillusion s'explique par le fait que la réalité finit toujours par l'emporter sur le rêve. C'est ainsi que le réel (matérialiste anglo-saxon) l'a emporté sur le mythe (culturel français) lors du référendum de 1980, d'où cette recherche du pays disparu constamment happé par le réel. C'est également ainsi que le roman s'achève sur le retour de la narratrice et de sa fille à la maison où elle a vécu autrefois, ce voyage est décrit de la façon suivante: "Nous n'avons pu résister à l'appel de l'irréalité. Nous sommes parties dans le pays incertain"(154). On nous dit cependant de la maison visitée que, bien que prémonitoire et symbolique, "ce n'est pas une maison pour y vivre"(161). La dualité du choix national se retrouve tout entière dans cette affirmation, le pays réel est invivable, mais le pays mythique demeure hors d'atteinte. Le mythe du pays est indispensable mais il est aussi insaisissable (il est en tout cas préférable à l'aspect réel (politique) comme l'indique la satire mordante des "grands révolutionnaires québécois" (164)). *L'Herbe et le varech* illustre ainsi à sa façon l'affirmation de Roland Barthes selon laquelle "l'écriture littéraire porte à la fois l'aliénation de l'histoire et le rêve de l'histoire" (1953, 64).

A l'image du pays dont elle est issue, la narratrice se trouve incapable de trancher et s'efforce de combiner de savants dosages pour échapper à l'emprise du réel: "j'ai toujours vécu la réalité si durement, si âprement malgré la densité du rêve" (165). L'amour est également condamné par cette indécision fondamentale à laquelle il n'y a aucun remède: "Notre amour est mort de n'avoir pu s'insérer dans la vie quotidienne mais il serait mort plus sûrement encore de s'y être inséré" (HV 165-6). Cette constatation clôt les incertitudes des années soixante-dix et le projet du "pays incertain" toujours recommencé jusqu'au prochain référendum. Comme le dit René Lapierre: "Il existera probablement toujours une contradiction assez grande entre le corps et l'esprit [...], entre la volonté agressive d'un pouvoir pragmatique vengeur et le regret d'une culture au sein de laquelle nous pourrions nous abstraire" (15). Comment s'étonner dès lors, de l'échec "d'une grande passion qui aurait dû être?". La seule gagnante est la femme qui y a gagné la possibilité de se définir: "Je tiens dans ma main, au creux de ma bouche qui enfin ose dire: **je**, la femme du présent et de l'avenir, ramenées au temps présent de l'être" (168).

Si cette phrase clôt le roman par la fin d'une grande passion et d'une époque révolue, elle anticipe le sentiment d'identités plurielles et d'une ère nouvelle pour les femmes.

University of Southwestern Louisiana   Bénédicte Mauguière

NOTES

1. Erikson définit l'identité comme un "processus" situé "au coeur de l'individu ainsi qu'au coeur de la culture de sa communauté" (1972, 18). La discussion sur l'identité ne peut dans ce cas *séparer la croissance personnelle des changements sociaux* pas plus d'ailleurs qu'on ne peut

dissocier la crise d'identité au sein de l'existence personnelle, des crises contemporaines inhérentes aux mutations historiques, car l'une come l'autre se définissent réciproquement, c'est-à-dire sont véritablement corrélatives" (Erikson 19). Dans notre perspective, c'est ce savoir sur soi-même qui est la source du sentiment d'identité personnelle (Codol, Touraine).

2. Voir à ce sujet Béatrice Didier quand elle dit que les femmes semblent retrouver leur véritable identité "comme dans une nostalgie de leur intégrité originelle" (Didier 33).

3. "Ils se sentent étrangers au monde qui les entoure et se sentent impuissants" nous dit Arguin (54).

4. Dans *la Noyante*, Hélène Ouvrard parle de: "la liquide frontière par où, si souvent au cours des siècles, s'était réalisée la malédiction féminine" (100). Sur ce thème, voir Mauguière 1995.

5. L'épisode politique des "Yvettes" est symptomatique de cette ambiguïté.

6. "Il y a en moi une étrangère" (HV 85).

7. Pour le thème de la maison, voir: Mauguière, Bénédicte. "Mythe, symbole et idéologie dans *La Noyante*". *The French Review* 65, 5 (Avril 1992): 754-764.

8. La partie à l'Est de la rue Saint-Laurent est consacrée à la prostitution.

9. Traditionnellement, l'Est de Montréal représente le quartier francophone plus pauvre.

10. Voir à ce sujet le numéro spécial de la revue *Liberté* intitulé "Haïr la France?" (1981) dont je m'inspire pour ce passage.

OUVRAGES CITES

Arguin, Maurice. *Le Roman québécois de 1944 à 1965*. Québec: Coll. Essais. Centre de Recherche en Littérature Québécoise (CRELIQ) n.1, 1985.

Didier, Béatrice. *L'Ecriture-femme*. Paris: Presses Universitaires de France. Coll. écriture, 1981.

Erikson, Erik. *Adolescence et crise: la quête de l'identité*. Paris: Flammarion, Coll. Champs, 1972. Traduction française de *Identity Youth and Crisis*. New York: Norton, 1968.

Freud, Sigmund. "The Anatomy of the Mental Personality." Lecture 31. *New Introductory Lectures in Psychoanalysis.* New York: Norton, 1933.

Lapierre, René. "Les desperados de l'Amérique." *Liberté* 138 (1981), 5-16.

Mauguière, Bénédicte. "La Noyante ou la subversion du mythe d'Ophélie" in: *L'eau, source d'une écriture dans la littérature féminine francophone.* Y. Helm, ed. Francophone Cultures and Literatures Serie. New York/London/Paris/ Berlin: Peter Lang Publishing, 1995.

————. "Mythe, symbole et idéologie du pays dans *La Noyante.*" *The French Review* 65, 5 (Avril 1992): 754-764.

Ouvrard, Hélène. *L'Herbe et le varech.* Montréal: Québec/Amérique, Coll. "Littérature d'Amérique," 1980.
Pratt, Annis. *Archetypal Patterns in Women's Fiction.* Bloomington: Indiana University Press, 1981

Ricard, François. "Choisir le relais français". *Liberté* 138 (1981), 17-22.

Van Schendel, Michel. "L'Amour dans la littérature canadienne-française" in *Littérature et société canadienne-française.* F. Dumont et J.C. Falardeau eds. Deuxième colloque de *Recherches sociographiques.* Québec: Presses de l'Université Laval, 1964.

Vers une nouvelle subjectivité?

"Transferts": transports, déplacements, croisements, mélanges, échanges, interactions, correspondances, traversées, intertextes, phénomènes transculturels, glissements, altérations. La liste des équivalences, son abondance même, illustre probablement plus que tout la facilité que nous avons aujourd'hui à faire surgir dans notre pensée des concepts qui concernent les passages, les entre-deux (ou les entre-plusieurs), qui disent l'espèce d'affection intellectuelle que nous avons pour ce qui bouge, pour tout ce qui ne trouve pas son assise en soi-même et n'a pas de lieu propre. Barthes et surtout Derrida ont laissé leur marque: le *sens* lui-même serait un incessant transfert, un infini déplacement, toujours ailleurs, toujours remis à plus tard. Habermas y a vu là, non sans paradoxe, un "concept mystique de la tradition comme processus de différence de la révélation" (216). Si l'on interprète la notion de "transferts culturels" dans l'optique déconstructionniste critiquée par Habermas, cela signifie que nous cherchons à décrire une littérature (et une culture), québécoise en l'occurence, comme jamais présente à elle-même, toujours différée dans d'incessants processus de déplacements. Une littérature et une culture "migrante", dans le sens le plus radical, ontologique du terme.

Je voudrais, très sommairement, adopter une attitude critique à l'égard de cette notion et de la perspective qu'elle développe. Cette critique, on le comprendra, je me l'adresse d'abord à moi-même, et je la considère comme un préalable. Non pas dans une attitude révisionniste qui consisterait à revenir en arrière, à rétablir platement, et paradoxalement, une problématique de l'identité et de l'homogénéité. Je suis à cet égard totalement d'accord avec les propos récents d'un Jean-Luc Nancy qui, à partir d'une réflexion sur le désastre de Sarajevo, affirmait: "L'éloge simpliste du mélange a pu engendrer des *erreurs*, mais l'éloge simpliste de la pureté a soutenu et soutient des *crimes*. Il n'y a donc à cet égard aucune symétrie, aucun équilibre à tenir, aucun juste milieu" (11).

Cela dit, le fait même que la notion de "transferts culturels" appartienne à un paradigme bien établi dans la culture et la théorie littéraire actuelle (celui-là même que décrivait mon énumération initiale), devrait déjà spontanément susciter une interrogation critique. Je poserais celle-ci en ces termes: qui, au juste, fait l'expérience des transferts culturels; quel type de subjectivité vit ces incessants déplacements, ces migrations, ces mélanges? Où et à partir de quels états de conscience cela se passe-t-il? N'y a-t-il pas un danger, ici, de décrire des processus impersonnels, globaux, qui ne tiennent pas assez compte de ce qui se passe dans les sujets concrets? Que disent les textes littéraires à cet égard?

Dans mes travaux précédents, notamment dans *L'écologie du réel* (1988), j'avais cherché à définir cette subjectivité en termes de "ritualisation", par opposition aux problématiques de la *fondation* et de la *transgression* qui avaient précédé. J'entendais par là que l'expérience fondamentale que fait le sujet du monde et de la culture actuels est celle du *chaos*, et que celle-ci entraîne des pratiques rituelles qui sont autant de mises en forme de l'expérience, des manières d'endiguer le gaspillage d'énergie vitale. Je voyais dans l'œuvre d'un Jacques Poulin, entre autres, un bel exemple de cette manière de poser la subjectivité dans le monde des choses et des signes.

Que la notion de "rituel" soit très populaire dans les milieux du Nouvel Age ne me paraît pas une raison suffisante pour la rejeter. Ce qui me semble important ici, c'est que ce rapport au désordre et au chaos ne puisse pas être pensé en termes *mythiques* (expérience d'un retour au magma originel, plongée dans un milieu archaïque en vue d'une renaissance—comme c'était le cas souvent à l'époque de la poésie du pays), ni en termes de *transgression* (la littérature comme pratique raisonnée du désordre, comme affirmation de l'inconscient souverain, comme pouvoir qu'à l'irrationnel de rajeunir, de renouveler un monde figé—conception qui a nourri les courants surréalistes, marxistes et jusqu'à un certain point, féministes, jusqu'au début des années quatre-vingt).

Non. Parler de "ritualisation", d'un sujet qui se définit dans des pratiques rituelles, c'est dire que le chaos est plutôt un horizon constant et même un milieu ambiant. On ne saurait le "surmonter", le "dépasser", ni le "mythifier": il constitue plutot le champ à l'intérieur duquel le sujet élabore des zones harmonieuses, des îlots d'ordre, des expériences aiguës mais non extatiques de conscience, de présence à ce qui est. Ces lieux, ces formes sont forcément éphémères, mais elles n'en sont pas moins authentiques, et elles ont une qualité éthique, faite de précision, de respect, de recueillement.

Ces remarques fort générales n'auraient à vrai dire aucune valeur si elles ne pouvaient se mesurer à un certain nombre d'œuvres qui, surtout depuis le milieu des années quatre-vingt, apportent indéniablement quelque chose de neuf dans le paysage littéraire québécois: une sorte d'intensité discrète, une sorte de douceur stylistique souvent liée à une intimité tantôt fragile, tantôt fervente. Ce sont des œuvres aux antipodes du baroque et du bariolage. Chez les aînés, André Major, avec *L'hiver au cœur* et Jacques Brault, avec *Agonie*, me paraissent appartenir à ce courant. Chez les plus jeunes, je mentonnerais entre autres Lise Tremblay, Pierre Gobeil, Elise Turcotte. Cette dernière retiendra surtout ici mon attention, car parmi ces écrivains, elle est sans doute l'une des plus remarquables. Les circonstances s'y prêtent d'autant plus que son très beau roman, *Le bruit des choses vivantes* (paru chez Leméac en 1991) a été traduit en anglais (*The Sound of Living Things*) et a fait l'objet d'un bref compte rendu dans le *New York Times*, au début de cette année.

Il est utile de rappeler qu'avant ce roman, Elise Turcotte s'était déjà imposée comme poète et qu'elle est à ce jour la seule à avoir obtenu deux fois le Prix Emile-Nelligan accordé chaque année à un jeune poète. *La terre est ici*, paru en 1989, deux ans avant le roman, pose déjà par son seul titre deux termes dont l'importance se vérifiera dans *Le bruit des choses vivantes*: la "terre", c'est-à-dire la planète, son Histoire avec un grand H, mais aussi sa géographie, ses paysages vus ou imaginés: et "ici", c'est-à-dire le plus proche, le plus intime: le Moi et sa demeure dans la ville. Les deux pôles, bien sûr, sont inséparables: le plus vaste est dans le plus petit, et il faut prendre ce "dans" au sens littéral, physique autant que psychique: "Ici, entre ces murs, les fiords dorment dans nos têtes" (*La terre est ici* 44), peut-on lire à la fin d'un poème, et plus loin: "La maison se remplit de corps et de ciels" (*La terre est ici* 50). Cet espace intime infiniment ouvert est le lieu d'une subjectivité fragile et rêveuse, qui cherche sa vérité dans la précision insensée des images, dans un enchantement tranquille qui est sa manière personnelle d'habiter le monde.

Le bruit des choses vivantes se situe essentiellement dans le même espace, mais envisagé constamment du point de vue de la relation d'une mère, Albanie, et de sa fille de quatre ans, Maria. Tout le roman se passe à la maison, autour de la maison, entre la maison et le lieu de travail (Albanie est bibliothécaire), la garderie, ou d'autres maisons toutes assez proches: celle du petit Félix et de son père qui habitent en face, celles de l'ex-conjoint, d'une amie ou d'un nouvel amant. Albanie et sa fille rêvent d'un voyage dans le grand nord, les "fiords de l'Alas/ça dorment dans leurs têtes", comme disait à peu de choses près *La terre est ici*. Mais nous n'assisterons qu'aux tout derniers préparatifs avant le départ et le voyage aura lieu au-delà du livre. En somme, il est difficile d'imaginer un roman qui soit plus sédentaire, où le monde soit autant perçu et imaginé à partir d'un seul et unique point de vue spatio-temporel: la maison et la vie quotidienne.

La toute première phrase du roman peut paraître désolante de banalité: "Plusieurs choses arrivent dans ce monde" (11). Cette ouverture à profil bas débouche pourtant sur une donnée essentielle, déjà pressentie dans le mot "plusieurs"; il s'agit de ce rapport au désordre et au chaos dont je parlais plus haut. "Le monde" dont il est question ici se définit par un effet de nombre : il y a trop d'images, trop de choses, trop d'histoires de toutes sortes, vues, entendues, inventées. La première image présentée par la narratrice est celle d'un bébé iranien à deux têtes vu dans un reportage télévisé. L'image suivante montre une femme dont un oeil pleure tandis que l'autre est sec. La tête, le visage, ces formes primordiales de la personne, sont d'emblée soumis à cette pluralité: surabondance, unité brisée, discordance.

La vie, la conscience d'Albanie entretiennent un rapport constant au pluriel et au désordre: jouets qui traînent, piles de linges, livres à classer par pays ou par ordre alphabétique à la bibliothèque, images télévisées qui ne montrent elles-mêmes que des perturbations, des dérèglements: tremblements de terre, enfants faméliques, soulèvement des foules en Europe de l'Est, juste avant l'écroulement du Mur de Berlin. Mais ce ne sont pas ces contenus, où nous n'avons pas de mal à retrouver notre propre expérience du monde actuel, qui donnent au roman d'Elise Turcotte sa couleur propre: c'est le traitement qui en est fait, l'insertion de cet horizon désordonné et surabondant dans un lieu extrêmement intime, plus précisément dans une pratique absolument inflexible de l'habitation, conçue non pas métaphoriquement mais au sens propre comme "le centre de l'univers" (80), un espace fermé avec des fenêtres et une porte, avec une télévision et un téléphone, et une enfant qui grandit et découvre le monde. Dans cet espace entre quatre murs, tout se déverse, tout converge, tout fait image.

"J'ai toujours aimé les maisons. On pourrait me définir comme une fille qui aime les maisons et les glaciers" (54), dit la narratrice, qui reconnaît s'être fréquemment adonné à ces visites libres de maisons annoncées par les agents d'immeubles, les dimanches après-midi, et qui aime passer l'Halloween avec sa fille pour la même raison: les maisons et le coup d'œil fugace que l'on peut jeter sur leur intérieur. A l'inverse, Agnès, une femme qui passe toutes ses journées à la bibliothèque, a vécu le drame terrible de l'incendie de son appartement et elle a longtemps traîné avec elle l'odeur du feu. Mais la maison est bien davantage ici qu'un abri ou un foyer, au sens traditionnel, familial, du terme. Ce n'est sûrement pas la "maison du père" qu'a décrite Patricia Smart dans son étude sur le sujet-femme dans l'écriture québécoise. La maison d'Elise Turcotte est plutôt le lieu psychique (autant que physique) où transitent toutes les images, toutes les nouvelles du petit et du vaste monde, ce qui veut dire aussi qu'elle est un lieu de *transferts*, de constants investissements émotifs dans des objets, des réalités, des personnes étrangères. L'omniprésence de la télévision, dans *Le bruit des choses vivantes*, va évidemment dans ce sens: au-delà de la position de voyeur ou de simple spectateur, la télévision est l'expérience d'une extériorité et d'une altérité totales qui habitent momentanément mon intimité, qui la forcent à s'investir psychiquement en elles. Je ne deviens pas autre, je deviens *témoin*, l'une des valeurs-clés à mon avis de tout le roman. Car être témoin, c'est être plus qu'une simple spectatrice, même si l'on parle trop souvent aujourd'hui de "témoins impuissants": être témoin, que ce soit d'une horreur lointaine ou d'un petit voisin mal aimé, c'est être présent, c'est participer au moment même où tout éclate ou s'effondre, c'est du même coup entrer dans une relation qui concerne les mots, le "témoignage", justement. Et il me semble que ce qui donne avant tout sa "beauté" au livre d'Elise Turcotte, c'est précisément ce travail de liaison, ce recueillement où le sujet cherche à s'"imprégner" (129) des images qui lui sont les plus extérieures. Faire en sorte que le dehors, le lointain, l'étranger deviennent mien, non pas au sens d'une connaissance ou d'une action, mais au sens d'un témoignage, d'un "être là" (209) qui est selon la narratrice la qualité essentielle que peut avoir une personne. Qualité modeste, certes, mais peut-être sommes nous plus que jamais dans un monde où l'on peut apprécier et même cultiver les affirmations modestes.

Une part de la présence dont je parle est une résistance à ce qui est le plus insupportable non pas dans le monde lui-même mais dans le discours que l'on tient ou que l'on entend sur lui. La petite Maria a ce commentaire suave qui dit tout là-dessus: "[...] la vie, c'est épouvantable, ils l'ont dit à la télévision" (69). La maison est ce lieu où la terreur pénètre mais où elle se trouve endiguée (bien que jamais définitivement) par le sujet-témoin, par ce qu'il peut recueillir d'impressions et d'images pour les transformer en paroles. En ce sens, cette maison est assez proche des très belles pages que le philosophe Emmaneul Lévinas consacre à l'habitation et à la demeure dans son maître-livre *Totalité et infini*. Lévinas écrit que "le recueillement et la représentation se produisent concrètement comme habitation dans une demeure ou une maison. Mais l'intériorité de la maison est faite d'extraterritorialité au sein des éléments de la jouissance dont se nourrit la vie", et il ajoute: "L'habitation et l'intimité de la demeure qui rend possible la séparation de l'être humain, suppose [...] une première révélation d'Autrui (161). N'ayant pas le temps de commenter en détail, je retiendrai simplement cette idée riche et lumineuse: la maison comme extraterritorialité, comme déracinement et séparation, mais aussi comme lieu d'accueil privilégié à autrui.

Le monde d'Elise Turcotte n'est pas un monde d'appartenance et d'identité; bien au contraire, on risque toujours ici de se retrouver dans l'irréel, de n'être plus qu'un personnage dans un film ou dans un vidéo, de redevenir un témoin "impuissant", simple spectateur ou spectatrice. Le monde médiatique est fort présent ici, beaucoup plus en fait que la littérature, malgré une citation de Joyce Carol Oates et la lecture d'un roman qui a pour titre *Frankie Addams*. Comme dans tous les livres d'Elise Turcotte, les allusions à la musique populaire sont nombreuses: Liza Minelli, les Rolling Stones, Bashung, etc. Nous sommes à Montréal mais le Québec n'existe guère ici comme référence, comme culture.

En ce sens, la maison est vraiment "hors territoire", lieu de séparation et de déracinement. Mais c'est justement par là que le roman élabore le lieu même de la subjectivité, dans le temps et l'espace rituels de la demeure, là où tout se déroule en se répétant, là où il faut toujours mettre de l'ordre, là où "la terre est [vraiment] ici". Toutes les dérives et traversées dont je parlais au tout début, tous ces "transferts", transactions et déplacements qui constituent notre monde empirique et conceptuel prennent dans *Le bruit des choses vivantes* une autre couleur, apparaissent sous un autre éclairage. Comme d'autres oeuvres parues au Québec depuis dix ans, ce roman échappe dans une grande mesure aux descriptions que nous avons cherché à faire du "roman québécois des années quatre-vingt". *Le bruit des choses vivantes* n'est pas un roman de migration réelle, de désastre ni de fête. Ce n'est pas un roman qui montre un désir d'action et de puissance en même temps qu'une soif de sacré, comme ces oeuvres qu'un Gilles Marcotte rattachait au "Temps du Matou". Le roman d'Elise Turcotte n'est pas davantage porté sur les jeux post-modernes qu'a étudiés une Janet Paterson: pas d'autoréférence ici, aucun jeu sur la pluralité des voix narratives.

Sans rien de tout cela, le roman se constitue comme un noyau psychique par où transite le monde entier, du plus proche au plus lointain. Il dit qu'habiter n'est pas nécessairement un repli ou un retrait, mais une séparation qui est en même temps une ouverture et aussi, comme dit Lévinas, "le contraire de l'extase". Cela est très important et inséparable du ton antilyrique, toujours retenu, du livre. Les images d'Elise Turcotte ne sont pas extatiques, ce sont des images errantes qui ont trouvé un "chez soi", qui disent que tous les voyages, tous les échanges, tous les croisements de cultures doivent bien, quelque part, trouver un foyer, se situer dans un sujet qui habite le monde.

Université de Montréal **Pierre Nepveu**

OUVRAGES CITES

Habermas, J. *Le discours philosophique de la modernité.* Paris: Gallimard, 1988.

Lévinas, Emmanuel. *Totalité et infini. Essai sur l'extériorité.* Le livre de poche, "Biblio/Essais", 1990.

Marcotte, Gilles. "Le temps du Matou". *Paragraphe,* 2, "Autrement, le Québec. Conférences 1988-1989". Université de Montréal, 1989. 33-49.

Nancy, Jean-Luc. "Eloge de la mêlée". *Transeuropéennes* 1 (automne 1993), 11.

Paterson, Janet. *Moments postmodernes dans le roman québécois.* Ottawa: Presses de l'Université d'Ottawa, 1993.

Turcotte, Elise. *La terre est ici.* Montréal: VLB éditeur, 1989.

———. *Le bruit des choses vivantes.* Montréal: Léméac, 1991.

Le "lieu commun" à redéfinir dans *Babel, prise deux ou Nous avons tous découvert l'Amérique* de Francine Noël: la ville, le verbe et le vertige

La Tour de Babel: un lieu commun peu commun

Le mythe de la tour de Babel connaît en ce moment une certaine popularité, grâce à sa pertinence indéniable pour des sociétés où des populations de langues différentes vivent en proximité géographique, le partage de l'espace les forçant à essayer de se comprendre pour éviter une confrontation douloureuse. Plusieurs auteurs ont ressuscité ce mythe, de Borgès à A.S. Byatt, en passant par Derrida.[1] L'accent peut être sur l'aspect perçu le plus souvent comme positif: la cohabitation paisible, utopique (mais éventuellement totalitaire) de la tour unilingue, intégrale et cohérente d'avant la chute. Mais on peut aussi souligner l'aspect perçu habituellement comme négatif: la diaspora polyvalente et polyglotte qu'un Dieu jaloux a imposée aux anciens habitants de la Tour.[2]

Quand Francine Noël a publié *Babel, prise deux* en 1990, elle n'était pas la première au Québec à choisir un titre semblable: son éditeur montréalais, VLB, avait déjà fait paraître en 1981 un texte de Renaud Longchamp désigné *Babelle I: Après le déluge*. Dans un entretien publié en 1993 dans un numéro spécial de la revue *Voix et Images* (18:2) consacré à son oeuvre, Noël exprime son espoir que son roman à elle, dans son ensemble, "montre assez bien la dérive dans laquelle nous sommes emportés collectivement" (233).

La Tour de Babel biblique a été construite par les fils de Noé après le déluge. Noël résiste à la tentation de rêver à une deuxième arche (de "Noël"?), réservée aux Québécois "de souche" ou "pure laine", pour échapper à l'inondation d'immigrants allophones (devenant vite anglophones) qui risque de les noyer. Au contraire, "... nous sommes tous dans la Tour refuge... nous avons tous découvert l'Amérique!" (364). Ce récit représente la ville de Montréal telle qu'elle est maintenant (cosmopolite, bigarrée, en re-construction) du point de vue d'une Québécoise "de souche". Selon le rêve de la narratrice, Fatima Gagné, dont le journal intime occupe les trois quarts du livre, cette nouvelle Babel devrait permettre aux différentes communautés de cohabiter sans se piétiner, de communiquer sans perdre leur hétérogénéité. Il s'agit d'un accueil au multiculturalisme qui va à l'encontre de ce qui est perçu dans l'ouest du Canada comme un certain intégrisme québécois—l'attitude qui a permis à Jacques Parizeau, après le dernier référendum, de rendre les minorités ethniques responsables du "non" à la séparation du Québec. Le sous-titre de Noël, "Nous avons tous découvert l'Amérique", renferme une allusion à l'étude de Todorov, *La Conquête de l'Amérique. La question de l'autre*.[3] L'Amérique représente ici la terre d'immigration par excellence, que ce soit l'Amérique du Nord ou l'Amérique du Sud, que la langue dominante soit le français, l'anglais ou l'espagnol: dans cette perspective, les Québécois sont des immigrants comme les autres. Sur une base composée des cultures autochtones plus ou moins enterrées, des couches successives se construisent. La substitution fait concurrence à la juxtaposition, l'axe vertical à l'axe horizontal; la métaphore de la tour l'emporte dans ce roman sur sur la métonymie de la mosaïque. C'est la confusion entre les deux axes—de la contiguïté et de la similarité—qui pose des problèmes. Ceux-ci sont reliés non seulement à la territorialité, mais à la langue: là où les deux se rencontrent se trouve la faille qui peut faire effondrer la Tour et rendre impossible la cohabitation paisible.

Différences et juxtapositions

Le texte, *Babel, Prise Deux*, constitue un commentaire sur les rapports entre ces deux axes, qui gouvernent l'organisation de l'espace et de la parole: la combinaison et la sélection. Le "lieu commun" se redéfinit non seulement comme le terrain partagé à la base, mais aussi comme le "lieu commun" verbal nécessaire pour établir la communication. Comme Gide a dit, "On ne s'entend que sur les lieux communs. Sans territoire banal, la société n'est plus possible".[4] La tour doit se construire sur une fondation commune. Mais tout comme l'horizontalité suppose un centre et une périphérie, ou une origine et des suites, la verticalité suppose aussi une hiérarchie: les étages de la tour risquent de devenir les rangs d'une échelle. Ou, conversement, les habitants du rez-de-chaussée, gardiens des fondations, peuvent s'ériger en propriétaires, reléguant les autres locataires à un état de dépendance ou de subjection. Il s'agit pour Noël de transformer les locataires en locutaires, mais pour ce faire il faut que tous puissent se rencontrer en terrain neutre. Pour défaire une hiérarchie il faut l'applatir, au risque de s'écraser. Pour trouver une langue commune il faut renoncer à l'unilinguisme, au risque de ne plus pouvoir parler sa propre langue.

Le défi à relever par Noël est d'autant plus difficile qu'elle veut relier les problèmes de communication et de cohabitation entre différents groupes linguistiques et ethniques à la différence entre les sexes. Cette autre division culturelle et physique est composée elle aussi d'une dimension spatiale et une dimension verbale. Il s'agit d'une opposition entre le domaine public et le domaine privé.

La patrie au nom du père / la maison et la langue maternelle

Dans le contexte du Québec, la masculinité est souvent associée à la langue anglaise dominante, la féminité à la langue française. Fatima compose le dialogue imaginaire suivant: "This country is mine", dit-il, "Ce pays est aussi le mien", she replies (180). Pourtant, il n'y a aucun personnage important anglophone dans ce roman. Le masculin est représenté plutôt par deux hommes québécois—les deux amants de Fatima—qui s'intéressent surtout à la construction physique (221, 233), étant l'un (Louis) architecte-sculpteur, l'autre (Guillaume) géographe-urbaniste. Les femmes, par contre, sont préoccupées par des questions de construction verbale, puisque Fatima elle-même est orthophoniste et travaille avec des personnes souffrant d'aphasie (137, 200), tandis qu'Amélia, sa meilleure amie et *alter ego*, est traductrice.

Amélia représente le métissage de naissance, étant moitié française (de France) et moitié espagnole (60). Son exil est volontaire, puisqu'elle a immigré au Québec, suivant un Québécois qu'elle a épousé. Malgré leur divorce elle a gardé son nom à lui, *Malaise* (44), qui est celui de leurs enfants. Fatima elle-même porte un prénom arabe, grâce à la prédilection de sa grand-mère catholique pour la Vierge de Fatima (objet de dévotion portugais, populaire au Québec à l'époque).[5] Chacune est marquée par des lieux et des signes culturels auxquels elle ne s'identifie plus. Elles illustrent l'observation de Fatima: "Ici plus personne ne ressemble à ses origines. C'est un lieu de mutations. Babel in progress!" (50). Pourtant chacune garde une certaine nostalgie (dans le cas d'Amélia) ou culpabilité (dans le cas de Fatima) envers sa famille et son milieu d'origine.

Le principe patriarcal de marquer l'appartenance à un endroit et à une famille par le Nom du Père, signe de la propriété et de la légitimité, paraît anachronique. Le nom de famille de Fatima, "Gagné", s'avère peu approprié, car son père (fort sur le partage) vient de perdre possession de son garage au profit d'un ancien employé appelé O'Sullivan (voir *Maryse*), plus habile que lui dans les affaires. Cette métaphore évidente de l'état du Québec se prolonge dans le refus de Fatima d'avoir des enfants, contrairement à sa voisine, la "grosse femme d'à côté", Canadienne française ("Cf") xénophobe à l'ancienne, qui est enceinte (comme celle du roman de Michel Tremblay *La grosse femme d'à côté est enceinte*, 1978). La légitimité de la famille traditionnelle est aussi mise en question par la garde partagée des enfants de parents divorcés, comme ceux d'Amélia. Déchirés entre leurs parents, comme les immigrants entre deux pays, ils passent leur temps entre deux maisons.

Ce modèle du domicile non-fixe est présenté ailleurs dans le texte comme préférable à l'enracinement immobilisateur et territorial. Amélia n'arrive pas à s'installer en permanence dans sa maison de Ville Mont Royal, où elle continue à vivre en gitane, dans des valises, n'occupant qu'une petite partie de l'espace libre (8, 85, 164). Elle fait le tour des maisons à vendre, n'arrivant pas à choisir définitivement un lieu de résidence permanente. Nomade de naissance, sa décision ultime d'adhérer au Québec s'avèrera impossible. Pour elle, la maison représente les souvenirs associés à la construction d'une identité personnelle, davantage qu'un refuge physique à protéger. Sa maison toujours ouverte ressemble à une auberge (164). Elle ne mangera jamais les tomates qu'elle plante, puisqu'elle n'arrive pas elle-même à s'implanter.

Pour Louis, l'ex-amant d'Amélia, la maison familiale est celle de sa femme Hélène, légitime et autocrate,[6] à Notre Dame de Grâce, d'où il voudrait s'évader (72). C'est la raison pour laquelle il s'établit provisoirement et à temps partiel dans l'appartement vide en face de chez Fatima. Contrairement à Amélia, les deux protègent leur lieu privé, surtout contre les personnes du sexe opposé (Fatima: 12, 38, 66; Louis: 124). Pour qu'ils se retrouvent, des espaces intermédiaires communs sont essentiels.

Le plan de la ville: la rue comme lieu commun

D'abord un café, La Croissanterie, devient leur "lieu commun" (106, 129-130), ensuite les musées et les hôtels. La rue entre les deux représente au début une frontière presqu'infranchissable. Pourtant, l'image dominante du journal de Fatima devient celle de Louis qui traverse la rue pour la rejoindre (291). Le fait qu'il a déjà été (à l'insu de Fatima) l'amant d'Amélia, qu'elle aime aussi, produit un effet de dédoublement basé sur la substitution de "l'étrangère" (Amélia) à la place de l'habitant et vice-versa. Ces changements de "case" (de place par rapport à l'autre et de maison) imitent la projection de l'axe vertical sur l'axe horizontal, associé par Jakobson à la fonction poétique. "Case" est le terme employé par Fatima, qui voudrait, d'un côté, savoir "chacun à sa case" (214), mais qui cherche aussi à démolir les cloisons.

Sa rue "limotrophe" (38, 266), la rue Hutchison,[7] divise le Plateau de Montréal (lieu d'origine pour Fatima, qui a grandi dans la rue Marie-Anne) du secteur d'Outremont où dominent les Juifs hassidiques. Ceux-ci provoquent chez elle un mélange de curiosité et de ressentiment: révélant son propre sens de propriétaire, elle commente: "Ils circulent dans nos rues" (37), mais elle a l'impression qu'ils croient que "le trottoir leur appartient" (268). La rue, le trottoir, autant de lieux communs où le partage ne va pas toujours de soi, puisque l'espace est étroit. Fatima raconte une confrontation avec des garçons hassidiques qui l'empêchent de marcher sur le trottoir, l'insultant en anglais. Ses tentatives de se rapprocher de Louis seront accompagnés d'un effort parallèle pour rejoindre une voisine hassidique qui finira par lui rendre son sourire un jour qu'elle est seule: signe d'espoir pour l'avenir? Noël avoue dans l'entretien cité plus haut qu'elle a eu peur de déplaire à la communauté juive.

La ville de Montréal, nouvelle Babel, est évoquée dans ce roman, aussi bien que dans les deux romans précédents de Noël (*Maryse*, 1983 et *Myriam Première*, 1987),[8] comme un espace concret intimement connu, mais aussi comme un texte, une série de toponymies qui inscrivent une ville mythique, intertextuelle (tissée d'allusions à Tremblay ou à *Bonheur d'occasion* de Gabrielle Roy). L'espace a une dimension linguistique et littéraire. Ici il s'agit surtout des noms de rue arpentées par Fatima, le jour et la nuit: Laurier, Lajoie, Stuart, Avenue du Parc: réseau qui constitue son "chez soi" autant que son appartement. Cette toile de fond sert aussi de filet de sauvetage, puisqu'elle s'y sent invulnérable, malgré la violence croissante du quartier. La familiarité de ces rues est mise en contraste avec des endroits exotiques, plus ou moins rêvés, tels que la Côte Nord, "l'île perdue" (180) ou le marais secret où Louis l'emmène. Le milieu de Babel est nécessairement urbain. Fatima a moins de mal à imaginer une grande ville cosmopolite en Europe ou en Amérique latine qu'une campagne perdue au Québec.

Le lieu commun verbal et vertical

Au cours de ses pérégrinations à travers la ville, Fatima rencontre un échantillon des habitants mixtes et bigarrés de la nouvelle Babylone, paumés, ou bien intégrés comme son ami juif, Allan, qui proteste, en réponse à ses questions sur les Juifs: "...je ne suis pas que juif

(...) pas juif à plein temps" (186). Elle est prête à l'accepter, lui, comme un Québécois, puisqu'il a adopté l'idiolecte du pays (186). Les différences d'origine, d'ethnie ou de religion s'estompent devant l'importance de la langue. C'est pour défendre son droit à vivre en français que Fatima appuie la Loi 101 et proteste que les immigrants doivent parler français, parce que "nous sommes leur lieu commun" (363). Pour elle, la communauté linguistique l'emporte sur la géographie. C'est pour cette raison que sa meilleure amie est une Française polyglotte, qui affirme la valeur du français tout en allant par la traduction vers les allophones, surtout les hispanophones qui partagent l'Amérique. Il s'agit de "faire le pont entre deux cultures" (26), capacité que Fatima envie mais qui condamne Amélia au "non lieu" de la mort.

Le progrès vers une utopie babélienne rêvée par Fatima (voir Potvin, 1993) achoppe quand les deux personnages qui semblent le plus près de l'atteindre rencontrent les dangers associés aux hauteurs. L'envolée d'Amélia tombe, littéralement, à l'eau. Le mythe de Babel se confond avec celui d'Icare (252, 339, 344, 354), autre tentative d'atteindre le ciel. Amélia-Icare (389) sombre dans l'Atlantique quand l'avion qui la ramène au Québec s'écrase, emportant avec elle sa traduction des écrits d'une écrivaine latino-américaine, Délia Febrero. La verticalité et le vol de la langue de l'autre s'avèrent également dangereux dans le cas de Linda, l'adolescente aphasique soignée par Fatima. Celle-ci, qui voulait devenir traductrice, a perdu la capacité de parler, suite à un accident (dans la voiture de Guillaume, qui devient l'autre amant de Fatima) sur le pont Jacques Cartier (18, 98, 224, 329). Ce pont relie l'île de Montréal à la banlieue de Longueuil, quartier associé au jeune Italien que Linda aime. Francophone d'une famille "péquisse", elle avait choisi d'apprendre l'anglais pour mieux communiquer avec lui. Sa thérapie ne fonctionnera qu'en anglais, au grand dépit de Fatima. Aller vers l'autre entraîne le risque de se perdre —de devoir renoncer à sa langue, peut-être à sa vie. On devient quelqu'un d'autre, sinon l'autre. Toute tentative de "planer" (179) au-dessus de la mêlée peut mener à une chute.

Fatima éprouve la peur du risque—le vertige—à partir de son balcon (311,321,340), d'où elle voit Louis. Comme le pont ou l'avion, le balcon se tient dans l'air, suspendu et précaire. Mais il représente également une partie de la maison qui est dehors, et une partie du dehors qui est apprivoisée (42-43, 131, 170, 177-178, 216). Montréal est connue aussi sous le nom de "Balconville" (183).[9] Sortir sur le balcon, c'est se livrer, se révéler, inviter le dialogue, tout en restant chez soi.

C'est être accessible d'en bas ou de l'intérieur, tout en étant encadré et protégé. Tel quel, le balcon représente la combinaison idéale entre l'accessibilité et la sécurité. Il offre aussi un point d'observation, comme le belvédère du Mont Royal (186), à plus petite échelle.

Pour surmonter les barrières entre les sexes et entre les communautés, il ne faut pas rester collé à la terre. Fatima se voit dans ses fantasmes comme Super Fatima, volant à la rescousse des démunis du monde (180). Sa tante Aline, marraine de conte de fées, apprend à léviter (179, 295). Linda compense son incapacité au niveau de la parole en faisant des dessins d'oiseaux. Pour sortir de sa cage, il faut devenir des voleurs ou des voleuses de langue, dans le sens de Claudine Hermann (dans *Les Voleuses de langue*, 1976), refusant la propriété linguistique et géographique. Mais le "village global" pose d'autres problèmes.

Les média comme absence de communication[10]

Le monde privé de Fatima est constamment envahi, non pas par la présence des autres (étrangers ou trop proches) mais par leurs voix, véhiculées à distance par les ondes du téléphone et de la télévision (209). Incapable de se "disconnecter" (88), malgré ses efforts de jeûne, elle est obsédée par les actualités mondiales qu'elle regarde de loin, et de près, puisque les Arméniens, les Russes, les Ethiopiens, ainsi que les Turcs illégaux et les Amérindiens d'Oka, sont tous présents chez elle, médiatisés par des personnalités de Radio Canada, à qui la grand-mère de Fatima avait l'habitude d'adresser la parole. Le pire, ce serait d'être condamné pour toujours à cette fausse présence, ce faux rapprochement: de vivre face à la télé dans une tour d'appartements, comme celui où Guillaume va s'installer. La décision qu'il prend de réintégrer l'espace familier et familial de l'île de Montréal, pour éviter la traversée du pont néfaste, est fort ambivalente.

A la fin du roman Fatima hésite encore entre, d'un côté, sa famille retrouvée et la cohabitation paisible avec Guillaume (son semblable qui veut un enfant "signé") ou, de l'autre côté, la continuation précaire de ses deux liaisons. Ce choix lui permet une certaine indépendance tout en favorisant le "partage" qu'elle revendique comme préférable à l'exclusivité. Abandonner sa relation avec Louis, ce serait renoncer à suivre les traces d'Amélia. En partant seule vers le sud en vacances—et par avion[11]—elle semble enfin choisir rester fidèle à ce double différent, de vouloir surmonter le vertige dont elle a hérité. Dans un sens, elle prend la place d'Amélia, pour continuer ce qu'elle faisait. Elle va aller vers l'autre, prête à essayer de parler d'autres langues si nécessaire. Le bilinguisme, pour cette orthophoniste, est le contraire de l'aphasie.

L'aphasie et le bilinguisme poétique du texte

Fatima a déjà appris un peu d'espagnol et de portugais, sans parler de l'anglais dont son journal est parsemé. Pourtant, selon Jakobson (1956: 56-62), le désir de parler plusieurs langues à la fois peut être symptomatique d'un des deux types d'aphasie qu'il discerne: celle qui est reliée à un trouble de la contiguïté, à une incapacité de contextualiser les mots et de les hiérarchiser. A la limite, le mélange de codes qui en résulte, comme dans certains passages du texte de Fatima, peut rendre le message difficile à déchiffrer. L'édition française de ce roman comporte, effectivement, un petit lexique de termes québécois ou autres qui peuvent mystifier le lecteur non-initié.[12] Paradoxalement, la compréhension de cette "babille" est, précisément, ce qui caractérise les habitants de "Babel. Prise deux". La langue bâtarde ou métissée peut devenir une *lingua franca*, le lieu commun d'une communauté mixte.

L'autre type d'aphasie, selon Jakobson, a ses origines dans un trouble de la similarité: l'aphasique possède les éléments d'un code commun, mais "il considère le discours de l'autre comme un baragouin" (Jakobson 55). L'aphasique de ce type n'ose pas manipuler librement la langue, de peur de perdre contrôle de la construction des mots et des phrases. Il se réfugie dans les syntagmes tout faits des lieux communs, se limitant à des modèles connus. Ce manque d'originalité décrit le journal de Louis, dont les extraits laconiques, juxtaposés au journal effervescent de Fatima, produisent un effet de contraste frappant. Sa prose sobre et réservée correspond à ses tentatives répétées, en tant que sculpteur, de faire des copies d'un modèle du musée, les "Trois femmes de Caughnawaga" (qui figure sur la couverture du livre)[13]. Ces trois femmes amérindiennes se ressemblent et ressemblent toutes à une image globale de la femme cachée derrière ses voiles. Louis les associe aux trois femmes de sa vie—Hélène, Amélia et Fatima—qui restent, toutes les trois, mystérieuses pour lui. Elles se suivent et changent de place, le condamnant à tourner en rond, incapable de choisir mais détestant le partage prôné par Fatima. Son lieu d'évasion est un marais. Amélia l'a quitté après avoir visité cet endroit, se rendant compte qu'il ne pourra pas partager son désir de voler vers l'inconnu.

Les deux journaux intimes qui constituent ce roman rappellent une distinction faite par Luce Irigaray dans *Parler n'est jamais neutre* (1985). Le mode de communication de Louis se rapproche de celui qui caractérise les obsessionnels: ils parlent sans tenir compte du locutaire. Celui de Fatima, par contre, est plus près du discours des hystériques, qui s'expriment en se mettant toujours à la place de l'autre.[14] Comment parler pour soi et pour l'autre? Le roman sous forme de journal "à deux mains" résoud ce problème. Louis et Fatima ne partagent pas leurs écrits intimes, mais le lecteur du roman a accès au métissage intercalé des deux. L'effet a été décrit par Caroline Barrett (1993) comme dialogique, en termes bakhtiniens. Etant donné l'importance de l'aphasie comme métaphore dans ce récit[15] (reliée à celle de la tour de Babel), on peut aussi voir ce contrepoint discursif comme un exemple de la fonction poétique, telle qu'elle a été définie par Jakobson: la projection du principe d'équivalence de l'axe de la verticalité sur celle de l'horizontalité.[16] Cet effet se produit à travers de nombreux dédoublements, parallèles et inversions dans le texte: surtout, la juxtaposition de deux textes hétéroclites permet leur transformation en un seul texte hybride, à la fois journal et roman. Cet archi-texte savamment construit de mots multiformes représente lui-même la Tour de Babel, prise deux, lieu de rencontre par excellence—la corde raide où on essaie de surmonter le vertige pour partager notre altérité commune.

Université de la Colombie Britannique   Valérie Raoul

NOTES

1. Borgès, "La bibliothèque de Babel" (Potvin, 303); Jacques Derrida, "Des Tours de Babel", in J.F.Graham (dir.), *Difference in Translation* (Ithica: Cornell University Press, 1985); A.S. Byatt, *Babel Tower* (roman anglais qui est en ce moment un "bestseller" au Canada, dont l'intrigue tourne autour d'un roman entitré "Babbletower").

2. Genèse, ch.11. La tour est construite par les fils de Noé. Le nom "Babel" serait relié au mot hébreu "balale" qui signifie "confus". Babel serait la ville de Babylone, dont les vestiges révèlent plusieurs tours ou ziggourats.

3. L'auteure mentionne ce texte de Todorov dans l'entretien cité plus haut (237), comme source de sa connaissance de la Malinche.

4. Cité dans *Le Petit Robert* sous "lieu commun".

5. Le personnage de Fatima avait déjà paru dans le premier ouvrage de Noël, la pièce *Chandeleur* (voir l'entretien avec Noël cité plus haut, 234). Fatima est le nom d'une ville au Portugal, au nord-est de Lisbonne, devenue un lieu de pélerinage à partir de 1917, quand trois jeunes bergers ont déclaré y avoir vu six apparitions de la Vierge.

6. Caroline Barrett (311) voit dans le personnage d'Hélène des traces de la mère "phallique" traditionnelle au Québec, phénomène analysé par Valerie Raoul dans *Distinctly Narcissistic. The Diary Novel in Quebec* (Toronto: University of Toronto Press, 1993).

7. La rue n'est pas nommée dans le texte, mais en quatrième page de couverture.

8. Pour une comparaison entre les femmes représentées dans ce roman et celles des autres romans de Noël, voir Lori Saint-Martin (1993).

9. *Balconville* est le titre d'une pièce du dramaturge montréalais anglophone, David Fennario (Vancouver: Talonbooks, 1980).

10. Dans l'entretien déjà cité, Noël explique qu'elle a voulu faire une critique des média dans ce roman.

11. Cela rappelle la fin de *Myriam première*, où Maryse s'envole aussi, mais plus spécifiquement vers le Nicaragua.

12. Il s'agit d'une co-édition (Leméac/Actes Sud). Le lexique est mentionné par l'auteure dans l'entretien déjà cité (236).

13. Cette sculpture de Marc-Aurèle De Foy suzor-Côté (1869-1937) existe et on peut la voir au Musée des beaux-arts de Montréal.

14. Irigaray (33-34) sur l'obsessionnel (aux paroles "prudentes et redoutables"): "Il vous ignore. Il se parle". Quant à l'hystérique, qui "ne tarit pas de paroles", "il se tourne vers vous. Car, de son discours, enfin il presse le sujet. C'est vous" (33).

15. Noël, dans l'entretien cité, observe que: "L'aphasie et l'itinéraire de la rééducation, ont été pensés comme une métaphore du Québec actuel" (233).

16. Dans "Linguistique et poétique" in Jakobson, *Essais de linguistique générale* (*op. cit.*): "La fonction poétique projette le principe d'equivalence de l'axe de la sélection sur l'axe de la combinaison" (220).

17. J'emprunte le terme à Janet Paterson, *Anne Hébert. Architexture romanesque* (Ottawa: Presses de l'Université d'Ottawa, 1985).

OUVRAGES CITÉS

Barnett, Caroline. "La voix dialogue: une lecture bakhtinienne de *Babel, prise deux*". *Voix et images* 18, 2 (1993), 254-261.

Irigaray, Luce. *Parler n'est jamais neutre*. Paris: Editions de Minuit, 1985.

Jakobson, Roman. "Deux aspects du langage et deux types d'aphasie" et "Linguistique et poétique" in *Essais de linguistique générale*. Paris: Editions de Minuit, 1956.

Noël, Francine. *Babel, prise deux ou Nous avons tous découvert l'Amérique*. Montréal: VLB, 1990.

———. "Je suis une femme dans un pays". Entretien avec Francine Noël. *Voix et images* 18:2, 224-238.

Potvin, Claudine. "De l'Eden à Babel: écrire l'utopie". *Voix et images* 18, 2 (1993), 287-303.

Raoul, Valérie. *Distinctly Narcissistic. Diary Fiction in Québec*. Toronto: University of Toronto Press, 1993.

Saint-Martin, Lori. "Histoire(s) de femme(s) chez Francine Noël". *Voix et Images* 18, 2 (1993), 239-252.

Passions dévorantes et satisfactions alimentaires dans *Une liaison parisienne* de Marie-Claire Blais

Plonger un jeune écrivain québécois dans un milieu parisien où l'on bafoue ce personnage venu d'ailleurs, voilà qui pourrait soulever bien des questions quant au message contenu dans *Une liaison parisienne*. Mais le tout n'est qu'un prétexte pour bafouer également, sinon dénoncer, et sans aucun ménagement, certains milieux parisiens. C'est là, dans un schéma très simplifié l'enveloppe extérieure de ce roman peu étudié à ma connaissance.

En effet, *Une liaison parisienne* n'a certes pas retenu l'attention de la critique au même titre que bien d'autres oeuvres de Marie-Claire Blais. L'aurait-on cru aussi naïf que Mathieu Lelièvre? ce personnage qui n'a même "pas la trace du plus petit accent même [s'il est] Québécois" (23), ainsi qu'on le lui a dit, comme si c'était là un suprême compliment.

Mon propos n'est pas toutefois de définir la fortune du roman mais bien d'en relever certaines caractéristiques. L'interêt de l'intrigue ne repose pas uniquement sur l'histoire d'un jeune écrivain, d'où qu'il vienne, dans un milieu antagoniste, mais ce roman représente également une diatribe contre les structures de toute société dont les principes demeurent exclusivement ceux du passé. De plus, et c'est là un aspect important, le roman dévoile impitoyablement le racisme, tel qu'il s'exprime ouvertement dans un milieu décadent. De même, on y condamne les moyens de répressions, parfois subtils, d'une société vis-à-vis d'une autre, d'un pays vis-à-vis d'un autre.

Marie-Claire Blais, on le sait, a quelque peu regretté le ton acerbe de son roman, et pour elle "c'est comme un nuage, un mauvais nuage". Le roman contient malgré tout, comme elle l'a admis, . . ."beaucoup de choses vraies".

Je me propose ainsi d'isoler ces "choses vraies" par le truchement de l'étude de quelques-unes des métaphores alimentaires. Dans la multitude des composantes d'un texte, comment choisir de façon valable celles qui puissent contenir une valeur microcosmique du roman? Il se peut donc que les nombreuses allusions à l'alimentation prennent en charge divers aspects thématiques contenus dans la trame du récit.

Par son ampleur, *Une liaison parisienne* est un texte pluriel constitué par un réseau fragmenté de métaphores très diverses apportant des couches de significations multiples. Les personnages, qu'ils souffrent d'isolement ou qu'ils soient marginalisés, sont victimes de "passion[s] dévorante[s]" (42) et sont ainsi à l'affût d'une gamme entière de satisfactions sexuelles et plus souvent encore de "satisfactions alimentaires" (129). Ces aspects se définissent les uns les autres.

Rappelons que Mathieu Lelièvre se rend à Paris pour assister à la sortie de son livre. Il est reçu dans un milieu parisien de l'île Saint-Louis où l'hôtesse, Yvonne d'Argenti, lui servira de conseillère et, soi-disant, de guide dans les méandres de la société. On songe bien entendu au rôle que joue Madame de Beauséant auprès de Rastignac à la différence que les traits des personnages sont à présent proches de la caricature et que l'hôtesse ne tardera pas à devenir la maîtresse du jeune homme. Déjà, nous pouvons relever le semblant de parodie, ou même parodie tout court, de la tradition du *Bildungsroman*.

Dès son entrée chez Madame d'Argenti, alors qu'il est invité à déjeuner, Mathieu Lelièvre est ébloui de façon béate: "Il contempla le feuillage cossu des murs drapés de velours comme pour le dévorer du regard,...' (13). Malgré la prise de possession sensuelle des lieux et le plaisir qu'il en ressent, Mathieu conçoit mal que cette charmante hôtesse puisse lui annoncer que le diner sera servi plus tard "à cause de [son] crétin de fils" (13), chargé de préparer les repas. Il ne se doute nullement que ce milieu si affriolant pour lui ne sera qu'un appât auquel il sera pris au piège. Il deviendra ainsi la proie de Madame d'Argenti, personnage monstrueux qui par sa presence crée une atmosphère infernale. Notre héros, ou antihéros venu tardivement, ne remarque pas qu'il a échoué dans un milieu sclérosé ou les personnages, aux dimensions balzaciennes malgré tout, sont consumés par leurs passions ou par leurs tares lesquelles sont explicitées par bien des aspects inquiétants. Ainsi, Madame d'Argenti expliquera à la bonne qu'il faudra laver les caleçons de son fils, "quel garçon dégoûtant, ajoute-t-elle, il y a bien un mois qu'il les a cachés sous le réfrigérateur,..." (29) La proximité des caleçons près de l'endroit où l'on conserve l'alimentation crée un effet perturbateur dont le sens ne peut nous échapper. Néanmoins, même Bonita, une bonne sans doute venue du Portugal ou d'Espagne, "on en trouve toujours de ces petites" (17) comme l'affirme Madame d'Argenti, donc même Bonita refuse de les laver. Le linge sale ne se lave même pas en famille. Dès le début, le texte dévoile aussi à quel point Madame d'Argenti exècre ses enfants, par contre ses intentions infanticides sont transposées dans son roman car, tout comme Mathieu, elle aussi est écrivain.

Mathieu, lui, poursuit "sa délectation intérieure . . . lui qui se voyait comme un esprit du passé qui se promène en jeans" alors que les d'Argenti "l'observaient . . . avec une consternation amusée, rien ne leur semblait plus neuf et plus barbare que cette créature échevelée qui venait d'atterrir dans leur salon . . ." (15). Le mari, Antoine d'Argenti, qui souffre d'être placé dans une situation fausse, étant homosexuel et n'attirant que de jeunes garçons, aura tôt fait, en jouant le rôle de proxénète, de jeter Mathieu Lelièvre dans les bras de sa femme. On en convient, Lelièvre n'est guère un gibier de premier choix, mais il se présente au moment opportun car "l'amour, disait Madame d'Argenti, était un combat, et ce combat souvent désespéré entre deux êtres avides des mêmes satisfactions, exigeait parfois des sacrifices, dans cette. chasse, aussi, le gibier était souvent innocent" (24).

L'union des êtres, on devrait dire l'union des corps, se fera par un rituel qui consiste en une dégustation d'huîtres. Ainsi la "délectation intérieure" (15) dont jouissait Mathieu, nourri de romantisme vis-à-vis de la maison où "il retrouvait sa place dans le temps parmi les vieilles choses,..." (15) ainsi donc cette délectation se transformera en satisfactions palpables. Comme premier geste, lors de sa visite suivante, Yvonne d'Argenti, préparant l'offrande de sa personne comme appât, prie Mathieu d'ouvrir les huîtres. Mathieu, dans son innocence, voyait dans cette "preuve de confiance culinaire . . . le signe d'un accueil authentique et bien français, . . ." (23). L'atmosphère liquéfiante semble ainsi avoir atteint le niveau le plus favorable aux débats amoureux alors que "la douceur du plaisir illuminait le visage de la femme encore trempé sous ses cheveux" qu'elle venait de laver et "dont les boucles ruisselaient sur ces épaules" (23). Dans sa joie, Madame d'Argenti, venant de recevoir un joli sac à main, de son hôte:

> ne voulait rien perdre de la substance des huîtres et s'en emplissant délicatement la bouche d'une main, nourrissait Mathieu, de l'autre: ce mouvement d'échanges ou de fiançailles à travers la nourriture était pourvu d'une telle grâce que Mathieu eut l'instinct de lui sucer les doigts, ce qu'il fit, mais qu'elle remarqua à peine tant elle avait faim (25).

C'est alors que le jeune homme, par un souci d'humanité très généreux, se demandait si le mari "était sensible comme lui aux arômes félins dont les coussins et le canapé avaient été à une certaine époque fort inondés..." (25).

Contrairement à Mathieu qui est "de la race des jouisseurs pensants" (27) Yvonne d'Argenti, elle, ne conçoit l'amour que par la satisfaction immédiate telle que procurée par la nourriture, laquelle est choisie en fonction de caractéristiques permettant diverses analogies avec le plaisir qu'offrent ces aliments. Les huîtres semblent la matière la mieux désignée pour entamer une relation sexuelle. Ainsi, en Tunisie, lors d'un séjour en famille, c'est-à-dire avec Mathieu, Madame d'Argenti fait la connaissance de Peter, un diplomate américain qui promet de venir la voir à Paris. Et comme elle entrevoyait déjà "d'étreindre sur son sein plein de feu une créature aussi flegmatique et qui par bonheur, avait la réputation de laisser partout de généreux pourboires" (93), elle accepte "la rituelle douzaine d'huîtres et la bouteille de champagne que lui offrait gracieusement Peter" (93). Pour cette femme vorace, Peter symbolise l'Amérique généreuse qui viendrait lui apporter une corne d'abondance. Ce n'était guère ainsi du Canada en la personne de Mathieu, le Canada avec "toutes ces prairies, tous ces lacs" (28). En fait, Mathieu a mal joué étant donné qu'il a peu retenu les conseils de son ami Pierre-Henri Lajeunesse: "Avoir l'air d'un riche Canadien, lui avait-il recommandé, ce qui n'existe pas encore comme mythe, tu comprends, on ne parle que du riche Américain, voilà comment on achète l'amour quand on est un Québécois colonisé!" (10). Quant à Mathieu, après la scène de séduction que je viens de mentionner:

Il voulut lui dire combien il aimait ses joues veloutées, ses épaules rondes, s'enivrer en paroles de toute sa personne à nouveau étreinte avec des mots, mais elle disparut vers la salle de bains et se penchant vers leur déjeuner il vit que l'abondance de leur repas romain, les seize huîtres, le fromage, le vin, que toutes ces merveilles avaient été englouties par son ogre menu et qu'il n'en prenait conscience que maintenant (27).

Pour Yvonne d'Argenti, la satisfaction alimentaire est prise au sens le plus prosaïque bien contrairement, comme on le voit, à celle conçue par le jeune rêveur qu'est Mathieu. Pour elle, la digestion est d'un tout autre ordre que ne comprend pas encore le jeune amant: "Une femme fantastique, pensa-t-il, quelle noblesse dans ses appétits, quel amour de la vie, c'est prodigieux!" (27).

Le contact entre les personnages ne se conçoit pas sans contact d'ordre alimentaire qui s'accompagne d'une intention d'achat, sinon de corruption. A Tunis, le mari, Antoine d'Argenti, attire et séduit Ashmed par la vision d'une vie à Paris, vision d'ailleurs très vague et lointaine pour ce jeune garçon. La destinée des peuples colonisés se trouve ainsi résumée en une seule remarque car Ashmed est "un être né pour la conquête de toutes les jouissances sur cette terre, mais peu destiné à la solide affection d'un seul maître" (90). Tout compte fait, Ashmed est le seul personnage libre dans ce roman, et il le déclare à sa façon:

Ashmed ira à Paris parce qu'il fait tout ce que veut Monsieur d'Argenti. Ashmed ira à Paris parce que lui, très gentil . . . Ashmed ira à l'école, toujours avec couteaux, Ashmed est fort et doit battre d'autres garçons. Ashmed, toujours le plus fort (88-89).

On comprend dès lors qu'après une crise de larmes d'Ashmed où celui-ci semblait condamner Antoine d'Argenti d'être "le complice muet de toute cette haine contre [sa] race" (103), on comprend qu'Yvonne ait conseillé à son mari pour calmer le jeune garçon et après avoir elle-même "dévoré son copieux petit déjeuner" de lui acheter le premier et le plus efficace des tranquillisants, c'est-à-dire "quelques sucettes" (103).

Les d'Argenti sont ainsi soumis à des passions destructrices dont ils souffrent chacun dans leur propre domaine affectif. Pour Madame d'Argenti la passion s'exprime dans le texte par une gamme de termes divers tels que "vorace", "faim", "insatiable", "bouche", "dents", "rôtir", "ogresse" et on pourrait prolonger cette liste très signifiante bien plus longuement. Tout se transpose pour elle en satisfactions alimentaires. Ainsi, dans une scène curieuse,

[Madame d'Argenti] avait pris l'habitude de manger dès l'aube son panier de fruits au lit, répandant ainsi autour d'elle avec son haleine et ses baisers, le baume de cette digestion fruitée dont Mathieu était envahi comme des parfums d'un jardin, lorsqu'il ne tournait pas le dos dans une grappe de raisins, il se réveillait, avec dans les cheveux des écorces d'oranges que Madame d'Argenti avait jetées sur lui plutôt que vers le balcon où dormait mollement contre le grillage son maillot de bain à deux pièces . . . (79)

Apparemment, à lire ce passage, Mathieu Lelièvre joue de mieux en mieux le rôle de gibier que lui aurait destiné son nom, et que son hôtesse garnit selon ses caprices. La nourriture devient pour cette femme insatiable un objet de culte qui console de bien des désirs non satisfaits car elle "sortait de l'amour comme de la turbulence d'une agonie sauvage, s'écriant: "J'ai faim, mon ami, un faim vorace . . . Allons, debout..." (50) et Madame d'Argenti d'envoyer Mathieu chez le boucher pour les meilleurs morceaux sans oublier le faux-filet pour les chats—

dont l'un, une femelle, s'appelle Victor--mais c'est là une nouvelle tentative illusoire d'assouvissement devant les déboires de la vie et en particulier par rapport au mari qui ne l'a aimée que brièvement:

le sexe peut languir de faim comme tout autre organe . . . , affirme-t-elle à Mathieu. Au fond, de quoi avais-je besoin dans la vie? D'amour, oui, voilà, c'est tout. Et c'est toujours la seule chose qu'on vous refuse! (39).

Il n'est guère surprenant que Mathieu ait songé "`aux deux bouches' du corps de Madame d'Argenti" (52).

Alors que se déroule la narration avec ses menus événements ou incidents, l'aspect pathologique d'Yvonne d'Argenti se précise. Qu'on ne s'y méprenne pas, Yvonne d'Argenti n'est pas la victime des grandes tragédies, seul Mathieu se laisse prendre à ses élans du coeur. Le mari, lui, lucide comme il l'est, y trouve son compte en assurant la présence de Mathieu auprès de sa femme. En fait, l'analogie cachée dans l'épisode de la partie de tennis ne manque pas de piquant:

L'air était de plus en plus étouffant, mais armé soudain d'une souplesse séraphique, bien que virulente, Antoine d'Argenti renvoyait à sa femme les balles de tennis, lesquelles claquaient contre sa raquette, comme une éclosion d'oeufs secs . . . (86-87).

Ainsi, cette comparaison rend peut-être compte de la valeur de leurs rapports conjugaux , sa virilité s'exprimant plus avec sa femme.

L'obsession de Madame d'Argenti prendra dans le roman une tournure qui dévoilera l'égocentrisme de la société qu'elle représente. Alors qu'elle revenait du cinéma avec Mathieu, ils avaient vu un noyé que l'on sortait de l'eau: "Mais ne regardez pas mon ami, vous voyez bien que cela vous trouble...Allons...venez...Je dois passer par le pâtissier..." (35). Pour elle en effet ce n'est pas "un homme" comme l'avait mentionné Mathieu: "C'était, mon ami, c'était..." (36). Entre voir un noyé que l'on repêche et une visite chez le pâtissier, le choix à faire ne pose guère de difficultés.

Pour Madame Colombe, une amie d'Yvonne d'Argenti—elle aussi romancière et "l'auteur d'un roman d'une admirable pornographie" (59), le problème de la famine aux Indes ne peut se résoudre—et elle l'affirme en découpant une escalope—"que par la bombe atomique, voilà ce que nous devons souhaiter à ces pauvres gens, et croyez-moi, avait-elle ajouté, ils sont si vils et si paresseux qu'ils le méritent bien" (58-59). En fait, à l'annonce de la famine aux Indes, Monsieur d'Argenti avait auparavant appris à Mathieu que dans un élan de générosité Yvonne avait eu l'intention de secourir ces malheureux, intention sans doute vite réprimée lorsque son mari lui a demandé comment elle pourrait "supporter la vie là-bas? Oui, auprès de ces misérables qui ne sont pas même de sa race" (59). Il la croit trop fragile et trop gracieuse pour faire face à ce genre de malheur. Mais à présent ce ne sont pas les soit-disant bons sentiments de sa maîtresse qui retiennent l'attention de Mathieu, car il avait peine à croire que l'on pouvait "prononcer à une table parisienne entourée d'oreilles que le salut d'un peuple était dans un bain de sang" (60).

Avec l'entrée d'Ashmed, personnage venu très visiblement et typiquement d'ailleurs, un malaise sera perçu et même de la part d'Antoine car il ne pourra pas se protéger des rumeurs quant à ses goûts sexuels et cela "dans une ville, où pourtant sans être dit, tout se fait" (102). Le racisme ne perdra pas ses droits:

Il remarquait pour la première fois, pendant que la tête crépue d'Ashmed se blottissait contre son épaule, que la peau de l'enfant qui lui paraissait à Tunis 'raisonnablement foncée', avait, dans la pénombre du soir parisien, 'une teinte plus chocolat', non que Monsieur d'Argenti se mit à aimer moins Ashmed pour cette raison, pensa-t-il, mais parce qu'il pressentait soudain pour lui toute une diversité de mortifications qu'il n'avait pas prévue, et qu'Ashmed, dans son innocence, semblait prévoir moins encore. (102)

Pour sa part, Mathieu craignait, après avoir été emmené par Yvonne dans une famille d'anciens collaborateurs, Mathieu craignait, puisque venu d'ailleurs et représentant celui dont on se méfie, "qu'il pouvait bien devenir lui aussi, comme d'autres, 'leur Juif', 'leur Noir'..." (140).

Mais je m'écarte de mon sujet, car enfin les conflits intérieurs des personnages ne sont peut-être pas si graves, si inquiétants pour chacun d'eux. Ne suffit-il pas d'un bon repas pour effacer le réel car nourriture est synonyme de divertissement et en même temps de refuge dans le milieu des d'Argenti: "Regardez-la danser, s'exclame Yvonne, quand ces gens-là sont bas, ils sont bas. Si elle n'était que noire, mais elle est putain en plus, c'est odieux! Venez Antoine, je ne peux pas supporter cela, allons déjeuner,... c'est inclus dans le prix de l'hôtel..." (103). Les vicissitudes de la vie sont effacées pour les uns par le foie de canard et pour Yvonne par l'indispensable fromage sans lequel elle ne peut pas vivre. Manger émousse la conscience des individus.

Enfin, profondément déçu par son expérience de la vie à Paris et de la piètre réception de son livre—"ce lièvre aurait dû rester dans son trou" (64) disaient les critiques—et après son contact avec Madame d'Argenti, le tout correspondant, au sens le plus large du terme, à une liaison parisienne, Mathieu entreprendra dans la deuxième partie du roman de voyager dans la France provinciale, la France aimable de ses ancêtres. Dans une famille bretonne où il est reçu, il appréciera la soupe bien chaude, les pommes de terre, le ragoût de lapin de la veille, la bouteille de mousseux, l'eau de vie et le cassis de la tante Angeline qui a..."le foie cuit par la gnôle" (158). Enfin, dans ce milieu où règne la misère et qui semble une reprise d'*Une saison dans la vie d'Emmanuel* (1966), Mathieu, enfin, même s'il est soucieux de la misère de ces pauvres paysans, dort avec bonheur.

On retrouvera Mathieu Lelièvre à Paris avant son retour au Québec, et lésé par son séjour en France, il fréquentera le milieu des cafés les plus pauvres, toujours à l'affût d'un passé évanescent. "Ah! se disait-il, si seulement Madame d'Argenti n'avait mangé qu'une partie de son âme et de son corps, mais non ses légers caprices d'ogresse lui avaient dérobé aussi 'les deux plus belles saisons à Paris, le printemps et l'été...'" (163).

En somme, du foie gras au ragoût de lapin arrosé d'un coup de cassis en passant par le couscous, sans oublier les tartines au fromage et les boulettes de pain, Marie-Claire Blais a fourni de quoi alimenter un univers romanesque.

University of Arizona   **Henri Servin**

Ouvrages Cites

Blais, Marie-Claire. *Une liaison parisienne*. Montréal: Quinze-présence, 1980.

Marcotte, Gilles. "Marie-Claire Blais: 'Je veux aller le plus loinpossible'". Entrevue. *Voix et Images*. VIII, 2, (hiver 1983), 191-209.

Carnivalization in the Post-colonial Texts of Lola Lemire Tostevin and Gail Scotts' Questions of Language and Identity[1]

The article focuses on the problems of language and identity in the texts of two Canadian feminist writers, the Franco-Ontarian Lola Lemire Tostevin, and the Anglo-Quebecer, Gail Scott. The texts of both women belong to the emergent postmodernist language-oriented canon of Canadian literature. The comparison of English Canadian and Anglo-Quebec feminist writers may entail studying differences between Anglo-American and French feminisms and their impact on Canadian literary discourse. Nevertheless, I want to avoid limiting the opposition, as a significant number of English Canadian and American critics have taken up and developed insights of French post-structuralist theory. Consequently, the terms "French" and "American" feminist theory, as Felski stresses, must be taken to refer to "a grounding in a particular intellectual tradition, rather than simply to the nationality of the individual critic" (Felski 20).

Historically, American feminism had an earlier impact on Canadian society. It is only later that post-structuralist and deconstructionist theories have been assimilated by Canadian women writers. The combination of the early positive reception of French feminist theory by Quebec feminist writers and critics, and the consequent spread of the new discourse to English Canada and its assimilation by the writers of the emergent language-oriented canon, is responsible for the present orientation of Canadian post-modernist discourse. An interesting and authentically Canadian phenomenon is the development of comparative English and French Quebecois critical theory and practice, illustrated, for instance, in bilingual *Gynocritics/Gynocritique*, the feminist journal *Tessera*, literary collaborations and national conferences. My choice of Tostevin and Scott, both bilingual writers, aims at showing that a current Canadian discourse tends in the direction of a dialogue between Anglo-American and French feminisms.

The texts of both writers can be discussed not only in the context of feminist discourse but also of post-colonial literature. Canadian post-colonial discourse aims at establishing a literature distinct from the colonial centres of Britain and France. Feminist texts have a distinct place in the post-colonial writing as the perspectives of both discourses overlap and inform each other. The passionate work on language in post-colonial texts, a result of a protest against the linguistic control by the colonizer, is intensified in writing by women who experience a double subjection, a double colonization, both by the dominant culture and by the patriarchal society.

In terms of Deleuze and Guattari's theories, post-colonial literature is deterritorialized and it belongs to the category of 'minor literature' which does not "come from a minor language; it is rather that which a minority constructs within a major language" (*Kafka* 16). The three characteristics of minor literature: "the deterritorialization of language, the connection of the individual to a political immediacy, and the collective assemblage of enunciation" (Kafka 18), can be easily traced in the feminist post-colonial texts. Deterritorialized literature can be reterritorialized through the transcoding of various levels of language, for instance, as proposed by Henri Gobard in his tetralinguistic models: the vernacular (maternal), the vehicular, the referential or the mythic (Gobard 34). This transcoding is a way of rewriting a text, a kind of translation.

The multivoicedness of language, its 'polyglossia,' reminds one of a Bakhtinian linguistic and cultural universe; a theory of translation is implicit in his general theory of discourse; translation for him is "all man does" (Emerson, "Translating" 23); Barbara Godard calls women's writing a "transformance" (Theorizing 46). The word emphasizes a process of translation, of constructing meaning through the transformation of discourses which always entails the rereading and rewriting of the already written ("Theorizing" 46). Consequently, the complexity of women's writing, with its emphasis on the multiplicity of languages, is better explained by the theories using a strategy of translation rather than representation. Transformation of meaning is a kind of performance staged on the "scene" of a polyphonic literature.

The concept of literary production as performance brings us close to the Bakhtinian notion of carnival re-enacted on the scene of literature. The carnivalesque structure is dialogical: "It is spectacle, but without a stage . . . drama becomes located language. . . . All poetic discourse is dramatization, dramatic permutation . . . of words (Kristeva Swords 79). The characteristic carnivalesque ambivalence "consists of communication between two spaces: that of the scene and that of the hieroglyph, that of representation by language, and that of experience in language, system and phrase, metaphor and metonymy" ("Word" 85).

The idea of a double-voiced discourse (both representation and its transgression) is developed in both the American and French models of feminist writing. In the American model, however, the emphasis has been placed on reading and rewriting of the "dominant" and "muted" story, the conventions of plot and character. There has been little concern with subverting rhetorical strategies, form, language or gender. Canadian feminist language—and theory—oriented writers, on the other hand, engage in the transformation of those formal codes of writing and also the problem of gender and identity.

The theory of feminist writing as translation in the feminine which uses Roman Jakobson's division of translation into the interlingual, intralingual, and the intersemiotic types (*Essais* 78-86), along with the Bakhtinian theory of "carnivalization," are the major frames of reference in the following discussion. The question asked here is: what kinds of translation and what translation strategies are used by the writers in order to "carnivalize" the dominant writing practices of the colonizer and the patriarchy?

What makes the writing of Tostevin and Scott specific lies in the interlingual translation between two official languages of Canada. Scott points to "the endless translation of ideas in her writing and speech which often forces the confrontation of reflexive and imaginary writing in the same texts" (*Spaces* 47). They deliberately mix both languages or write fragments of their texts in French. This strategy relativizes meaning and questions many concepts whose meaning is based in language. The interlingual translation is often fused in their texts with the intralingual and the intersemiotic in order to problematize the question of feminine identity and thus create new subversive narratives with women as subjects of enunciation. Scott and Tostevin reread and rewrite various types of texts, including the biographical, the literary, and the text of culture. Their writing questions the concept of genre. It may be identified as 'life writing', fiction/theory or a "roman" or "novel" understood by Kristeva as an intersection of genres and a generalized form of intertextuality which encompasses both the novel and poetry ("Interview" 283).

Language is the major tool of Scott's and Tostevin's transformative strategies. A theory of language is the basis for understanding the problem of subjectivity; Kristeva points out that: "every language theory is predicated upon a conception of the subject that it explicitly posits, implies or tries to deny " (*Desire* 124).

For Tostevin, language has the "power to *express* the most fundamental dimension of both personal and universal realities" and also "the power to transpose, transform" ("breaking" 391). This statement points to a concept of language which merges the America expressive and the French signifying theories of language. Neither Tostevin nor Scott agrees with the exclusive expressive theory of language which posits a universal grammar and consequently a universal, transcendental subject. Scott opposes the concept of a "unary subject" by stating "However small my differences are as an Anglo-Québécoise vis-a-vis the dominant culture in the pan-Canadian context . . . asserting them is offering yet one more challenge to the bland assumptions of *sameness* . . . which is the hallmark of patriarchy and the dominant cultures everywhere" (*Spaces* 51). In the same text she also asserts her interest in the "writing subjects" in-the-feminine. Not the "self" as a . . . predetermined figure, but a complex tissue of texts, experience, evolving in the very act of writings" (*Spaces* 11).

Both writers invoke several kinds of translation in the feminine. Tostevin's *Gyno-text* features as an example of an intersemiotic translation; here she works on her gyn/ ecological memories—which means she reterritorializes the patriarchal language through the maternal, the language of the body. Tostevin inscribes a woman's space, as defined by Kristeva, the semiotic, a woman's unexpressed libidinal potential, her supposedly inarticulate corporeality. The "body" functions as text and the text as body which lives, feels, and writes. It is a text with a high interdependence of parts, the textual body as intertextuality, "united/we can speak now/ of penetration" (no pagination). The semiotic is a different level of language "a/different/tongue/ to/pen/a/trait. Through the subversion of syntax in the line: "V/notch / of I/dentity" Tostevin deconstructs the concept of unitary identity forced on women by a patriarchal discourse in such a way that it causes a "dentity," a hollow , a wound, in "I", in a woman's psyche. This unitary concept is just "a/ legend/at/leg's/end" (*Gyno-Text* no pagination).

Tostevin's translation here is under the realm of metonymy; it is the translation for the signifier, a translation with a subversive ironic intent. The emphasis is on sound and its generation of meaning. The semiotic processes can be detected, in the melodic, rhythmic, and alliterative devices such as in the lines: "&/belly/bells/in/abdominal/dome"; "hymen/hyphen/gender"; "language bled/lampblack/black leads" (*Gyno-text*, no pagination); Tostevin performs here an intersemiotic transcoding which inscribes female libidinal rhythms in language. She replaces what Kristeva describes as "the descriptive and traditional symbolic language of communication (the phenotext)" with "the generative language of poetry (the genotext)" (*Desire* 74-75).

Scott's translating for the maternal operates in a similar fashion. It is "writing focused on language where words, syntax, are the real material of writing" (*Spaces* 24). Her project involves the combination of the intralingual and intersemiotic transcoding; In *Spaces Like Stairs* she explains it as "a double sided movement: both opening the floodgates of possibility (letting the play of images, the writing be an exploration of the undersides of words); then imposing another kind of sentence (vision, rhythm) on them" (*Spaces* 24).

Another text by Tostevin, *Color of Her Speech*, interestingly combines three types of translation, the interlingual, the intralingual, and the intersemiotic. Tostevin inscribes the process of losing one language and entering another, losing French and being introduced or rather consciously choosing English. She transcribes it as "unspeaking" the mother tongue "the unbinding of Umbilicals," and entering the language of the father; the process is similar to the semiotic entering the symbolic; both French and English inscribed in intense melodic and rhythmic, semiotic patterns are mixed in the text. Any unspeaking of language sets meaning adrift. The unspeaking, the undoing of language results in an endless slippage of signifiers, the impossibility of fixing meaning, and thus deconstructing and transforming all monological patterns.

The intralingual translation shows the economy of a monological patriarchal language with its fixed binary; it is language which imposes stereotypes and myths on women, language filled with patriarchal values, and thus language with a universal grammar, a masculine grammar and epistemology. This language translates a Sanskrit word *kedesha*, an independent woman, into "harlot" (no pagination); but Tostevin says ironically: "after all the reading/mankind speaks/but one language" (*Color*, no pagination). This language makes Scott push "on the edges of the blanks in discourse, the gaps in history, the spaces between the established genres of male dominated canons" (*Spaces* 10). Tostevin and Scott transcode numerous stereotypes, myths, and clichés: woman as a siren, la belle dame sans merci, Penelope, Helen, or the Virgin Mary. Scott stresses that she translates stereotypical images like "a silly wedding car", for instance, into "something even more fictional and carnivalesque" (*Spaces* 19). The subversive translations of Tostevin and Scott operate under the reign of both the metaphor and the metonymy.

An excellent example of intralingular translation with an

emphasis on the reterritorialization through myth and symbol is provided by Tostevin in *"Sophie."* Both the translation for the signified under the reign of metaphor and for the signifier intermingles in the ambivalent space of the text. Tostevin transcodes in a subversive manner the space given to women in a patriarchal discourse of philosophy, history, and myth. In this discourse woman is nothing but "an apostrophe in mid-air." The symbols and myths explored in the text are open to many interpretations. The polyvalent meaning of the word "Sophie" leads, through various associations, to such signifiers as muses, music harmony, lyre, goddess Sophia as Wisdom, or Philo-Sophia, or Universal Mind, number seven, Seven Pillars of Wisdom, seven branches of learning, arithmetic, geometry, astronomy, rhetoric, dialectic, and music, which are explored in the text, both through the representation by language and the experience in language.

In Tostevin's texts the negative spaces which reflect the binary logic and a masculine economy of language are transcoded, through a logic of difference, into a different feminine space. For her it is a new conceptual space, a "pregnant pause," a fertile break. For Scott it is a space in a shape of a spiral (spaces like stairs). Both spaces point to "a writing of excess, a surplus of reality, *écriture féminine* which exceeds and subverts usual linear (phallic) writing" (Tostevin "Pregnant" 74). In such space, Tostevin explains, "The subject escapes through a sieve of meanings. . . . Different languages begin to invade one another . . . metaphoric/metonymic slips accidently and exquisitely connect . . . puns, repetition, rhythm, breath, wordplay, word association, parody, neologisms, new coinings that suspend, *corps charnel, corps spatial* (Tostevin, "Pregnant" 75-76). In short, it is a translation for the signifier which produces a dialogical, carnivalized meaning, never unitary, always "in-between," forever deferred. In *écriture féminine* the position of the subject cannot be fixed, the problem of identity is not ontological (one of being) but rather one of location or positioning.

Scott and Tostevin also explore intertextuality, another type of translation and transcoding which poses a problem of an "I." They understand "intertextuality" in the manner of Kristeva who deduces the concept from Bakhtinian theory of language. Kristeva stresses that a "textual segment, sentence, utterance or paragraph, is . . . the result of the intersection of a number of voices, of a number of textual interventions ("Interview" 281), which are combined in the semantic, the syntactic, and the phonic fields of the utterance. What is important here is that "the discovery of intertextuality at a formal level leads . . . to an intrapsychic or psychoanalytic finding" concerning the status of the writer who places himself or herself "at the intersection of this plurality of texts on their very different levels" ("Interview" 281). Kristeva understands subjectivity as a "subject in process" or "polyphony" in Bakhtin's terms. In an interview with Janice Williamson, Tostevin reveals a parallel view on the issue. She stresses her interest in the multiplicity of the selves, in the "polyphonic presence of the self, where we have many versions of the "I," many stories to tell" ("Sounding" 34). She realizes that "ultimately the exploration of language leads back to the self, or preferably to different selves" ("Sounding" 33).

Tostevin and Scott believe, along with Kristeva, Cixous, and others, that the place of a subject is in language, that "language creates the identity of a speaking agency" (Kristeva, *In the Beginning* 8). Tostevin explores the problem in a series of poems on the identity of "I". Writing as a space marked by woman's absence in a patriarchal discourse, the muted space, is translated into a new female conceptual space,"the pregnant pause," the fertile space of écriture féminine: "I am not a woman I am a poem"; "I am not a woman I am words/on the prowl"; "I am not a woman I am not sequence/dismembered each organ fastened/to a verb"; "I am not a woman/I am a woman/a space in space" (*Double*, no pagination). Thus for Tostevin there is no identity prior to its enunciation in language or, as Butler states, "identity is performatively constituted by the very "expressions" that are said to be its results" (Butler 25). This negates the essentialist concept of woman in favour of the performative femininity, as created in language working at the intersection of various discourses.

Similarly, for Scott, identity and gender do not "exist prior to their articulation in historically specific, and situational, discursive contexts" (Butler 9). Scott's subjects are multiple, linguistically and discursively constructed. The issues of race, class, and religion are of primary importance in her texts. In *Heroine* Scott shows how various Quebecois discourses of the 1970s and 1980s, such as nationalism, leftist politics, feminism, and lesbianism, influence the formation of individual identity. The text is a type of "life writing," "fusion between the creative act of writing and the act of living creatively, between the textual and the biological" (87). Scott is interested in the "psychic aspect of writing as trace of a dialogue with oneself with another . . . as a splitting of the writer into subject of enunciation and subject of utterance" (Kristeva, "Word" 74). The narrator's name in

Heroine is Gail and her initials are G.S., the same as those of Gail Scott. The narrator writes a novel about a female character who also engages in writing. The boundary between these two subjects is blurred, and so is the boundary between the author and the narrator. "Life writing" emphasizes the fluidity of the self and it corresponds with Bakhtin's theories of the dialogization between the writer and her/his autobiographical subject-character, the dialogic conception of intersubjectivity, the transgression of the boundaries between self and the other, between the inner self and outer self. Scott asserts that her "heroine is not only a woman of many self-images, but is also part of the other women she is close to. The women she loves and hates" (*Heroine* 95).

In the ambivalent space of Tostevin's and Scott's text, where language functions both as representation and signification, all identities are performance and they are articulated in the intersection of gender, race, class, and sexual ideologies. It is a carnivalized world where, in Scott's words, women adopt masks in their "various roles: mother, writer, militant, lover, friend" (*Spaces* 34). In Scott's carnival subjects keep dividing into actor and spectator, or as in *Heroine*, into the writer/ reader/ translator. In her version of the carnival the emphasis is on "a performance of subjects of new sort" (*Spaces* 134): self-reflexive, polyphonic selves, "dressed up for the explosion . . . in robes of stunning irony" (*Spaces* 134), selves living at the intersection of the real and textual world.

To summarize, the texts of Tostevin and Scott are written at the intersection of Anglo-American and French literary discourses. They do not follow exclusively any of these traditions but they enter into a dialogue with them. Writing functions for them as translation and performance, "performance as process of transformation of bodies and languages" (Godard, "Performance" 14) used for the construction of femininity and the new woman-centred discourse. Identity is constructed in language over which they are gaining a partial control through the translation in the feminine combining the intersemiotic, the intralingual, and the interlingual transcoding. The uniqueness of their writing lies in the merging of the American and French approaches to language and identity. It inscribes the Bakhtinian theory of language which offers a solution to the current impasse in feminist critical thought which subscribes either to the absolutist textual theories of post(structuralist) linguistically based formalism or the sociological theories of Anglo-American gynocentric school.

Similar to Bakhtin, Scott and Tostevin are sensitive to textual processes of literature but they never dissociate them from social and historical contexts; they simultaneously embrace the textual, the intertextual, and the contextual.

Memorial University of Newfoundland   Eugenia Sojka

NOTE

The title of the article may be misleading as it points to my exclusive interpretation of Canadian feminist literary discourse along the lines of Bakhtin's theory of language and culture. Nevertheless, I do not treat this theory as an authoritative method of interpretation. I follow the advice of Helène Cixous who, in order to avoid the mastery of a text, insists "on the notion of a path to be traced, rather than that of the beautiful road, or the method to be applied" (Conley, "Introduction," *Reading* xii-xiii). Having this advice in mind, I treat the Bakhtinian theory as one among many ways of approaching the production of meaning in a literary text.

WORKS CITED

Butler, Judith. *Gender Trouble: Feminism and Subversion of Identity*. New York and London: Routledge, 1990.

Conley, Verena Andermatt. "Introduction." *Reading with Clarice Lispector*. Ed. Helene Cixous. Trans. Verena Andermatt Conley. Minneapolis: University of Minnesota Press, 1990, vii-xviii.

Deleuze, Gilles and Felix Guattari. *Kafka. Toward a Minor Literature*. Trans. Dana Polan. Foreword: Réda Bensamaia. Minneapolis and Oxford: University of Minnesota Press, 1991.

Emerson, Caryl. "Translating Bakhtin: Does His Theory of Discourse Contain a Theory of Translation?" *University of Ottawa Quarterly*. 53, 1 (January-March 1983), 23-32.

Felski, Rita. *Beyond Feminist Aesthetics. Feminist Literature and Social Change.* Cambridge, Massachusetts: Harvard University Press, 1989.

Gobard, Henri. *L'Aliénation linguistique: analyse tétraglossique.* Prefaces: Gilles Deleuze. Paris: Flammarion, 1976.

Godard, Barbara. "Theorizing Feminist Discourse / Translation." *Tessera* 6 (Spring 1989), 42-53.

————. "Performance/Transformance: Editorial." *Tessera* 11 (Winter 1991), 11-18.

Jakobson, Roman. *Essais de Linguistique Générale.* Paris: Les Editions de Minuit, 1963.

Kristeva, Julia. *Desire in language: A Semiotic Approach to Literature and Art.* New York: Columbia University Press, 1980.

————. "Word, Dialogue, and the Novel." *Desire in Language: A Semiotic Approach to Literature and Art.* New York: Columbia University Press, 1980, 64-91.

————. "An Interview with Julia Kristeva." Margaret Waller. Trans. Richard Macksley. *Intertextuality and Contemporary American Fiction.* Ed. Patrick O'Donnell and Robert Davis. Baltimore and London: The Johns Hopkins University Press, 1989, 280-294.

————. *In the Beginning Was Love. Psychoanalysis and Faith.* Transl. Arthur Goldhammer. New York: Columbia University Press, 1987.

Scott, Gail. *Heroine.* Toronto: Coach House, 1987.

————. *Spaces Like Stairs: Essays.* Toronto: The Women's Press. 1989.

Tostevin, Lola Lemire. *Color of Her Speech.* Toronto: Coach House, 1982.

————. *Gyno-text*. Toronto: Underwhich Editions, 1984.

————. *Double Standards*. Edmonton: Longspoon, 1985.

————. "The Pregnant Pause as Conceptual Space (or Gimme a Break)". *Open Letter* 6, 7 (Spring 1987), 74-76.

————. *Sophie*. Toronto: Coach House, 1988.

————. "Breaking the hold on the story the feminine economy of language". *A Mazing Space*. Edmonton: Longspoon, 1986, 385-391.

Williamson, Janice. "Sounding the Difference. An Interview with Smaro Kamboureli and Lola Tostevin." *Canadian Forum* 66, 765 (January 1987), 33-38.

Franglo théâtre—esthétique et politique: Reaching Out to a Bilingual Audience, ou quoi?

This paper will attempt to examine the rather recent emergence in Canadian theatre history of bilingual-bicultural theatre.

Theatre in which bilingual actors perform in English one night and in French the next as they did in a recent production of *Les Mis* in Montreal shall not be considered. Nor shall a reference be made to the more common phenomenon of playing the same show for successive performances with two different casts, one English and one French. This sort of thing has been going on in Montreal for years and is hardly bilingual-bicultural theatre for bilingual bicultural audiences. The only productions considered are those which contain relatively equal amounts of dialogue in both languages and are played to a more or less bilingual audience.

In January 1979, what has been termed Canada's first real bilingual play, David Fennario's *Balconville*, opened at the English-language regional theatre in Montreal, the Centaur, and brought French-Canadian actors speaking French onto the stage beside English Canadian actors speaking English. Coincidentally or not, at the time this play appeared, Quebec was facing the impending PQ referendum on sovereignty. Between 1989 and 1992, paralleling the buildup in tension to the October 1992 referendum on the constitution, there have appeared a spate of bilingual-bicultural productions, most notably in Montreal, as one might expect, but elsewhere in the country also. At both times, Canadians and Quebecers faced the real possiblility of separation.

Theatre is a political act as well as an artistic endeavour. The question of whether and to what degree the choice and concept of a production is motivated by political or artistic considerations is always murky territory. However, because critics have addressed both these points to varying degrees in their reviews, it is important to look upon the stated intents of the artists, the processes followed, as well as the products themselves.

The summer of 1989 saw a bilingual production of *Romeo & Juliette* staged by Nightcap Productions for the Shakespeare on the Saskatchewan Festival in Saskatoon. Artistic director Gordon McCall invited Quebec director Robert LePage and his company, Le Répère, to join him in mounting a bilingual production in order to take advantage of a funding criterion within a Saskatchewan government grant application for "extra funds." McCall claimed that this was "the first time that we know of that . . . an anglophone company and a francophone company have joined forces in collaboration to present Shakespeare."[1] He is right and he is wrong.

Ontario's Stratford Festival staged *Henry V* in 1956 using members of Le Théâtre du Nouveau Monde to play the French court. It was a unilingual production however. In fact many of the French Quebec actors could not speak English and had to learn to speak the lines by rote, as nonsense syllables. Stratford does not have a bilingual audience (unless one considers American a second language); Saskatoon does—or at least it has communities representing the two cultures who do not easily get along.

The stated intent of Shakespeare on the Saskatchewan is to present "uniquely Saskatoon versions of the Bard's great works." Another of their stated intents, as part of their first five-year plan, is to develop a national component within their productions.[2] *Romeo & Juliette* filled both criteria. It was performed in a huge tent on the banks of the Saskatchewan river. The set was a dusty stretch of the trans-Canada highway running down the centre. The audience sat on each side. The Montague's were beer-guzzling English-speaking prairie boys. The Capulays were Franco-Saskatchewanians. Both roar around on motorcycles. Juliet's balcony speech was played in a pickup truck. Seated inside the cab after the party, she hears a noise. She shines a flashlight through the rear window. It's Romeo, she's heard. He says, "What light through yonder window breaks?" The Prince is an RCMP officer. He arrives in a police cruiser, lights flashing, siren wailing. All part of "the two hours 'traffic' of our stage," intoned by the Prince at the beginning of the play. Saskatoon audiences loved it and gave it standing ovations. "You don't understand every word but you certainly know what's going on," was one response. "It's Shakespeare. Even in English it's not easy to understand." was another.[3]

In the course of its seven-week run it played to 95 per cent capacity. Many people returned to see the play more than once. Even the artistic director was surprised that there was a less than 1 per cent rejection of the show owing to French being spoken by the Capulet family (McCall 41). This is remarkable in a province that has lagged in support and implementation of francophone rights and privileges. It obviously struck close to home.

In the summer of 1990 it toured Ontario, sending critics into fits of apoplexy while attracting solid audiences from both language groups. "The directors have willfully ignored the esthetics of the play. It's one thing to update the classics, it's another to indulge oneself in unscholarly silliness" stated Robert Crew in a *Toronto Star* article under the headline "Wherefore art thou, Romeo, Juliet?" He called the directorial choices "plain dumb," stating "the text has been butchered and the play discarded." In their drive to popularize Shakespeare," he concludes, "someone forgot to bring *Romeo and Juliette* [sic] along for the ride."[4] Tellingly, there is not one word given to the political context of the production nor to the production's relevance for its audiences.

The *Globe and Mail's* reaction was similar. Its headline read "A Case for the Esthetic Police." "It should be against the law to people an aristocratic play with mouth-breathing dimwits" railed Ray Conlogue. Conlogue gives six words to political and social context and spends his energies comparing the only cultural clash of importance to him: that of the two directing styles, preferring LePage's input to McCall's.[5] The audiences evidently recognized themselves in the show and once again gave the production standing ovations, the critics be damned.

Critics in Toronto, we may infer, basically view theatre as an artistic, aesthetic business venture; political and social contexts just aren't considered part of it.

The same cannot be said for the French critics in Quebec who cannot conceive of theatre without political intent. Elaine Nardocchio makes this clear in her 1986 book, *Theatre and Politics in Modern Quebec*, published by the University of Alberta Press. The language, sponsorship, venue, and audience of these performances, she explains, are as intensely sociopolitical acts as are their content. They provide eloquent testimony to continuing cultural sovereignty.[6]

Herbert Whittaker, longtime theatre critic and doyen of Canadian criticism, has pointed why he feels this is so. The French and English language critics at mid-century were part of a national organization. For their own reasons, French critics decided to form their own body. "The days of the Quiet revolution were upon them, and many Quebec critics sided with the artists who proclaimed it so vigorously. . . . In French Canada, then, the cause of nationalism often came first. In English Canada, the state of the art was still of prime concern."[7]

It came as no surprise, therefore, when the reaction of the French critics to Marianne Ackerman's bilingual *L'Affaire Tartuffe, or The*

Garrison Officers Rehearse Molière, a 1990 production of Montreal's Theatre 1774, differed markedly from the response of the English critics.

The play is predicated on a single historical fact: in 1774 British garrison officers in Montreal performed a play by Molière in French. The playwright imagines the rest, peopling her stage with French, Swiss, coureurs de bois, English, Scottish, Irish, and Americans, each with their own accents, each with their own personal histories, each with their own agendas. Ackerman explores Quebec's multi-ethnic, multi-class, multi-lingual, far from pure-laine, very rich cultural heritage, past and by extension, present. At the same time she parallels historical events with contemporary events.

It is not entirely surprising that the company which has received the most political attention is Theatre 1774, despite its claim to be working simultaneously in English and French for purely artistic reasons and not as a political act. Officially Theatre 1774 exists expressly "to create projects in which anglo- and francophone artists can work together and through their work, to explore both cultures, their perception and influence upon each other."[8] Co-artistic directors, Ackerman (a former Montreal drama critic turned playwright) and Clare Schapiro, both continually reaffirm, "This company is not a political act."[9] By this they mean that there is no hidden agenda. There is no pre-determined point of view to be espoused or policy to be implemented. They are open to exploration, pure and simple, of Quebec history and the human condition to find out what common roots there are, what bridges exist as well as what divisions, and what it means in human terms to live sharing two cultures.

1774's initial production of *Echo,* an imagistic staging almost entirely in English with some German, under the direction of francophone director Robert LePage of poet Ann Diamond's book *A Nun's Diary* in 1989, came under attack from the French press solely on political grounds. "Qu'est donc aller faire Robert LePage dans cette galère?" demanded *La Presse* critic Gilles Lamontagne in his headline. Why, he wondered, was the hottest French Canadian director working for two anglophones. He accused 1774 of piracy, not collaboration, for seeking to rob the "vitality of our theatre" in order to give life to an artistically impoverished anglophone culture.[10]

Leonore Lieblein, in an article in *Canadian Theatre Review* saw this as his "doubt that the anglophone and francophone communities could interact on any but unequal footing. Hence he experienced the production of *Echo* as an aggression by one linguistic theatre community against another, "[11] she asserts. The sin committed by 1774, suggests Lieblein, its statement of intent notwithstanding, was to break new ground by inserting itself into the cultural politics in Quebec.

With *L'Affaire Tartuffe,* the French critics again reviewed the play in the political contexts of the ongoing language debate (Bills 101 and 178) and the then-occurring constitutional crisis. They differed, however, in their assessments of the play based on their personal feelings about the English and French communities' relationship to each other. For Louise Blanchard in *Le Journal de Montréal,* the production was very important culturally. She welcomed the play as a breach in the wall between two sides which remain hidden from one another to each other's detriment.[12] Alain Pontaut in *Le Devoir,* considering the two solitudes to be impenetrable, saw the play only as a superficial gesture.[13]

Once again English newspaper critics focused almost exclusively on the artistic aspects of the play and failed to relate it to current events in Quebec. Myron Galloway, writing in the *Suburban,* called it "A theatrical achievement of epic proportions" and "an important milestone in the history of theatre in Montreal . . .".[14] The milestone and the achievement he identified were that of artistic collaboration between English- and French-speaking actors. If he thought there might be contemporary political implications he kept it to himself. Pat Donnelly of the *Gazette* described it as "a play of sweeping scope, Shakespearean ambition, worthy intentions and delicious flashes of sniping wit." She and Galloway both agreed on the play's weaknesses: too long, too many issues to deal with. They both viewed the play's context solely as an illumination of history. Donnelly went so far as to title her review "Local history is cue for *L'Affaire Tartuffe.*" The furtherst she ventures from purely artistic analysis is to wonder why "a city so wealthy in history and theatre has inspired so little historical play-writing" before.[15]

The Toronto critic Stephen Godfrey of the *Globe and Mail* also focuses on the artistic aspects of the play in his review "Lurching awkwardly across linguistic lines."[16] While he notes "there are deliberate anachronisms: one scene is called The Swim in Lake Meech, and the barmaid sarcastically suggests her father put his sign outside in French," he, too, fails to associate these obvious clues to contemporary Canadian events.

Lieblein excuses the oversight, observing, "Perhaps it was too obvious to be worth mentioning" and postulating that "in the climate of the Bélanger-Campeau hearings [the critics] had withdrawn from overt political comment but were [nevertheless] grateful that the play . . . had re-inserted the English into Quebec history" (69).

A more reflective review by Montreal allophone, Pauline Abarca, for the Canadian theatre magazine, *Theatrum*, did call attention to context although it also focused primarily on the artistic aspects. Agreeing with her colleagues from the newspapers, Abarca cites an ambitious script, great comic effect, sharp and witty dialogue, visually interesting direction, moving performances. She calls the production a wonderful vehicle for great bicultural ensemble work, but adds, "some scenes are positively riveting in their relevance to Montreal's current reality."[17]

January 1992 saw a remount of Fenarrio's *Balconville* at the Centaur, thirteen years after it was originally presented there. Featuring a cast of English- and French-speaking characters, *Balconville* is a socio-political statement about working class existence in Montreal. In it, Fennario uses English and French conflict as well as conflict between men and women, the young and the old, and between dreams and realities, not to highlight historical, linguistic, cultural, and gender-based differences so much as to exploit them to address his overriding and more universal concern: the human degredation of poverty and the powerlessness it breeds.

When the show first played in 1979 Fennario stated the big problem isn't language, it's class. "The workers must control the industry. Working class people in our society—and by that I mean everyone who gets hired and fired—are slaves," he is on record as saying. For Fennario, when he wrote the play, the only answer was getting together politically. Despite their differences, the characters recognize that they have a common *interest*.[18]

Some of the questions that concerned those involved in the remount were: what differences has time made, is there a common interest anymore, and is it the same one. Back in January 1979 the economy was in a mess, taxes were high, and it looked as if the country were about to split up. As they say in Quebec, "plus ça change . . .".[19] For the remount, Fennario made no changes to the script "because times really haven't changed." One of the actors, who also played in the original production disagreed, but only slightly. "The situation is worse than when we presented it the first time," he is quoted as saying, implying the show is even more relevant today.[20]

Audience reaction bears them both out. The show was extended twice and played to full and enthusiastic houses through its final performance on a Sunday. If anything, English audiences accepted the 40 per cent French dialogue more easily this time round, and probably understood more of it too. French audiences, getting used to finding their way to this bastion of English language culture, increased in numbers also.

During the spring of 1992 Ackerman rewrote *L'Affaire Tartuffe* in an attempt to "finalize the script." She felt she did not have enough time before it opened in 1990 to resolve enough of her own questions. She sought to simplify and shorten the script (the weaknesses cited by the critics) and at the same time to make historical events more resonant with contemporary events in Quebec. The production opened May 1 and this time round played in a French-language venue, Théâtre La Chapelle. Although the production that had played in the English-language venue had had a French-language director, this one, playing in a French-language venue, had an English-language director. 1774 chose Guy Sprung, the director of the original version of *Balconville* and former artistic director of Canadian Stage in Toronto, to direct.

L'Affaire Tartuffe II was not merely a different production; it was a completely different play. Many of the same characters peopled both versions, but the time frame, the concerns of the characters, and the nature of the action were far removed from the first version. The first version was set in 1774 in a variety of locales. It had a two-level set. It had a strong through line. The second version was set in a dining room of a mansion in Westmount in 1992. The set was on one level only. It was episodic. The first play was driven by the personal and conflicting objectives of its characters. It was emotionally charged and the action was complex. The second version entailed a discussion around a dinner table about making a film set in 1774. It was driven by its characters' need to reach a common perspective. The 20th-century characters (a minister of culture, a brewery magnate, an actress, a filmmaker, and so on) donned pieces of period costume and role-played *les personnages d'antan* in imagined situations as they explored their subject matter. It was a play within a play within a play and became an intellectual exercise. Despite some well-written individual scenes and remarkable insight into Quebec society (then and now), as drama it was disappointing. If the first play suffered from having too many conflicting plot lines to follow, the second suffered from not having any.

Ackerman did succeed in one respect: getting the critics on both sides to look more deeply at the political and social contexts of

English/French relations, although once again the critics were divided in their response along linguistic/cultural lines. Their responses this time, though, like the play itself, were more muted, and more thoughtful.

Liam Lacy in his *Globe and Mail* review entitled "A Political Parable" states "the play serves as a vehicle for a series of meditations on the relationship between language and identity" and "makes a good case for bilingualism." Despite the recognition of the issues he does not go into them, however. He is concerned with the effectiveness of the presentation and finds it lacking. "Overall the story is obstinately earthbound," he states. "When the characters speak and move, we are often acutely aware that this is a very talky costume show in which the actors serve as two dimensional agents in a political parable."[21]

Pat Donnelly of the Montreal *Gazette* agrees with him. She headlines her review with "*Tartuffe* more likely to win literary prize than audiences." "We are asked to care," she writes, "about a myriad of historical currents which have flowed through Quebec politics since the mid-18th century." Like Lacy in the *Globe and Mail,* while identifying the topic for her readers, she gives neither analysis nor comment. She too frames her criticism solely on the artistic merits of the presentation and spends most of her review criticizing the acting, concluding that the production "never quite transcends the anti-climactic . . . this version is simply not as much fun as the original presented at Centaur in September 1990."[22]

Le Devoir's Gilbert David titles his review "A happy detour from history: a plea for cultural enrichment." He spends as little time as possible on the artistic merits of the piece—one praiseworthy sentence at the beginning and two at the end, instead choosing to address the implications of the play's message. While he finds Ackerman's idealism excessive and argues strongly against her point of view, he gives her position a positive exposure. "Throughout a deliciously frothy play, possessed of a bitter-sweet irony," he writes, "Ackerman, without trumpets or drums, inclines in favor of a reconciliation of distinct peoples, not on the basis of an imposed bilingualism, but by way of a cultural enrichment freely chosen, that despite differences in culture and language, the life of each would know only the limits of imgination."[23]

Is there then a future for further bilingual ventures? Perhaps it depends on the need to demonstrate and avow some sense of national unity. Although at present one can sense, in the post-referendum period, a more settled atmosphere and an increased degree of receptivity between French Quebecers and other Canadians, still both French and English communities feel under seige by the other and everyone is treading carefully. As example, 1774's current production, while continuing to mix francophone and anglophone artists and boldly incorporating aspects of both cultures to create a quite exciting aesthetic experience, thus demonstrates once again the values of cross-cultural collaboration. The play is a rigorously cut version of Shakespeare's *Measure for Measure* and is performed in English only.

Certainly it might be pushing the point too hard to ascribe the phenomenon of bilingual-bicultural theatre activity solely to the tensions preceding the PQ's referendum at the time Fennario's *Balconville* was written, and to the tensions leading up to last fall's national and Quebec referendums on the constitution which coincided with the most recent manifestations. Still, it is interesting to speculate that there probably is a significant relationship. If there is an identifiable pattern to be discerned, it may well reappear should we have to gear up yet again for yet another referendum—presupposing the fall of the present Liberal government in Quebec and no softening of Parizeau's separatist rhetoric. For the moment there is a lull and subtly though ever more openly, francophone and anglophone artists are continuing to collaborate to create theatre as a reflection of their joint cultural reality.

Since theatre reflects the society which breeds it, as theatre history demonstrates, one can safely assert, at least, that what happens on stage will be indicative of the future of the country.

Concordia University   **Philip Spensley**

NOTES

1. See Bob Cox [Canadian Press], "Bilingual Shakespeare a hit in Saskatchewan," *The Gazette*, July 19, 1989. F10.

2. See Gordon McCall, "A Bilingual Romeo & Juliette in Saskatoon," *Canadian Theatre Review* (Spring 1990), 35.

3. See Bob Cox [Canadian Press], "Romeo and Juliet goes bilingual for Saskatoon's Theatre Festival," *Vancouver Sun*, July 15, 1989. p. A12. also Jamie Portman, "Radical version of Romeo-Juliet wins audiences," *Vancouver Sun* July 4, 1990.

4. See June 13, 1990.

5. See June 13, 1990.

6. See Barry Wellman, *Canadian Review of Sociology and Anthro-pology* 25 (4), November 1988, 677.

7. See "Canadian Theatre Criticism," in *Contemporary Canadian Theatre*, Anton Wagner. Toronto: Simon and Pierre, 1985, 340.

8. "Theatre 1774." Statement explaining company's name and mandate. n.d.

9. Personal conversation. n.d.

10. September 14, 1990.

11. See "Political Reflections on *L'Affaire Tartuffe*," Summer 1991: 66.

12. See "*L'Affaire Tartuffe*: Aussi drole que le Lac Meech." September 20, 1990.

13. "L'hypocryte et les habit rouges." September 14, 1990.

14. See September 12, 1990, 54.

15. See September 11, 1990. F1.

16. See September 15, 1990. C6.

17. See "L'Affaire Tartuffe or The Garrison Officers Rehearse Molière." Winter 1990/91, 42, 43.

18. See Maureen Peterson, "Fennario: The politics of plays," *The Gazette*, December 29, 1978, p. 27.

19. See "plus ça change, plus ça reste": the more things change, the more they stay the same.

20. See Pat Donnelly, "Fennario's Big Hit puts working class back on centre stage," *The Gazette*, December 28, 1991. E1, E2.

21. See Saturday, May 9, 1992. C9.

22. See Saturday, May 2, 1992. C3.

23. See "Un heureux détour de l'histoire: Plaidoyer pour l'enrichisse-ment culturel," samedi, le 9 mai, 1992. C4.

Conjonctions et disjonctions dans *Chronique de la dérive douce* de Dany Laferrière ou poésie de la condition immigrante

Le dernier ouvrage de Dany Laferrière, *Chronique de la dérive douce* (1994), a reçu un accueil plutôt tiède de la critique, et curieusement, c'est sa forme qu'on lui a reprochée, cette juxtaposition de 365 petits poèmes en prose qui raconte la première année d'un immigrant haïtien à Montréal, une forme assez semblable à celle que l'on retrouvait dans *L'Odeur du café* (Laferrière 1991).

Cette chronique est difficilement dissociable de l'oeuvre antérieure de Laferrière, notamment de *Comment faire l'amour avec un nègre sans se fatiguer* (1985) et de l'auteur lui-même. Laferrière dans une entrevue à *Plaisir de lire* passait directement du narrateur à sa personne, mais pour ma part, je l'envisagerai comme une oeuvre littéraire où le "je" est fictif, car je ne veux pas être amené à identifier certains personnages qu'il nomme et décrit dans sa chronique. Nous savons tous et toutes que la genèse des personnages littéraires est complexe, composite et ce n'est pas ce point de vue génétique qui m'interesse.

Comme l'indique le sous-titre, "Poésie de la condition immigrante", je veux plutôt montrer que les disjonctions et conjonctions que cette chronique nous donne à lire s'achèvent et se subsument en la naissance d'un écrivain immigrant, rejoignant ainsi une recherche que j'ai entrepris depuis quelques années sur la littérature et la culture immigrante au Québec (Thérien, 1993, 1991).

Disjonctions

L'année que traverse le narrateur est marquée par cinq formes principales de disjonctions : les différences de comportement, un autre espace et une autre température, les aléas de ce que j'appelle ici la promiscuité et qui en fait la misère, la discrimination raciale et la discrimination immigrante. Le narrateur est un Haïtien débarqué à Montréal en 1976 au moment des Jeux Olympiques et fuyant la dictature de son pays, soit cinq ans avant l'action décrite dans *Comment faire l'amour avec un nègre sans se fatiguer*.

A peine descendu de l'avion, le narrateur est saisi de l'indifférence des voyageurs devant une scène, qui à Port-au-Prince, écrit-il, aurait provoqué une émeute:

Un couple en train
de s'embrasser
à l'aéroport.
Un baiser interminable.
La fille est en
mini-jupe rouge [...].
Je suis le seul à m'intéresser
à ce baiser rouge. (11-12)

Un peu dans le même ordre d'idées, le narrateur fuira un bar de
filles pour immigrés, non parce que la plus jeune aurait 65 ans, mais
parce qu'il ne supporte pas leur froideur.

Je laisse passer un moment avant de partir.
Pas parce qu'elles sont vieilles.
À cause de leur yeux.
Un regard froid (20).

Sous la différence qui se lit entre l'espace montréalais et l'espace
haïtien, et dans la liberté sexuelle que permet le premier, la prose
efficace de Laferrière donne aussi à lire la différence des fortunes.

A Port-au-Prince, quand une fille rancontre un gars, le
problème c'est de trouver un endroit pour être à l'abri
du million de paires d'yeux qui ne vous lâchent pas une
seconde. A Montréal, les deux partenaires ont chacun
leur propre clef (29).

Au-delà du froid, qui, quelque part, écrit le narrateur, est
supportable, au-delà du fait de se réveiller dans un pays d'hiver où tout
le monde est blanc, ce qu'il ne peut tolérer, ce sont les arbres nus:

Il me semble que c'est la forme
que prend la mort pour manifester
sa présence parmi nous (97).

On conviendra que le dénuement qui caractérise ces paysages urbains
d'hiver s'accepte assez mal quand on a connu la luxuriance tropicale.
Liée à sa misère d'immigrant qui, de chambre d'ami le conduit en
maison de chambres, le narrateur doit vivre ici aussi, pourrait-on dire,

les conséquences de la promiscuité.

Parmi les ébats amoureux d'un voisin (36) qui rappellent ceux de Belzébuth dans *Comment faire l'amour*, les policiers qui passent leur temps dans l'escalier de son immeuble (36), certaines fois un coup de feu qui fait la manchette dans le journal (36), on ne peut pas dire qu'il a la vie facile. Et le rire désespéré que ce geste entraîna ne cessa que quand le voisin de gauche "se mit à taper contre le mur" (39).

Une fois, que par mégarde, il s'assit sur une femme dans l'autobus, tout le monde lui demanda d'enlever son chapeau. Cette réaction, assez bon enfant, on en conviendra, est moins cruelle que celle qu'il déclencha pour avoir mangé un bol de salade et bu un verre de vin dans l'escalier de son immeuble:

> Les gens me regardent avec
> des fusils dans les yeux.
> Je ne sais pas si c'est à cause
> de mon bonheur ou du fait
> qu'aujourd'hui c'est mardi et
> qu'un type normal devrait être
> au boulot à l'heure qu'il est (63).

Plus graves que ces difficultés dues à la misère sont les manifestations de la discrimination raciale. D'abord, c'est le choc de se retrouver seul noir au milieu d'une population blanche.

> Je le savais déjà
> pour l'avoir lu.
> Pour l'avoir vu au cinéma.
> Mais c'est différent dans
> la vraie vie.
> Je suis noir
>
> et tous les autres
> sont blancs (14).

Le narrateur nous montre bien, que c'est lui qui eut le choc! Il n'en est malheureusement pas ainsi pour la police. L'événement vécu par le narrateur—où l'on voit ce dernier plaqué contre le mur et fouillé en règle pour la seule raison qu'on cherche un noir (49)—ne laisse pas doute dans l'esprit du lecteur. En fait, pire que la discrimination raciale, la disjonction plus grande, c'est la condition immigrante que nous appelons ici la discrimination immigrante.

Plus que la faim, plus que le froid, plus que la solitude, les conditions de travail de l'immigration sont insupportables parce qu'elles sont voulues par ceux qui les imposent et les créent volontairement. Quand il se présente au Bureau de la Main-d'œuvre, le narrateur est vite ramené à sa condition d'immigrant. À la case "Salaire esperé," il inscrit $18 l'heure:

> Le conseiller à la Main-d'œuvre l'a effacé
> pour écrire trois dollars dix,
> le salaire minimum,
> sans même lever les yeux vers moi (66).

Les conditions de travail qu'il connaîtra à l'usine sont particulièrement odieuses, alors qu'il remplace un ouvrier qui a eu l'avant-bras broyé:

> Au lieu de changer la machine défectueuse, qui coûte
> une fortune, faut le dire, la direction a préféré donner le
> poste à un immigrant. Les gars font tout ce qu'ils
> peuvent pour qu'il m'arrive quelque chose (67).

Parce que, s'il arrivait un deuxième accident, on changerait peut-être la machine! En fait, ce sont Joseph et Josaphat qui illustrent le plus tristement le sort fait aux immigrants.

Ils n'arrêtent même pas de travailler pour manger. "Quelqu'un leur a dit que s'ils ne travaillent pas comme des bêtes, on les renverra chez eux" (119). Ce sont des illégaux, qui travaillent au noir, en deçà du salaire minimum et qui doivent verser la moitié de leur salaire à celui qui leur a procuré ce travail. La fin de leur histoire est particulièrement cruelle et la portée de l'épisode, sans ambiguïté:

> Ils ont dit aux nouvelles
> qu'un des Haïtiens s'était pendu
> et qu'on craignait que son frère
> ne suive son exemple.
> Si Josaphat écoute la télé
> en ce moment, il sait ce qu'on
> attend de lui (130).

Heureusement pourtant, *Chronique de la dérive douce* ne se referme pas sur cette forme ultime de disjonction. Avant d'aborder les manifestations de la conjonction, nous allons traiter la forme intermédiaire que nous avons appelée "Conjonctions-Disjonctions."

Conjonctions-Disjonctions

Dès son arrivée, le narrateur perçoit intuitivement à la fois les différences et les ressemblances entre son pays et le pays d'accueil.

D'une certaine façon, ce pays
ressemble le mien.
Il y a des gens, des arbres,
un ciel, de la musique, des filles,
de l'alcool, mais quelque part, j'ai
le sentiment que c'est totalement différent
sur des points très précis: l'amour,
la mort, la maladie, la colère, la
joie, le rêve ou la jouissance (14).

Les manifestations des conjonctions-disjonctions peuvent se regrouper autour de cinq ensembles narratifs: les amis retrouvés, Antonio, Julie et Nathalie, l'Indien et le vieux du 5e.

Manger et dormir, ou plutôt trouver à manger et un endroit pour dormir sont les premières quêtes du narrateur. Deux fois, il trouvera à dormir chez un ami retrouvé, vraisemblablement un compatriote, et les deux fois, il devra partir. La première fois, parce que la femme lui fait la gueule (21) ; la seconde, parce qu'il a fait celui qui ne comprend pas: "La dernière fois, sa femme m'avait reçu en robe de chambre avec des yeux de nuit et j'avais fait semblant de ne pas comprendre" (27). Il en sera à peu près de même avec Antonio.

Habitant dans le quartier italien, le narrateur s'était lié avec Antonio: "Il me traite comme si j'étais son fils/ alors que je couche avec sa fille" (41). Ce dernier voulait comme gendre un certain Marcello. Le narrateur aimait bien Maria et Antonio, mais il préférera partir plutôt que de s'encombrer de Maria.

J'ai dit calmement à Maria
de ne pas se servir de moi
pour faire face à son père.
Je marche seul (42).

Il marche seul! C'est une façon de parler, puisqu'on le retrouve entre autres, entre Julie et Nathalie.

Julie, c'est sa "flamme vacillante au bout de ce tunnel de glace" (103). Elle ne supporte guère qu'il aime toutes les femmes (103). Si, par contre, Nathalie semble mieux le supporter, elle n'hésite pas à plaquer le narrateur toute une soirée avec un Sénégalais qu'elle a retrouvé à la porte du bar (71). Elle partira finalement au Brésil avec un musicien brésilien (123). L'amitié avec l'Indien conduira aussi à la séparation.

Cette amitié est née à l'usine. Le narrateur s'en était bien défendu.

> L'Indien veut qu'on fasse équipe.
> J'ai dû lui expliquer calmement
> qu'un nègre et une Peau-Rouge ensemble,
> ce serait pas bien vu en Amérique (73).

Quoi qu'il en soit s'est progressivement tissé entre eux un lien d'amitié, un rapprochement de leur condition.

> L'Indien est venu à la maison
> et nous avons discuté
> de nos clichés respectifs.
> Lui, c'est l'alcool.
> Moi, le sexe (79).

Finalement, l'Indien partira aux Etats-Unis avec la fille du patron de l'usine (122). Sorte de vengeance de l'opprimé, certes, mais aussi solitude accrue pour le narrateur. Il en sera de même pour le Vieux du 5e.

La forme concise et elliptique de *Chronique de la dérive douce* donne à certains épisodes une force concentrée et poignante. Il en est ainsi de la mort de la petite souris (126), à laquelle, comme le narrateur, nous étions attachés, mort annonciatrice en quelque sorte de la fin du vieux du 5e, entr'aperçu au fil de la narration:

> Le vieux du 5e m'a fait
> entrer dans sa chambre
> pour me montrer son
> album de photos (76).

La juxtaposition de l'annonce de suicide de Joseph et le départ en ambulance du vieillard:

le brancardier me fait signe
qu'il n'a aucune chance (131).

tisse un autre lien de solidarité entre les homme. Au-delà des disjonctions, il y a bien, dans cette chronique, des conjonctions.

Conjonctions

Les manifestations de la conjonction peuvent s'organiser autour de cinq axes: les ressemblances entre les deux pays, les différentes expressions de sympathie, d'amitié et d'amour, la solidarité, la connivence et l'écriture comme une décision libre d'écrire son destin.

Le bruit des voitures (17), le soleil (21), le ciel bleu (47) et plus encore, les rumeurs de la ville transportent parfois le narrateur en pleine créolité:

Les voix des gens massés
le long de la rue Sherbrooke,
encourageant les coureurs du marathon,
me parviennent comme un chant créole (21).

En fait, ce sont bien davantage les manifestations de sympathie, d'amitié et d'amour qui illustrent la conjonction dans cette chronique.

Que ce soit à l'Accueil Bonneau où on lui donne un bol de soupe chaude et une paire de chaussures (26) ou au Bureau de dépannage des immigrants où le préposé lui offre trois fois plus d'argent que celui auquel il aurait droit (27), le narrateur connaît dès son arrivée des manifestations de sympathie et d'accueil.

Il en sera de même de la jeune fille qui l'amène chez elle, rue St-Dominique (28) et de celle qui lui fait un strip-tease à sa fenêtre (44). Il en sera de même aussi du vieil alcoolique qui lui donne une recette si utile de pigeon (33) ou de ce policier assez bon joueur:

pour (les) avertir
de faire attention au type du 16 (38).

Semblablement, les deux bonnes vieilles qui lui louent une chambre, sans s'inquiéter comment il fera pour payer le loyer (43), ou la concierge qui l'invite à réveillonner chez elle, lui manifestent beaucoup de sympathie. Le narrateur écrit avec émotion :

Ce n'est que maintenant que je prends conscience que
cette femme de 78 ans qui ignorait tout d'Haïti avant de
me connaître sait aujourd'hui qui est Duvalier et même
combien coûte la livre de riz au marché de Port-au-
Prince (99).

Entre Julie et Nathalie, se place une troisième protagoniste: la
grosse femme de la buanderie. Non seulement le narrateur répond-il à
ses avances, mais avec elle, c'est du solide. On la voit arriver chez lui
avec deux gros sacs de provisions (110) et il découvrira un mois plus tard
dans un bouquin un billet de $10 (125). Il semblerait qu'il appliqué avec
elle la règle d'or du Haïtien rencontré dans le parc:

[...] ne quitte jamais une femme en hiver [...]
- Ici, mon vieux, dès la fin d'octobre, tout le monde est
casé... Il faut attendre le printemps quand tu passe
ton tour (113).

Au-delà du gîte, de la bouffe et du sexe, le narrateur se sent bientôt
solidaire. Solidaire de ce voisin de palier, qui partage le même espace
que lui:

Tu ne voles pas, tu ne prends de drogue, tu n'as
pas de filles qui travaillent pour toi, comment fais-tu
pour vivre, Man?
Le ton d'un grand frère anxieux (37).

Solidaire des autres immigrants qui partagent la même condition
que lui:

Haïtiens, Italiens et Vietnamiens
des quartiers pauvres
entassés comme des sardines
dans ces wagons qui filent
vers l'est de la ville
toutes couleurs confondues.

Tous ceux qui prennent
le métro vers cette heure
reviennent de l'usine (74).

Mais c'est peut-être dans la musique et la littérature, ou plus précisément par la musique et la littérature que le narrateur retrouvera la plus profonde connivence:

> Doudou Boicel m'a présenté
> a Dizzy Gillepsie qui m'a
> regardé comme si j'étais
> quelqu'un.
> Comme c'est étrange! (48)

Dans *Chronique de la dérive douce*, le jazz est loin de jouer le rôle essentiel qu'il a dans *Comment faire l'amour*... Par contre, on y retrouve les Borgès, Bukowski, Baldwin, rappelé aussi dans *Cette grenade*—"le seul écrivain en qui j'ai pleinement confiance" (165)— Baldwin, Salinger. Le narrateur passe ses journées à lire dans la librairie de son amie: "Tous les copains sont là: Borgès, Bukowski, Limorov, Baldwin, Miller, Gombrowicz, Salinger" (50). Il n'est pas exagéré de lire dans ce passage à la fois l'univers privilégié du narrateur, les autres les plus souvent cités dans les romans de Laferrière, et comme la voie le conduisant le narrateur à l'écriture.

La forme la plus achevée de conjonction, nous la retrouvons dans le désir d'écrire du narrateur:

> Je suis allé voir le boss,
> après le lunch
> sur un coup de tête,
> et je lui ai dit
> que je quitte à l'instant
> pour devenir écrivain.
>
> Je vais donc retourner
> au parc, traîner, regarder
> les filles, noter mes impressions
> et, bien sûr, essayer d'autres recettes
> de pigeons (136).

On peut dire qu'il mettra cinq ans à écrire *Comment faire l'amour avec un Nègre* . . .

Que nous dit *Chronique de la dérive* douce si ce n'est que de cette boue . . . l'écrivain a su faire de l'or.

En fait, non seulement la chronique nous révèle l'avant de *Comment*

faire l'amour mais nous donne mieux à lire l'œuvre de Laferrière où semblent se dessiner trois axes :
-l'axe québécois avec *Chronique* et *Comment faire l'amour*
-l'axe américain avec *Eroshima* et *Cette grenade*
-l'axe haïtien avec *L'Odeur du café* et *Le Goût des jeunes filles,*
une œuvre typique de la culture immigrée avec les deux pays d'accueil et le pays en allé, une œuvre contribuant à définir une nouvelle identité québécoise.

Université de Montréal   **Michel Thérien**

Ouvrages Cites

Laferrière, Danny. *Comment faire l'amour avec un nègre sans se fatiguer.* Montréal : VLB, 1985.

————. *Eroshima.* Montréal : VLB, 1987.

—————. *L'Odeur du café.* Montréal : VLB, 1991.

—————. *Le Goût des jeunes filles.* Montréal : VLB, 1992.

—————. *Cette grenade dans la main du jeune Nègre est-elle une arme ou un fruit?* Montréal : VLB, 1993.

—————. *Chronique de la dérive douce.* Montréal : VLB, 1994.

Thérien, M. "L'enseignement de la littérature dans un contexte pluraliste". *Construire un espace commun, Pluriethnicité, éducation et société.* Eds. F. Ouellet et M. Pagé. Québec : Institut québécois de recherche sur la culture, 1991, 453-466.

————. "Littérature immigrée et didactique du français." *Sens des didactiques et didactique du sens.* Eds. Y. Lenoir et P. Jonnaert. Sherbrooke : CRP, 1993, 333-338.

The Ontario Protestant Novel

A great deal of Canadian fiction, popular enough in its own era, has been consigned to oblivion. One such body of literature could broadly be termed the Protestant novel, a genre popular in the late nineteenth and early twentieth century.[1] In Ontario alone, many writers were directly connected to the Protestant ministry—ministers, ministers' wives and children; these writers used their fiction to focus on religious and moral issues.[2] Dozens of these novelists and hundreds of their works are mentioned in literary histories such as Carl Klinck's *The Literary History of Canada* (1965),[3] but their fiction is seldom read today. Tastes change. There is no longer a great demand for moral tales, and stories by Ralph Connor, Marian Keith, Mack Cloie, W.H. Withrow, and R. and K.M. Lizars, to name only a few, sit gathering dust on library shelves. Yet a study of these works yields some interesting results. On the one hand, novels written by a Presbyterian, a Methodist, or an Anglican[4] feature the religious faith and biases of the writer. On the other hand, the same novels demonstrate the removal of the narrow doctrinal barriers which hitherto had created dissension both within and between Protestant denominations.[5] A basic paradox is established then, as the writers both uphold and undermine doctrinal bias. Ultimately, however, the similarities of religious ideas and fictional themes become more striking than the differences, pointing the way to the formation of the United Church of Canada in 1925.[6]

Originally in Ontario there were at least six separate Methodist sects;[7] some had ties with American Methodists; others were more directly linked with the British Methodists (Cooper, passim). W.H. Withrow's *Barbara Heck* (1895) is a fictionalized account of the arrival in Ontario of Loyalist Methodist preachers, and his *Neville Trueman, The Pioneer Preacher* (1880) features an itinerant American Methodist preacher who chooses to stay in Canada during the war of 1812-1814. The paths which led to Ontario came from a number of directions, and the original differences between the various Methodist groups were both doctrinal and political. Despite initial divisiveness, the Methodist church in Canada showed an early propensity to heal division through union. From 1832 to 1833, for example, the Episcopal and the Wesleyan Methodists in Upper Canada united to form the Wesleyan Church. Then, in 1884, all remaining sects were joined in the Methodist Church. In this we see what becomes a typical pattern in

Canadian church history—the general movement towards the resolution of doctrinal strife through union.

The works of W.H. Withrow, himself a Methodist minister, reflect his time and place. *Barbara Heck, Neville Trueman,* and *The King's Messenger; or, Lawrence Temple's Probation* (1879) capture in fiction the beliefs and religious practices of Methodists in Upper Canada. For one thing, his novels are written in the style of Christian biography, drawing on the popular tradition of "lives" of well-known Methodists. For another, his male protagonists carry on the practice of circuit riding—spending much of their time on horseback to reach widely scattered settlements. This indirectly points up the movement towards Methodist union; division into sect seems pointless when there are neither enough people to fill a church nor enough ministers to go around.[8] Finally, Withrow's work features basic Methodist beliefs, as for example, the intense, joyful, and personal realization of God (Hopper 107-108; Westfall, "Order" 14-18). When Lawrence Temple converts a sinner, he bursts into "that grand exultant strain of Charles Wesley" (96).

The Anglican novels offer the reader a glimpse into the beliefs and the practices of another particular Protestant church. Like the Methodists, the Anglicans had developed inner doctrinal strife which they brought with them to the New World[9]—a division most commonly manifested in the split between "Low" and "High" Anglicanism. The problems concerning theology and policy were inherited from the English and Irish settlers (Moir, *Canada West* 4-5), but because of the scarcity of ministers and the impracticality of building two churches in one small town, initial differences tended to disappear. In Slowford's Anglican church, in *Committed to His Charge* (1900), there are Low Church and High Church adherents who co-exist in an uneasy truce. The choice of a new minister splits the congregation:

There would be war. Everyone knew that. The High Church party in the congregation, those who wished to stand during the offertory and have an alms basin, who longed for a surpliced choir and a floral cross on the altar at Easter, would make a desperate effort to put in a man of progressive views. This party consisted of the bankers and others who were not Slowford people proper . . . (3)

The Low Church party were for a man of purely evangelical type . . . [M]embers who had determined in years gone by to be true till death to their purely Protestant principles. The members still lived and they still protested. (4)

One point of the Lizars' gently comic satire is that both groups stand upon tradition for their differences and seem unsure of the reasons for their beliefs. The minister—once he is finally chosen—must walk a tightrope between "Low" and "High." The lucky man, Tom Huntley, finds it especially difficult to choose sermon topics:

[H]e had given two sermons every Sunday, appropriate to the season, of sufficient variety in subject, and sound enough in doctrine to satisfy those wishing to be dubbed "High," as well as those who, as "Low," said they required "spiritual sustenance." (12)

Yet it is important to remember that here in Slowford, the two groups have united, uneasy as that union may be; the minister, Huntley, serves as mediator.

A sense of superiority comes across in Anglican novels—arguably related to a higher social standing. For many years, the Anglican church was the only officially recognized Protestant church in Upper Canada (Millman 17) and clung to a number of rights and privileges (clergy reserves, control of education).[10] Even after these perks were rescinded, the knowledge of privilege marks Anglican writing. In the Lizars' conservative town of Slowford, in *Committed to His Charge*, society is built on policies of exclusiveness and exclusion; the true church (Anglican) is separate from all others (outsiders):

[T]hese outsiders comprehended all Jews, Turks, infidels and heretics; their money was exchangeable, but there their usefulness ceased. There was absolutely no interchange of anything else between the Anglican church and outside Slowford. (57)

These same Anglicans would rather send bales of used clothing to far away Indians and Eskimos than help needy Slowford residents.

The other major Protestant group in Ontario, the Presbyterian church, was deeply divided when it first arrived—the result of doctrinal differences in Scotland.[11] The original question had been whether or not the church ought to be aligned with the state: the Free

Church was formed as a body separate from the state. There were also Presbyterian evangelical groups which had formed during the eighteenth century in an attempt to reach the new working class in the cities. Such doctrinal and political differences seemed irrelevant, even "exotic" (Smith, *Short History* 51) in Canada despite the fierce loyalty of many Scots to their homeland (Smith 28-51). Accordingly, the Canadian Presbyterians declared themselves free of Scottish control and formed their own presbytery as early as 1818. After a number of small unions, by 1875 Canadian Presbyterians had created a single Presbyterian Church.[12]

Calvinism is the primary theological legacy handed down through the history of Scottish Presbyterianism: it has been claimed that Presbyterianism without Calvinism is like a pail without a bottom. A rather strange phenomenon occurs in Ontario Presbyterianism as it is expressed in the Presbyterian novels, however. The Calvinist theory of predetermination (whether one is saved or doomed from birth) is almost entirely absent.[13] What takes its place is the central doctrine that all men are flawed and must turn to Christ to be saved. This is a gloomy view of a human as a depraved creature, but it is also hopeful in its promise of a better world to come for those who are prepared. Ontario Calvinism presents "the basic Christian paradox of the depravity of man and the overflowing abundance of the grace of God in Jesus Christ the Redeemer" (Reid, "Background" 5). It is entirely possible, depending on the circumstances, to accentuate either the "depravity" or the "grace" in this doctrine. A confrontation between the two possibilities occurs in Ralph Connor's *The Man From Glengarry* (1901). At the funeral of young Mack Cameron, the kirk elder, Peter McRae, "man of iron" (22), terrifies the mourners by preaching the depravity of man and pointing out the unlikelihood of salvation. It is McRae's fear that Mack has not been brought to Christ, that Mack, like all humanity, is flawed and therefore doomed:

" 'There is none righteous, no, not one, for all have sinned and come short of the glory of God. He that believeth shall be saved, and he that believeth not shall be damned.' That is my message, and it is laid upon me as a sore burden . . . to warn one and all to flee from the wrath to come.". . . Then, raising, his voice, he cried aloud: "Woe is me! Alas! It is a grievous burden. The Lord pity us all, and give grace to this stricken family to kiss the rod that smites." (180)

The family, quite naturally, is horrified at the suggestion of hellfire and damnation. Fortunately, the speech is tempered by an address from a man more disposed to see that the light of salvation is available to all. After this second oration, "the hearts of all were comforted" (183). But even Connor's McRae is a watered-down version of earlier Calvinism. There are few examples of an absolute belief in predestination in the Ontario Presbyterian novels. One exception occurs in Robert Knowles' *St. Cuthbert's* (1905) where a certain Mr. M'Phatter does not go to church because "Ance saved, aye saved. That's ma doctrine" (53).

Since the supreme head of the Presbyterian church is Christ the King, the individual should desire to do God's will at all times (Reid, "Protestant" 120). A sense of divine calling can result, as in Marian Keith's *Duncan Polite* (1905) where Duncan Polite, the spiritual watchman of Glenoro, gives up his life to save others. Closely related to divine calling is the Presbyterian emphasis on conversion. All humanity must recognize inherent weakness and turn to God, "seeking his grace, mercy and forgiveness through Jesus Christ" (Reid, "Protestant" 133). There are numerous examples of major Presbyterian revivals in Ontario, the most notable in Glengarry where an intense emotional response was awakened in the community.[14] While this type of emotionalism would seem more typical of Methodism (and is one example of the way that the various Protestant faiths began to grow together in Ontario), in his *The Man From Glengarry*, Ralph Connor attempts to fit the Glengarry revival within traditional Presbyterian doctrines. Connor's version carries on in a series of nightly meetings for a year and a half. Many people respond emotionally—"women and men would break down in audible weeping" (264) and listen with an "unusual" intensity (264)—but Connor (a Presbyterian minister himself) is quick to point out that this is not merely an emotional and unthinking response to fervent appeals:

No fictitious means were employed to stir the emotions of the people or to kindle excitement among them. There were neither special sermons nor revival hymns. The old doctrines were proclaimed, but proclaimed with a fullness and power unknown at other times. The old psalms were sung, but sung perhaps as they had never been sung before. (266)

The Presbyterian concept of conversion, as Connor presents it, seems almost a paradox: there must be an intense personal experience, but one must not be too conspicuous or emotional about the whole thing.[15]

These are only a few of the distinguishing features of the three dominant Protestant traditions in Ontario, especially as they are depicted in fiction. While all of the novelists are quite explicit about the faith of their protagonists and emphasize the unique beliefs and practices of that faith,[16] it should already be apparent that there are certain areas of similarity between what ought to be quite dissimilar forms of worship. Although many Ontario novelists used the novel form to promote a particular religion, doctrinal biases frequently are removed or ignored. In both fiction and fact, in the frontier environment of Upper Canada, strict lines of doctrinal difference between and within sects began to dissolve. As has been noted, individual Protestant groups began to resolve differences which they had brought to Canada with them. The High/Low Anglican split in the Lizars sisters' *Slowford* is welded together by an uneasy but workable compromise. Neville Trueman, Withrow's itinerant American preacher, cuts off his ties with the United States to stay in Canada during the war of 1812-1814. The Presbyterians in Connor's *The Man From Glengarry* show an ability to mediate between various points of view with respect to Calvinism. Finally, though, the movement towards church union was a larger force than that which resolved intra-denominational strife. Certain common themes and motifs are used by writers of all Protestant faiths, lessening the doctrinal and/or political gaps between them and pointing the way to the possibility of Protestant church union.[17]

A sense of Christian evangelical zeal, the missionary spirit, the need to convert the heathen and to save souls are prevalent themes in the literature of all churches. This common area of discussion supersedes denomination.[18] The missionary figure takes one of two possible forms: a strong, untiring, muscular Christian, or a gentle, usually female, sweetly persuasive soul. Each has particular qualities to which it adheres fairly rigidly. There is seldom a clash between the two divergent types, however, since the division into masculine and feminine Christianity is a split which is often resolved by marriage, or at least by close friendship. The spirit of compromise and unity in Christ is achieved metaphorically in the novels when the missionary figures are united in love.

One example is found in Ralph Connor's *The Man From Glengarry*. Reverend Murray and his wife are quite different even though they work towards the same goal. The minister, a stalwart Christian hero, is physically strong, able to endure the rigors of the Ontario backwoods life and capable of breaking up fights between the young men at church. He is intelligent and well-educated, with a Presbyterian sense of his calling as a minister and of his duty to admonish error in others. While he is often hasty to accuse (acting too swiftly, for example, to condemn the wild young Ranald MacDonald), he also can admit his mistakes. Reverend Murray strikes fear into the hearts of his parishioners with his ability to dominate them physically and emotionally. Yet he genuinely cares for his people, and they recognize his concern:

Old and young, absent and present, the sick, the weary, the sin-burdened—all were remembered with a directness of petition, and with an earnestness of appeal that thrilled and subdued the hearts of all, and made even the boys, who had borne with difficulty, the last half-hour of the prayer, forget their weariness. (133)

In contrast, Mrs. Murray is gently persuasive; her sweet personality wins souls. She, too, is well-educated; her upper-class family considers her talents wasted in the bush. But Mrs. Murray works with her husband to aid "the sick and the sorrowing and the sin-burdened" (47). Her genuine love of service and sacrifice provides an example for the other women who grow "to adore her as a saint, and to trust her as a leader and friend, and to be a little like her" (48). The men are won by her beauty and gentle goodness, yet self-sacrifice and happiness are the real keys to her success:

She lived to serve, and the where and how were not hers to determine. So, with bright face and brave heart, she met her days and faced the battle. And scores of women and men are living better and braver lives because they had her for their minister's wife. (48)

Although Connor never makes explicit his personal preference with respect to the missionary spirit, Mrs. Murray often seems the more effective in a smaller, personal context: she is the dominant influence in Ranald MacDonald's spiritual life, reaching him when her husband cannot.

In Marian Keith's *Duncan Polite*, the polarization of Christian endeavour is clear in the friendship of two devout and dissimilar old men—Duncan Polite and Andrew Johnstone. Duncan Polite is the self-appointed spiritual watchman of Glenoro and is an example, despite his gender, of the gentle, feminine Christian. He watches over Oro as a mother watches her children, so that:

> everything that brought discredit upon it gave him deepest pain,
> everything that tended to raise its moral tone was, to him, a personal
> favour and joy. (14)

Keith describes Duncan in feminine terms—both in his physical
appearance and in his personality. Gentleness and self-sacrifice are his
most notable traits. He brings people to Christ by means of personal
example and loving words. Young Jessie Hamilton turns to Duncan in a
time of spiritual confusion; he explains the old Presbyterian doctrines
to her, and she joins him in an inner awareness of salvation and a
personal knowledge of a living God. Then Duncan makes the ultimate,
loving sacrifice for his people when he gives up his own life to save
others. Duncan's best friend, "Splinterin' Andra" Johnstone, is different,
a forceful and opinionated elder of the Presbyterian church. The
quality he most admires in a minister is strength, and the new minister
of Glenoro greatly disappoints him in this respect. Johnstone is "a terror
to evil-doers and so prone to carry out the law and the prophets by
physical force that he had earned, among the irreverent youth of the
community, the name of 'Splinterin' Andra'" (15). One unexpected result
of Duncan Polite's final sacrifice is that Andrew Johnstone becomes
much more subdued. Moreover, the gentle spirit of his friend Duncan
seems to have entered Andrew and lives on through him.[19] This might
imply that to Keith the stronger force in Christianity is the feminine
loving spirit, a belief which is echoed in other Presbyterian novels.
Trends such as these must surely have hastened the demise of the old
strict Calvinism.

In *Committed to His Charge*, the Lizars sisters provide an
Anglican minister and wife combination, another example of the
unification through love of the rival Christian types. Helen Huntley is
beautiful and approachable, with kind words for all, while her
husband, Tom, is more formidable, tending to maintain his dignity as a
clergyman. The qualities of leadership, strength, and good health as
well as the ability to inspire fear are less pronounced in Tom than in
many other muscular Christians, but, of course, the novel is satiric
rather than morally didactic. Helen lacks the devoted slaves which
throng around the female missionary in other novels, but she is still
admired. The women find little to criticize (even though at one point
she forgets the words of the Lord's Prayer). Helen Huntley acts as her

husband's emotional prop: her first duty is to her husband. In this she is typical of the female Christian who devotes her life to the service of others.

Lawrence Temple, W.H. Withrow's preacher in *The King's Messenger*, tackles evil in the rough lumber camps of northern Ontario. Lawrence is a "strong-limbed warrior" (43) who is engaged in battles on two fronts. One battle is physical, as Lawrence pits his strength against the forest:

As Lawrence stood with his foot on the fallen trunk of the first tree, but a moment before standing grand and majestic and lordly as a king's son, like Saul among the prophets, he seemed guilty of sacrilege . . . but after a time his conscience became seared and calloused to this tree murder, and as he swung his axe . . . a stern joy filled his soul. (41-42)

On another front, Lawrence battles against sin, using his physical prowess to bring the most hardened sinners to Christ:

Lawrence, a fine athletic specimen of muscular Christianity, turned to with a will, and swung his axe and rolled his logs with the best of them, as "to the manner born." He won thereby the profound respect of several of the young men, who were more impressed with his prowess with the axe than by his eloquence in the pulpit. (211)

Lawrence is also eloquent, though, and this ability brings many more young men to God. Much later in the narrative, almost as an afterthought, Lawrence meets the girl he will some day marry. Her character is not clearly defined, but we know that she is pretty, intelligent, and devoted to her parents. It is indicated that she will not shrink from hard work. Once again two Christian types unite in love.

Generally, the religious services and beliefs of all Protestant churches show a common movement towards praising and glorying in the Lord. The Presbyterian church softens perceptibly, for example, especially with respect to the doctrine of predestination which becomes an historical rather than a living belief. Christianity, in the context of the Protestant novels (regardless of the writer's own biases), offers the promise of salvation rather than the threat of damnation. This spiritual trend can probably be linked to the missionary zeal exhibited by many of the early religious leaders. The lack of churches and the great number of "heathen"—Catholics, Indians, Americans, and the like—made it a common goal to reach as many people as possible with the healing light of salvation (Grant, *Canadian Experience* 9). These noble aspirations tend to transcend denominational barriers and are certainly reflected in the missionary zeal of the protagonists of the Protestant novels.[20]

Another important thematic concern of the Protestant novels is a confrontation between old and young. Young people represent a driving force of change; old people stubbornly attempt to keep things as they were in the old country—possibly looking for a sense of security in a strange new land. The young seem to have acquired the spirit of the new land and seek progress and change; customs from their parents' world no longer matter. Time and again, the young people clash with their elders. The confrontation often comes when the youth want to change the form of the church service. These proposed changes, which generally indicate the possibility of church union, also threaten the basis of religious denominational difference and represent a frightening collapse of order in the lives of the older settlers—therefore, they vehemently oppose new ideas.

A young and innovative couple confronts the older Anglican parishioners in *Committed to His Charge*. Tom Huntley, the youthful new minister, wishes to inaugurate a "harvest home" church service, but when he carries out his plan, the consequences are disastrous. After the Sunday morning service, he is warned to remove the decorations. Before he can get to them, they are forcibly torn down. All changes are resented in Slowford merely because they are changes. Huntley has considered himself moderate in his views until his arrival in the ultra-conservative town of Slowford where, much to his dismay, he becomes "progressive to the extent of Radicalism" (56).

In Robert Knowles' *St. Cuthbert's*, the minister's daughter and her friend Angus approach the Presbyterian elders for permission to sing hymns in church. Their request is denied. The winds of change are blowing, however, and one of the most stubbornly traditional elders relents on his deathbed, telling the minister that he was too hard on the young rebels. Marian Keith's *Duncan Polite* has a young minister, Mr. Egerton, who, like the Lizars' Tom Huntley, arrives in a tradition-conscious community. In this Presbyterian church the debate over the singing of hymns is also raised. The young people want hymns; the old folks think that hymn-singing is blasphemous.[21] With the arrival of the new minister, things begin to happen:

A new party with alarmingly progressive ideas, suddenly came to life. They were fain to introduce many improvements into the church service which the fathers of the sanctuary considered unsound and irreverent. They wanted a choir and an organ like the Methodists; they desired to sing hymns as did their sister congregation over on the Tenth; and, most of all, they considered it imperative that they should stand to sing and sit to pray, as did all respectable people. (36)

While a conflict between youth and age is a standard literary theme, the focus of the conflict in the Protestant novels—and the typical resolution in favour of change—anticipates church union and the arrival of a happier age.

It has been suggested that the creation of a federated Canada helped to make possible the union of Canadian Protestant churches; at any rate, there is at least a parallel movement (Morrow 284; Vipond, "Canadian" 19). As H.H. Walsh says in "A Canadian Christian Tradition,"

After Confederation the urge for church union became particularly strong. The new Canadian nation was artificial, its unity a tender plant that required constant cultivation. Patriots soon recognized that religious controversy was a luxury in which they could indulge only at the peril of national disintegration. (158)

An ideal federation involves the removal of small-group prejudices, ethnic as well as religious, and in the years following Confederation, Canadian churchmen consciously sought to emulate the political event (Wilson 11). Arguably, the impulse behind federation in both church and state is related to conditions of life in the colonies where neighbourliness was necessary for survival. Also, to the children of the pioneers, the mother country was a far-off place; their perception of place was linked to Canada (Reid, *Canadian Experience* 9). Consequently, allegiance shifted to Canada and to Canadian ideals. The disintegration of old ties and old conflicts is described in the Ontario Protestant novels as a necessary fact of pioneer life. There is, in fact, a heady optimism in the literature of the late nineteenth and early twentieth centuries: the more euphoric writers talk of church union as a herald of the millennium.[22]

The most violent racial-religious battles in the Ontario novels are Irish-Scottish and Orange-Green (Protestant Irish—Catholic Irish); there are a few Scottish Lowland—Scottish Highland confrontations as well. The original nature of the conflict in early battle scenes is physical violence which can result in injury and even death. Often the impetus is the annual Orange parade;[23] later the protests become more subdued and much less violent. The movement away from violence which seems to denote the beginning of a more tolerant age is perceived as inevitable in Ontario. First, the children of the new land, who meet in the one-room school[24] every day, find the old tales of religious persecution strange and unlikely. Next, the rigours of pioneer life force persons of different races and religions to work together. With increased social contact, increased understanding must follow.

In *Committed to His Charge*, the Lizars sisters comment on some of the typical prejudices in Slowford:

In the old days of the first settlers there had been battles royal betwixt the Scotch and Irish, the latter with shillelaghs, both with whiskey. But the Orange-Irish got on with his Scotch neighbour; all he bargained for was to be free of the little men in broadcloth and silk hats. (38)

In this we see the movement away from violence towards a kind of toleration (the "little men" are the Irish Catholics). The sole addition to the list of Protestant martyrs in *Committed to His Charge* occurs when an old Irish Catholic woman throws an orange cat into a pot of boiling potato water, saying "Bad scran to yez for a divil of a Prodestant cat" (39). So, although a death does occur, the unfortunate one is feline rather than human, and the scene is grimly comic rather than tragic.

Catharine Parr Traill's *Canadian Crusoes: A Tale of the Rice Lake Plains* (1852) is both idealistic and visionary in its use of a federation motif. Traill, herself an Anglican, creates a protagonist, Catharine Maxwell, the product of the harmonious marriage of a French Canadian woman and a Scottish soldier, both Roman Catholics. To her ethnic mix, Traill adds an Indian girl, Indiana, whom Catharine, her brother, and her cousin convert to Christianity. Further, it is intimated that Catharine's brother, Hector, will marry Indiana.

Not all immigrants were as tolerant or as visionary as Catharine Traill. Accordingly, some novelists, rather than creating an ideal world, document the early conflicts. Throughout Marian Keith's novel *The Silver Maple* (1908), there is a recurring tension between the Orange Irish and the Presbyterian Scots. A crisis occurs when Callam

Fiach MacDonald (Scottish) falls in love with Nancy Caldwell (Irish). Since neither family is willing to allow their marriage, even though both are Protestant, the two young people run away together and are killed during the elopement. There is a double lesson here. First, we see the disappearance of the old prejudices in the union of the lovers, who have met in school. Second, the lovers become a sacrificial offering, serving as an atonement for the sins of their elders and showing them the error of their ways. Keith points out that the desire for change is not always doomed when the Irish Dan Murphy and the Scottish Scotty MacDonald become lifelong friends and comrades in arms. These children are Canadian; through them, the spirit of universal love makes federation possible.

In his story of a Methodist preacher in *The Preacher of Cedar Mountain* (1917), Earnest Thompson Seton includes an Orange-Green brawl. The young minister's father dies in a fight at an Orange parade before his son's birth. The father, an Irish Catholic, is the leader of a gang which entertains itself by throwing whitewash at the parade's participants. The fighting is described by Seton in terms of hearty fun, but the consequences are deadly. The death comes in an ironically simple way, as the wagon overturns during the whitewash attack, killing its occupant. Obviously, there is a lesson here; our Protestant novelists are seldom subtle.

The geographical expanse of Ontario and the initially sparse settlement made it next to impossible for the settlers to maintain several different churches in any one area. Roads were terrible (if there were roads), and a minister had to ride long miles to reach his congregation. Out of necessity, early Ontario residents welcomed any preacher who reached them. Religious tolerance was easier to implement when the devout Christian had few choices about which church to attend. There are many reports—both fact and fiction—of men and women switching allegiance merely for the sake of worshipping in fellowship (Grant, *Canadian Experience* 7). In her account of backwoods life, *Roughing It in the Bush* (1852), Susanna Moodie makes fun of "Old Thomas," an uneducated man who feels compelled to preach the gospel:

Old Thomas was a very ambitious man in his way. Though he did not know A from B, he took it into his head that he had received a call from Heaven to convert the heathen in the wilderness; and every Sunday he held a meeting in our loggers' shanty, for the purpose of

awakening sinners, and bringing over "Injun pagans" to the true faith.
(316-317)

Although Moodie's tone is condescending, it is worth noting that
she (and apparently everyone else) attends the meeting. In Marian
Keith's Glenoro of *Duncan Polite*, Duncan Polite finds that he is
"driven to the extremity of seeking comfort in the Methodist Church"
(38) while a new Presbyterian minister is being sought. The previously
unthinkable has become the present reality. Duncan realizes that he
wants the company of other Christians and is pleasantly surprised by
the quality of the Methodist service. Furthermore, he notes that other
Presbyterians have defected:

Mr. Ansdell, the Methodist minister, was a benign old gentleman
with an angelic face and a heart to match. He noted the mingling of the
different religious sects in Glenoro with a humble joy, and regarded the
fact that a Presbyterian elder's son should lead the singing in the
Methodist church as a mark of the broad and kindly spirit of the age
and one of the potent signs of the millennium. (39)

Mr. Ansdell is, perhaps, rather too optimistic in his apprehension
of the millennium, but he is sensitively aware of the great ecumenical
spirit of Ontario.

Another common feature in the various Protestant novels is the
movement towards a personal experience of religion. While the form of
Christianity still relies on the structure and community spirit of an
established church, the religious experience becomes very personal.[25] A
knowledge of God and salvation is important in the works by writers of
all denominations; the most intense confrontations with God occur
during the many dramatic deathbed scenes. (It seems that no novel is
complete without at least one deathbed conversion.) Ralph Connor uses
this motif in *The Man From Glengarry*. As he is dying, the recently-
converted MacDonald Dubh asks his son Ranald to forgive LeNoir, his
murderer. Once Ranald has given his promise, MacDonald Dubh is able
to die in peace. Many characters in the Protestant novels possess an
inner light and serenity which is remarked upon by the other, less
Christian souls. This attribute is especially pronounced in the feminine
missionary—as, for example, Ralph Connor's Mrs. Murray in *The Man
From Glengarry*, the woman who converts MacDonald Dubh. The
spiritual journey or quest of the hero or heroine, also connected to the

personal experience of God, is a prominent theme in the religious novels, often the narrative thread which strings together a series of anecdotal but unrelated stories. As happens with Connor's MacDonald Dubh and his son Ranald, the growth to spiritual awareness culminates in a time of crisis and doubt. Then, a revelation leads to knowledge of God, resolving the doubt and leading to perfect peace.

The so-called social gospel movement of the late nineteenth and early twentieth centuries is reflected in the novels of the period.[26] A number of organizations were closely linked to Protestant churches but remained outside of denominational bias. The temperance movement, Bible societies, and young people's clubs ignored religious barriers and worked towards common ends.[27] A Bible society which was non-sectarian would be invaluable in finding common areas of belief among those belonging to different churches. The YMCA and the YWCA also aided the movement to church union. The YMCA, which is not affiliated with any particular denomination, has a club-like atmosphere that is echoed in the inner-city club organized by the young Methodist minister in Earnest Thompson Seton's *The Preacher of Cedar Mountain*. Mr. Egerton, the new Presbyterian minister in Marian Keith's *Duncan Polite* promotes several non-denominational groups: the Young People's Society of Christian Endeavour; the Young Men's Christian Association; the Sons of Temperance; the Ladies' Aid Society; and a group which unites with the Methodists, holding meetings alternately in both churches. Mr. Egerton tends to fall short in some of his ministerial duties (hence the need for the "watchman" Duncan), but his tolerance of other Protestant faiths is exemplary.

Another factor in the removal of religious prejudice is the formation of non-denominational universities (Moir, *Canada West* 82-128); the fictional heroes who attend are often surprised to discover that those from other religions are not the devil incarnate. The Reverend Fergus McCheyne in Hugh Pedley's *Looking Forward* (1913) is brought up in a strict and old-fashioned Presbyterian family in eastern Ontario (his father is the minister). For the young Fergus, Presbyterianism means the following:

The church where psalms were sung without choir or instrument, and both sermon and prayer were unstinted in length; the Bible with its absolute inerrancy from cover to cover; the Shorter Catechism with its incisive questions and sonorous answers; the Sabbath with its absolute separation from all worldly influences; the Presbyterian order with its still rooting in the past, and its bold appeal to the Scripture. (18)

Added to this is the belief that "the Presbyterian order was the one true model for the Church of God" (20). But Fergus leaves this environment to study at McGill University in Montreal and, as a result, many of his attitudes change:

By an intercollegiate arrangement he found himself taking lectures from a Congregational professor who seemed to be quite a sane and well-balanced individual. In his McGill philosophy course he was thrown into close contact with a Methodist student whose intellectual vigour he was able to test in more than one keen discussion; not over the five points of Calvinism, but over the legitimacy of the Ritchlian Philosophy. And, further, in undertaking work among boys in the rougher parts of the city, he found himself put to shame by the self-denial and spiritual energy of a young fellow from one of the Anglican churches. With such experiences as these it was inevitable that his prejudices should be modified, and his views on the church be greatly enlarged. (21-22)

Pedley's novel argues for church union: the reader is expected to learn tolerance along with Fergus McCheyne and to see that the views of an earlier generation are outdated.

An important part of Ontario history is the temperance movement. The temperance league was non-denominational, and elements within all Protestant churches supported temperance.[28] As a result, the religious novels frequently become mouthpieces for the prohibitionists. The tavern becomes synonymous with hell; the tavern keeper is the devil. Appropriately enough, the tavern often goes up in flames, and the owner may burn to death along with it. In the eyes of such writers as Marian Keith and Ralph Connor, alcohol inflames the blood and destroys the drinker. The heroes of the temperance novels either swear off drinking or never drink at all. Drinkers come to a bad end or, occasionally, are allowed to repent on their deathbeds. Drinking causes fighting—sometimes to the death (as with Connor's LeNoir and MacDonald Dubh in *The Man From Glengarry*), and the fighting Scots, when they are drinkers, are irrational. E. Ryerson Young's *Duck Lake* (1920) has a missionary minister, one of our muscular backwoods preachers, who is strongly against alcohol. The tavern is a trap for the idle young men, so the preacher and the schoolmaster offer night classes as an alternative. The villain—a cheat, a liar, a wife-beater, a drunkard—is Dodge, the tavern owner. When the tavern burns down,

Dodge is almost killed in the fire. Fortunately, however, Dodge is rescued by a brave Christian and lives to repent his evil ways. Less lucky is the tavern keeper in Mack Cloie's *The Old Orchard* (1903). The hellish tavern burns down, and all the drunkards die horrible deaths: Mrs. Martin, an alcholic, dies in a house fire; Hedley Stenson, the son of the tavern owner, dies while trying to save Mrs. Martin; Dave Stenson, the tavern owner, burns inside his own building; Mrs. Stenson drinks herself to death in a sordid city slum. The message is obvious—drink and you will die a painful death. The alternatives are equally clear. As in *Duck Lake*, in *The Old Orchard* the schoolmaster and a friend offer substitutes for tavern entertainment in the form of night classes and debating societies. The church and the school are the proper community meeting places. Moreover, it is possible to reform: Steve Fitzhugh, a local bully who likes to drink, is saved by a Salvation Army girl. Drink is a powerful force of evil in W.H. Withrow's *The King's Messenger*, in which the young Methodist hero attempts to save souls in a rough lumber camp. He converts a Catholic and an uneducated youth by showing them a better way of life. But he fails to save Evans, an upper-class Anglican Englishman, educated at Oxford. Evans has succumbed to the deadly evil of strong drink and is no longer able to control his actions—nor does his Anglican upbringing permit him personally to experience God's mercy. Evans tells Lawrence that his problem results from the overindulgence of his aristocratic parents who gave him wine to drink when he was young. Evans, as can be expected, comes to a bad end. There is little hope for a drinking man or woman in the temperance novels.

In their insistence on abstention and in their use of a number of other common themes and plot patterns, the Ontario Protestant writers reflect the religious and moral preoccupations of the society around them. These writers cannot be dismissed as merely evocative of an era, however, for as William Westfall points out in "Order and Experience," Protestantism shaped the society of Ontario: "It was religion that imparted a distinctive character to this region" (5). And our long-forgotten novelists help to create a distinctive Protestantism which rises above initial denominational differences:

By the last decades of the nineteenth century, a number of Protestant denominations had come to share a common set of institutional and intellectual features. Anglicans, Methodists, and Presbyterians had developed similar administrative structures, they relied upon similar methods of evangelism and they conducted similar forms of worship within churches that shared a common architectural style. And most importantly, they agreed upon the character of the God they worshipped—upon his design for man and the world. (Westfall, "Order" 5-6)

The Protestant novelists transpose these areas of agreement (as well as the remaining dissension) into fiction; they remind us that the church was a central aspect of Ontario life not so very long ago. Moreover, they set standards, isolate modes of perception, and define preoccupations which remain with us today. Finally, many of the religious novels are quite good, humorously and sensitively (albeit erratically) delineating experiences which are definitely Canadian. Whether from the point of view of literary criticism, social history, or entertainment, then, these novels deserve a better fate than oblivion.

University of Toronto   **Elizabeth Thompson**

NOTES

1. For one of the few critical works in this area, see McLean's article on evangelical and ecclesiastical fiction.

2. For an example of a writer who reluctantly consented to the general desire for moral messages, see Montgomery 73.

3. See Roper's "The Kinds of Fiction" and "Writers of Fiction."

4. Westfall notes four dominant Protestant bodies in Ontario: Methodist, Presbyterian, Baptist, and Anglican in *Two Worlds* 10-11.

5. On changes in Canadian doctrines see the following: Westfall, "Order and Experience" and *Two Worlds*; Grant, *Canadian Experience of Church Union, Church in Canadian Era*, and *Profusion*; Caldwell, "Unification"; Smith et al. *Short History*; and Moir, *Church and State in Canada West*.

6. In 1925 the Congregationalists, Methodists, and some Presbyterians joined to create the United Church. While the Anglicans did not become part of the new church, they were instrumental in beginning the union discussions.

7. There is some disagreement about the number of Methodist faiths. See Caldwell 3; Grant, *Church in Canadian Era* 6; and Pidgeon 12.

8. Interestingly, circuit riding lasted even after churches were built; Bush, "Reverend James Caughey."

9. Grant calls the two groups Anglo-Catholics and evangelicals in *Church in Canadian Era*. Moir defines the split as "Low" and "High" Church Anglicans who differed on liturgy, education, social issues— gambling and drinking, for example—in *Church and State in Canada West* 4-5.

10. See the documents reproduced in Moir, ed., *Church and State in Canada: Basic Documents*.

11. See Neil Smith et al. 50-51; and Grant, *Canadian Experience* 18.

12. Pidgeon isolates "nine unions culminating in 1875"(12-13).

13. See Moir's *Enduring* 181 for changes in Canadian Calvinism,

14. For a first-hand report, see Balfour 40-41.

15. See Moir's *Enduring* 172 for further discussion of this type of thing.

16. Space limitations prevent a more thorough analysis of the unique aspects of each form of Protestantism as these aspects appear in the fiction.

17. Not everyone favoured union. See Clifford, passim; and Campbell, passim.

18. Grant calls the Canadian Protestant evangelical movement, found in all churches, an "aggressive religious activity"; *Profusion* 104.

19. See Allen on "the triumph of evangelism over the more sober concepts of Calvinism" (5).

20. Westfall analyzes the destruction of an old religious structure to make way for a new Protestant alliance in *Two Worlds*, passim.

21. Moir contends that changes in Presbyterian worship reflect the greater wealth of the country, *Enduring* 171.

22. See Brown and Cook, passim; and Westfall 196, 199.

23. Grant discusses the importance of parades and ceremonial walks in Ontario in *Profusion* 235.

24. Although Ontario schools were officially non-sectarian, they were still strongly Protestant; see Westfall, *Two Worlds* 6-7.

25. Two opposing views of God existed in nineteenth-century Ontario: God was "a distant and superintending rational intelligence"; God was "an active and interventionist power who continually transformed people and the affairs of the world"; see Westfall, *Two Worlds* 41.

26. For the social gospel movement see Allen; also Smith et al.; and Vipond, "Blessed are the Peacemakers."

27. For a list of such organizations see Silcox 73-102.

28. For information on the temperance movements see Clemens; also Decarie; and Garland and Talman.

Works Cited

Allen, Richard. *The Social Passion: Religion and Social Reform in Canada 1914-28.* Toronto: University of Toronto Press, 1971.

Armour, Leslie, and Elizabeth Trott. *The Faces of Reason: An Essay on Philosophy and Culture in English Canada, 1850-1950.* Waterloo: Wilfrid Laurier University Press, 1981.

Armstrong, F.H., H.A. Stevenson, and J.D. Wilson, eds. *Aspects of Nineteenth Century Ontario: Essays Presented to James J. Talman.* Toronto: University of Toronto Press, 1974.

Balfour, R. Gordon. *Presbyterianism in the Colonies.* Edinburgh: Macniven and Wallace, 1900.

Broughton, Karen MacLean. "Symbolism of the United Church." Unpublished essay, 1992.

Brown, Robert Craig, and Ramsay Cook. *Canada 1896-1921: A Nation Transformed.* The Canadian Centenary Series 14. Ed. W.L. Morton. Toronto: McClelland and Stewart, 1976.

Bumsted, J.M. *Canadian History Before Confederation: Essays and Interpretations.* Georgetown, Ontario: Irwin, Dorsey, 1972.

Bush, Peter. "The Reverend James Caughey and Wesleyan Methodist Revivalism in Canada West, 1851-1856" *Ontario History* 79, 3 (Sept 1987),231-250.

Caldwell, J. Warren. "The Unification of Methodism in Canada, 1865-1884." *Bulletin* 19 (1967), 3-61.

Campbell, Rev. R. *The Relations of the Christian Churches to One Another, and Problems Growing Out of Them, Especially in Canada.*

Toronto: William Briggs, 1913.

Chown, Rev. S.D. *The Story of Church Union in Canada*. Toronto: Ryerson Press, 1930.

Clark, S.D. *Church and Sect in Canada*. Toronto: University of Toronto Press, 1948.

Clemens, James M. "Taste Not; Touch Not; Handle Not: A Study of the Social Assumptions of the Temperance Literature and Temperance Supporters in Canada West Between 1839 and 1859." *Ontario History* 64, 3 (Sept 1972), 142-161.

Clifford, N. Keith. *The Resistance to Church Union in Canada, 1904-1939*. Vancouver: University of British Columbia Press, 1985.

Cloie, Mack. *The Old Orchard*. Toronto: William Briggs, 1903.

―――. *The Pancake Preacher*. Toronto: William Briggs, 1906.

Cody, H.A. *The Frontiersman, A Tale of the Yukon*. Toronto: William Briggs, 1912.

Connor, Ralph. *Glengarry School Days: A Story of Early Days in Glengarry*. Introd. S. Ross Beharriell. NCL 118. Ed. Malcolm Ross. Toronto: McClelland and Stewart, 1969.

―――. *The Man From Glengarry*. Toronto: Westminster, 1901.

―――. *The Man From Glengarry*. Intro. S. Ross Beharriell. NCL 14. Ed. Malcolm Ross. Toronto: McClelland and Stewart, 1969.

Cooper, Elizabeth. "Religion, Politics, and Money: The Methodist Union of 1832-1833."*Ontario History* 81, 2 (June 1989), 89-101.

Decarie, Graeme. "Something Old, Something New...: Aspects of Prohibitionism in Ontario in the 1890s." *Oliver Mowatt's Ontario: Papers presented to the Oliver Mowatt Colloquium*. Toronto: MacMillan, 1972, 154-171.

Dooley, D.J. *Moral Vision in the Canadian Novel.* Toronto: Clarke, Irwin, 1979.

Duncan, Sara Jeannette. *The Imperialist.* Introd. Claude Bissell. NCL 20. Ed. Malcolm Ross. Toronto: McClelland and Stewart, 1971.

Elgee, William Harris. *The Social Teachings of the Canadian Churches.* Toronto: Ryerson, 1964.

Fraser, W.A. *The Lone Furrow.* New York: D. Appleton, 1907.

Garland, M.A., and J.J. Talman. "Pioneer Drinking Habits and the Rise of the Temperance Agitation in Upper Canada Prior to 1840." *Aspects of Nineteenth-Century Ontario: Essays Presented to James J. Talman.* Ed. F.H. Armstrong, H.A. Stevenson, J.D. Wilson. Toronto: University of Toronto Press, 1974, 171-193.

Gauvreau, Michael. *The Evangelical Century: College and Creed in English Canada from the Great Revival to the Great Depression.* Montreal: McGill-Queen's University Press, 1991.

Gordon, Charles W. *Postscript to Adventure: The Autobiography of Ralph Connor.* New York: Farrar and Rinehart, 1938.

Grant, John Webster. *The Canadian Experience of Church Union.* Ecumenical Studies in History 8. Eds. Rev. A.M. Allchin, Rev. Martin E. Marty, Rev. T.H.L. Parker. London: Lutterworth Press, 1967.

————. *The Church in the Canadian Era: The First Century of Confederation.* A History of the Christian Church in Canada 3. Toronto: McGraw-Hill Ryerson, 1972.

————, ed. *The Churches and the Canadian Experience: A Faith and Order Study of the Christian Tradition.* Foreword David W. Hay. Toronto: Ryerson, 1966.

————. *A Profusion of Spires: Religion in Nineteenth-Century Ontario.* The Ontario Historical Studies Series. Toronto: University of Toronto Press, 1988.

Henderson, J.L.H. *John Strachan 1778-1867*. Toronto: University of Toronto Press, 1969.

Hilts, Rev. Joseph H. *Among the Forest Trees: or, How the Bushman Family Got Their Homes*. Toronto: William Briggs, 1886.

Hopper, Mrs. R.P. *Old-Time Primitive Methodism in Canada*. Toronto: William Briggs, 1904.

Ivison, Stuart. *The Baptists in Upper and Lower Canada Before 1820*. Toronto: University of Toronto Press, 1956.

Keith, Marian. *Duncan Polite, The Watchman of Glenoro*. Toronto: McClelland, Goodchild & Stewart, 1905.

Keith, Marian. *The Silver Maple*. Toronto: Westminster, 1908.

King, Basil. *The Street Called Straight*. London: Methuen, 1914.

Klinck, Carl F., ed. *Literary History of Canada: Canadian Literature in English*. 2nd ed. Vol. 1. Toronto: University of Toronto Press, 1976.

Knowles, Robert E. *The Handicap: A Novel of Pioneer Days*. Toronto: Fleming H. Revell, 1910.

Knowles, Robert E. *St. Cuthbert's, A Novel*. Toronto: Fleming H. Revell, 1905.

Langtry, Rev. Dr. *Presbyterianism, A Lecture*. Toronto: Timms & Co., 1893.

Langtry, Rev. John. *Come Home: An Appeal on Behalf of Reunion.*Toronto: The Church of England Publishing Company, 1906.

Lizars, R. and K.M. *Committed to His Charge*. Toronto: George N. Morang, 1900.

MacGillivray, Royce. "Novelists and the Glengarry Pioneer." *Ontario History* 65.2 (June 1973), 61-68.

McLean, Ken. "Evangelical and Ecclesiastical Fiction." *Journal of Canadian Fiction*21 (1977-78), 105-119.

McNeill, John T. "Religious and Moral Conditions Among the Canadian Pioneers." *The American Society of Church History* 8 (1928), 65-122.

Millman, T.R. "Tradition in the Anglican Church of Canada." *The Churches and the Canadian Experience: A Faith and Order Study of the Christian Tradition.* Ed. John Webster Grant. Foreword David W. Hay. Toronto: Ryerson, 1966, 14-24.

Moir, John Sargent, ed. *Church and State in Canada 1627-1867: Basic Documents.* Carleton Library 33. Ed. Robert L. McDougall. Toronto: McClelland and Stewart, 1967.

————. *Church and State in Canada West: Three Studies in the Relation of Denominationalism and Nationalism, 1841-1867.* Toronto: University of Toronto Press, 1968.

————. *Enduring Witness: A History of the Presbyterian Church in Canada.* 2nd ed. Toronto: Presbyterian Church in Canada, 1987.

Montgomery, L.M. *The Green Gables Letters.* Ed. Wilfrid Eggleston. Toronto: Ryerson, 1960.

Moodie, Susanna. *Roughing It in the Bush; or, Life in Canada.* Afterword Susan Glickman. NCL. Ed. David Staines. Toronto: McClelland and Stewart, 1989.

Morrow, E. Lloyd. *Church Union in Canada: Its History, Motives, Doctrine and Government.* Toronto: Thomas Allen, 1923.

Neill, Stephen. *Anglicanism.* Great Britain: Penguin, 1958.

Oliver, Edmund H. *The Winning of the Frontier: A Study in the Religious History of Canada.* Toronto: The United Church Publishing House; Ryerson, 1930.

Pedley, Rev. Hugh. *Looking Forward, The Strange Experience of*

The Rev. Fergus McCheyne. Toronto: William Briggs, 1913.

Pidgeon, Rev. George C. *The United Church of Canada: The Story of the Union.* Toronto: Ryerson, 1950.

Porter, Jane. *The Christian's Wedding Ring, Written by a Lady With the Sincere Desire of Sowing the Seeds of Union in the Christian Church.* Montreal: Lovell, 1874.

Reid, W. Stanford. "The Scottish Background." *The Scottish Tradition in Canada.* Ed. W. Stanford Reid. Toronto: McClelland and Stewart, 1976, 1-14.

————. "The Scottish Protestant Tradition." *The Scottish Tradition in Canada.* Ed. W. Stanford Reid. Toronto: McClelland and Stewart, 1976. 118-136.

————, ed. *The Scottish Tradition in Canada.* Toronto: McClelland and Stewart, 1976.

Roper, Gordon, Rupert Schieder, and S. Ross Beharriell. "The Kinds of Fiction (1880-1920)." *Literary History of Canada.* Ed. Carl F. Klinck. 2nd ed., Vol. 1. Toronto: University of Toronto Press, 1976, 298-326.

Roper, Gordon, S. Ross Beharriell, and Rupert Schieder. "Writers of Fiction (1880-1920)." *Literary History of Canada.* Ed. Carl F. Klinck, 2nd ed., Vol. 1. Toronto: University of Toronto Press, 1976. 327-353.

Sanderson, J.E. *The First Century of Methodism in Canada.* Toronto: William Briggs, 1908.

Seton, Ernest Thompson. *The Preacher of Cedar Mountain: A Tale of the Open Country.* Doubleday, Page, 1917.

Silcox, Claris Edwin. *Church Union in Canada: Its Causes and Consequences.* New York: Institute of Social and Religious Research, 1933.

Smith, N.G. "The Presbyterian Tradition in Canada." *The Churches and the Canadian Experience.* Ed. John Webster Grant. Foreword David W. Hay. Toronto: Ryerson, 1966, 38-52.

————, Allan L. Farris, and H. Keith Markell. *A Short History of the Presbyterian Church in Canada.* Toronto: Presbyterian Publications, 1965.

Thompson, Elizabeth. *The Pioneer Woman: A Canadian Character Type.* Montreal: McGill-Queen's UP, 1991.

Traill, Catharine Parr. *The Backwoods of Canada: Being Letters From the Wife of an Emigrant Officer, Illustrative of the Domestic Economy of British America.* Afterword D.M.R. Bentley. NCL. Ed. David Staines. Toronto: McClelland and Stewart, 1989.

————. *Canadian Crusoes: A Tale of the Rice Lake Plains,* ed. Rupert Schieder. CEECT, ed. Mary Jane Edwards. Ottawa: Carleton University Press, 1986.

Vipond, M. "Blessed are the Peacemakers: The Labour Question in Canadian Social Gospel Fiction." *Journal of Canadian Studies* 10.3 (1975), 32-43.

Vipond, Mary. "Canadian National Consciousness and the Formation of the United Church of Canada." *Bulletin* 24 (1975), 5-27.

Walsh, H.H. "A Canadian Christian Tradition." *The Churches and the Canadian Experience.* Ed. John Webster Grant. Foreword David W. Hay. Toronto: Ryerson, 1966, 145-161.

————. *The Christian Church in Canada.* Toronto: Ryerson, 1956.

Westfall, William. "Order and Experience: Patterns of Religious Metaphor in Early Nineteenth Century Upper Canada." *Journal of Canadian Studies* 20, 1 (1985), 5-24.

————. *Two Worlds: The Protestant Culture of Nineteenth-Century Ontario.* Montreal: McGill-Queen's University Press, 1989.

Wilson, Rev. R.J. *Church Union in Canada After Three Years.* Toronto: The United Church Publishing House, 1929.

Wise, S.F. "Sermon Literature and Canadian Intellectual History." *Bulletin* 18 (1965), 3-18.

Withrow, W.H. *Barbara Heck, A Tale of Early Methodism.* Toronto: William Briggs, n.d.

————. *The King's Messenger; or, Lawrence Temple's Probation. A Story of Canadian Life.* Toronto: Methodist Book and Publishing House, 1881.

————. *Neville Trueman, The Pioneer Preacher, A Tale of the War of 1812.* Toronto: William Briggs, 1900.

Workman, H.B. *Methodism.* Cambridge: Cambridge University Press, 1912.

Young, E. Ryerson. *Duck Lake, Stories of the Canadian Backwoods.* London: The Religious Tract Society, 1920.

————. *Oowikapun: or, How the Gospel Reached the Nelson River Indians.* Chicago: Eaton & Mains, 1896.

Relative(ly) Politic(al)s:
Comparing (Examples of) Québec/Canadian "ethnic"/"immigrant" writings

This essay emerges[1] from a question that has arisen in my ongoing study of writing by women in Québec and English Canada.

I have been comparing women's writings in French and English in our country since the mid-1970s. In recent years, my focus has been on work by writers of racial or ethnic-minority group identification. The terminology is problematic, but generally speaking, I am referring to writing by women whose identification, imposed or chosen, is with groups having minority status on the basis of race or ethnicity. Writers of this identification have been producing work that poses many challenges and questions. The one that interests me here is an apparent difference in what I will term "political edge" in the two bodies of work, one written in French, another in English.

From its headwaters in the politically-inspired writing of Québec's *Révolution tranquille* in the 1960s, through its interaction with French feminist writing of the 1970s, the work of Québec women writers has manifested a political edge which has not been as striking in the work of colleagues in English Canada. This is not to suggest that English Canadian women's writing is devoid of social critique and political protest! Nonetheless, works such as Michèle Lalonde's *Speak White* (1974), Louky Bersianik's *The Euguélionne* (1976), Nicole Brossard's *L'Amer, ou le chapitre effrité* (1977), or France Théoret's *Bloody Mary* (1977), to name only a few, enjoined readers toward social critique and political commentary. This project impacted on the work of English Canadian writers like Daphne Marlatt and Gail Scott, through their dialogue with Québec women writers. In the late 1980s and early 1990s in English Canada, authors like Marlene Nourbese Philip, Dionne Brand, Himani Bannerji, Lee Maracle, again, to name only a few, drew readers' attention with sharp-edged works which were more politically provocative than earlier writing. Not only did they deal with issues of gender within Canadian experience, they introduced racial issues and considerations as well.

The first part of the essay offers sample works as a foundation for the question that I wish to probe further: is there an equivalent body of work to be found amongst women writers of racial or ethnic minority identification in Québec? And, if so, what is its political character?

This will be the focus of the second part of the essay. A third and final section will consider very briefly some sociopolitical factors which underlie these literary observations.

I

Language and representation are not neutral, but rather the site where social and political meanings are produced. They are, as well, vehicles for the ideologies behind these meanings. This has been the key insight of contemporary cultural movements such as feminism, postmodernism, and postcolonialism. Writers like Brand, Bannerji, Philip, and Maracle consciously locate their work at the intersection of language and society. They take up the struggle over meaning and representation, and their work has the potential to disrupt the ideologies that dominate contemporary Canadian society. In her recent *Bread Out of Stone* (1994), Dionne Brand writes that "the English Canada that I live in is always surprised by and resistant to cultural intervention from people it does not recognise as fitting into its imposed forms" (179). English Canadian culture, Brand elaborates:

is not an oppressed culture and can impose this stasis on all discussion also, so we have the situation where in 1994 its artists and social commentators refuse to admit the existence of an ideology some five hundred or more years old through which their ancestors arrived and prospered . . . we are unwilling and unable to be filled by this, just as we are unable inevitably to qualify for the grant of 'whiteness.' (*Bread Out of stone*, 180)

In questioning societal assumptions, revealing injustices, and imagining new possibilities, works by Brand, Bannerji, Philip, Maracle, etc. reveal that the tools of their writing are not only literary, but also political. This writing often prominently features political events or concerns—as in Afua Cooper's poem *The Power of Racism*[2] in which the poet asks how "the ROM could mount an African exhibition/without consulting Black people." Cooper is referring to the 1990 Royal Ontario Museum exhibit, "Into the Heart of Africa," which met articulate protest from many members of Toronto's (and Canada's) black communities. Among these was poet and novelist Marlene Nourbese Philip whose fiction and essays highlight facts of racial prejudice within Canadian experience. "I wish them to know the contempt which the literary establishment of this country has for

Black writers like myself," Philip writes in her collection of essays Frontiers, citing by way of example:

> George Bowering, one of the preeminent members of this establishment, writing and publishing in the Globe and Mail that he had read my poetry and was very surprised to see that I was a good poet! I want them to know that racism is alive and kicking shit all across this country; that in Toronto, for instance, four Black people have been shot by the police in the last two years, in situations that didn't warrant those shootings; that similar shootings take place in Montreal; not to mention the long history of racism in Nova Scotia against the oldest Black population in this country (264).

The conjunction of political and theoretical concerns relates to the authors' very position and identities as writing subjects. Writing as a black or an aboriginal Canadian woman becomes a political act in and of itself. Thus writing as a process and practice is seen to be inherently and necessarily political. It is part of a larger political struggle which often involves political action, frequently around women's issues or race relations. A well-known example of this is Marlene Nourbese Philip's involvement with Vision 21[3] and the latter's intervention at the PEN international meeting in Toronto in 1990. This writing thus frequently bursts beyond the limits of "literature." To quote Dionne Brand again:

> I've had moments when the life of my people has been so overwhelming to bear that poetry seemed useless . . . At times it has been more crucial to wield a scythe over high grass in a field in Marigot; at times it has been more important to figure out how a woman without papers in Toronto can have a baby and not be caught and deported; at times it has been more helpful to organise a demonstration in front of the police station at Bay and College Streets. Often there's been no reason whatsoever to write poetry. There are days when I cannot think of a single reason to write this life down. (*Bread Out of Stone*, 182)

Another notable example is the work of dub poet Lillian Allen, who in *I Fight Back* gives voice to the familiar/unfamiliar "foreign domestic":

Here I am in Canada

bringing up someone else's child
while someone else and me in absentee
bring up my own

AND I FIGHT BACK

[. . .]

They label me
Immigrant, law-breaker, illegal, minimum wager
refugee
Ah no, not mother, no worker, no fighter

I FIGHT BACK
I FIGHT BACK
I FIGHT BACK
Women Do This Every Day, 139-140

Numerous other illustrations exist, and happily are represented in a series of collections that have appeared recently, including Makeda Silvera's *The Other Woman: Women of Colour in Contemporary Canadian Literature* (1995); Arun Mukherjee's *Sharing Our Experience* (1993); Carol Morell's *Grammar of Dissent* (1994); and Carol Camper's *Miscegenation Blues: Voices of Mixed Race Women* (1994).

Compelling, controversial, instructive and sobering, these writings have less-readily-identifiable equivalents in Québec. The sounding board provided by *La Parole métèque*, a review featuring immigrant women writers established in 1987, no longer exists. Work by Régine Robin (notably *La Québecoite*) stands out, but is relatively isolated, as is that of writers such as Gloria Escomel and Ying Chen, for example. A sense of collective critique is harder to locate in Québec than in English Canada, but not impossible to find. Groups of South Asian, black, or Italian women writers are simply not as visible in Québec as in English Canada. There does, though, appear to be an emerging group of Québec writers of Arabic background—and a concomitant "racialization" of this group of writers (as witnessed by the recent rash of debates and publications around the issue of wearing the hijab/tchador). In the second part of this paper, I will focus on a few writers of Arabic background, including Andrée Dahan, Mona Lattif Ghattas, Nadine

Ltaif.

II

Andrée Dahan's *Le printemps peut attendre* (1985) is critical of
the life newcomers experience in Québec. Dahan conveys her critique
through the experiences of her protagonist, thirty-year-old Maya.
Maya is both happy and successful in her career as a biology teacher in
Egypt, when the notion of immigrating to Canada is presented to her.
Given encouragement and expectations of teaching opportunities, Maya
makes the difficult decision to emigrate to Québec. Upon arrival, her
life heads in unanticipated and unhappy directions.

First, Maya encounters numerous and incomprehensible delays in
securing the teaching job she was led to believe awaited her.
Eventually, she lands a part-time position in a trade school near
Québec City. The school is a microcosm of Québec society, and its norms
and values. Maya is not given the chance to teach her speciality,
biology; rather she is assigned a course on commercial transactions to be
taught to a class of problem students Symbolically, life (science) has
been replaced by commerce for Maya, which seriously closes down her
options. Ultimately, the story illustrates that her failure stems less
from any inability to master her new assignment than from her
disadvantaged relationship to language and its particular usages in
the school and local milieu. "They did not speak the same language,"
Maya realizes. "Different words, different bodies."[4] "Puns . . . exclude
and isolate her more and more in her peculiarity."[5] As she struggles to
"decode signs of communication which are not really identical to
hers,"[6] Maya only "falls into the trap of her own culture, which is her
only possible reference."[7]

Le printemps peut attendre corroborates Dionne Brand's claim that
no language is neutral, as Dahan skillfully expresses the personal
ordeal of a minority experience that is conscious of the images and
stereotypes projected onto it. Thus Maya "sees clearly the
unfathomable gulf growing deeper, and something tragic in the idea
that the image she has of herself does not coincide at all with the
image the class holds of her";[8] "she was a itinerant in a city coded
with forbiddens, where just walking about created suspicion and
feelings of strangeness."[9] Dahan's novel uncovers the school's faults and
injustices, and in the process exposes the inequities of society, its
leaders, and their processes. Thus for example, in response to Maya's
teaching performance, "management used its latest cure-all—group
dynamics with no specialist present."[10] Maya is brought before a school

committee, headed up by the vice-principal Madame Roy. "From the heighth of her authority" and through "a kind of imperialist power,"[11] the aptly-named[12] Madame Roy informs Maya that "her difficulties stem from her deafness."[13] So stunned is Maya by this declaration that she literally is rendered speechless. For Maya is neither deaf nor hearing-impaired. Rather, she is unheard by those around her, and silenced by the injustice of her treatment. From the depths of her anxiety, Maya is forced to ask herself "why wait for spring?"[14] to leave a hopeless situation. Indeed, she does not wait. Readers are left to speculate whether Maya's death in a quintessential Canadian-Québécois snowstorm is merely an unfortunate accident or rather the desperate act of a lucid immigrant.

Other works by writers of Arabic background portray Québec society in a critical and political perspective. In *Le double conte de l'exil* (1990), Mona Latif Ghattas presents a poetic narration of similar encounters, this time in the city of Montréal. Madeleine is "an Elder from 'Kébec,'"[15] that is to say an aboriginal person. Her life has not been easy. By age twelve, she was already working in a beer parlour and had been raped by one of the customers. Coming to Montréal, she finds work in one of the city's east-end laundries. Madeleine leads a lonely life until the day she helps a refugee from Anatolia, known only as Fève. The laundry becomes the stage for a critical commentary on Québec society. Key figures in this scrutiny are Madeleine's co-workers, "the three Claras"[16], whose long years at the laundry and likemindedness confer "privilege": "With the strength of their seniority and in common accord, they take it upon themselves to stare down all the newcomers, commenting on their behaviour, pointing fingers at their differences, watching their misery, spoiling their beauty, minimizing any qualities that might bring out their own deficiencies. In other words, they were in the business of making and breaking reputations".[17] They focus their criticism on a young Asian man who, like Madeleine, works hard and keeps to himself. "Clairette Légaré announced that he smelled of egg roll, Clarence Lindsay declared that she did not like Asian people, and Clara Leibovitch, after hesitating as usual, finally added that he did not speak well and she could not understand anything he was saying."[18] Through the three Claras, author Latif Ghattas underlines the mistrust, indeed the hatred[19] of "the other" in the milieu her novel depicts. Latif Ghattas also evokes the harsh reality of the underground economy and the need for its labourers to work and live in hiding. If Fève expresses a willingness to work "underground" (in the sewers of a wealthy west-end suburb, a two-hour bus ride from his home), it is because there "he was less at risk of being caught"[20] than when working at street-level. In keeping with Maya's observation in *Le printemps peut attendre* that "to be immigrant is to live in parenthesis,"[21] Mona Latif Ghattas's novel shows that newcomers to Québec can be bracketed by the milieu in which they are supposed to live.

Le double conte de l'exil exposes the existence of discrimination and stereotypes within Québec society. In a particularly revealing section of the novel[22] the author lists the various groups which experience racial discrimination: Moroccans, Sikhs, Haitians, Egyptians, Chileans, Salvadoreans, Colombians, Iranians, Jews, Turks, "and who else, who else," Latif Ghattas's protagonist Madeleine asks, "the emergency rooms of crowded hospitals, the subway like the tower of Babel, God, oh God."[23] Madeleine believes that her friend Fêve will receive landed immigrant status. However, as its title suggests, *Le double conte de l'exil* is a story of exile. Fêve is deported, and Madeleine is forced to acknowledge at last that her own ancestors have long experienced exile within their land.

Writers such as Andrée Dahan and Mona Latif Ghattas depict racial and ethnic minority experience in Québec from a critical perspective. They do not imply that these conditions are exclusive to Québec. In *Entre les fleuves* (1991) poet Nadine Ltaif presents the horrendous reality of war in Lebanon. Memories of the war haunt the narrative. 'T,' a poet now living in Montréal, which has become an "island for shipwrecked survivors,"[24] a "magical island"[25] "between roaring rivers"[26]:

> Here I am now coming back to the site
> of pain,
> and looking at myself.
> And watching Montréal.
> And I see double: East and West.
> I hold my head between my hands
> I believe I'm seeing Beirut.
> Shreds between the two.
> And horror and exile,
> a war between my two hearts. [27]

By superimposing the international and the local, Ltaif makes the point that Québec is neither unique nor exempt in matters of conflict and violence rooted in racial or ethnic differences. *Les Métamorphoses d'Ishtar* (1987) searches for and finds a way to perceive conflicts based on racial and cultural differences: "I am Arabic. And oh, you are Jewish," the poet observes on the last page of the text: "How heavy it is, the heart, the heart weighs when I sing, it is the heart of love, it is the ancient land in love, and hate between Agar and Sarah is actually love."[28]

Québec writers of ethnic or racial minority identification—notably those of Arabic background under discussion here—express a keen political consciousness as well as a social commentary in their work. Theirs are strong voices. If they appear to be relatively isolated cases, rather than part of a communal chorus, it is because additional influences on the expression of strong collective minority identities in Québec. Such factors require extensive political and sociological analysis, and the third and final section offers some preliminary observations on their possible nature.

III

A useful starting point is an essay published in the voluminous *Ethnicity and Culture in Canada: The Research Landscape* (1994), entitled "Quebec research on ethnic writing." In it, David Leahy and Sherry Simon declare: "there is no direct relationship between a writer's sociocultural background and the reach of her/his writing. In addition, the overall 1980s intellectual context tends to mistrust identity certainties."[29] In general, Leahy and Simon note, "critical studies are concerned with emphasizing the points in common between the writing emerging from cultural communities and the literary tradition in place, such that the pertinence in the issue of origin is put into question."[30]

But is this really what Québec ethnic and racial minority writing reveals, particularly in the case of women authors?[31] Leahy and Simon assert that "while the cultural specificity of a writer's origin is indeed important material to explore, in no way does it determine the nature of the writing."[32] How can this position be reconciled with the following lines from Nadine Ltaif, for example, in *Les Métamorphoses d'Ishtar*:

But how can I confess that my inspiration comes from elsewhere, that I'm not from here, even if I love a Montreal wolf, that my language comes from elsewhere, that writing is from elsewhere, that my own rhythm is not the rhythm of winter, but that my passion for you leads me to change my language, and I speak and I tell stories, as an Arabic woman to another Arabic woman.[33]

Leahy and Simon's overview of studies on Québec ethnic or racial minority writing highlights the strong tendency of this critical work towards a "reappropriation of a Québecity which is already transcultural."[34] This tendency subsumes the problematics of ethnic or racial minority writing within the domain of Québec literature at large. It generates analyses according to which "it is less ethnic writing per se which should be the focus of research than concepts of cultural identity conveyed by literary texts."[35] However, such stances lack resonance when reading ethnic or racial minority texts themselves, such as those considered above. Through their critical observations of society, these texts establish parallels with the writing of women such as Brand, Philip, Bannerji, and others in English Canada. Work by authors such as Dahan, Latif Ghattas, and Ltaif formulates a critique of the ideology presented by majority language and discourse in Québec: "You make me switch language and what I used to say in Arabic, I now say in French,"[36] writes Nadine Ltaif in *Les Métamorphoses d'Ishtar*. "What have you done with my language? How have I been able to preserve my voice? You are powerful beyond pain, beyond death!"[37] Andrée Dahan's protagonist asks similar questions: "What have they done to her authenticity? To be or to appear to be? Her life? Nothing more than appearances . . . . To appear or to disappear."[38] The writing of women such as Dahan, Latif Ghattas, and Ltaif expresses a will to be, to exist as a member of society and not as an exile. It is writing which affirms difference. As such, it parallels the writing of women from minority groups in English Canada. Comparative study of these two bodies of literary works would suggest that each has "political edge," expressing difference—differently!

Trent University   **Christl Verduyn**

NOTES

1. Translated from the original French, this is a modified version of an article which forms part of the proceedings of the August 1995 Trent University "Windy Pine Colloquium" on ethnic and racial minority writing and literary criticism in Québec and English Canada,

forthcoming in the *Journal of Canadian Studies*.

    2. In *Memories Have Tongue*, p. 73. The full text of the poem is "The power of racism/the power of racism/the power of racism/is such that Neville who is six foot two and weights [sic] 210/could be threatened with assault by three white children//The power of racism/the power of racism/the power of racism/is such that a Yusef Hawkins was killed in Brooklyn/due to the colour of his skin//the power of racism/the power of racism/the power of racism is such/that the ROM could mount an African exhibition/without consulting Black people."

    3. Described by Philip, in interview with Janice Williamson, as a multi-disciplinary, multi-racial, group "committed to making sure that the practice of art in Ontario is free of racism, sexism, and economic disparity." *Sounding Differences: Conversation with Seventeen Canadian Women Writers*, 242.

    4. "Ils ne parlaient pas la même langue. Ni celle des mots, ni celle du corps" (78).

    5. "les jeux de mots . . . l'excluent et l'isolent de plus en plus dans sa singularité" (25-26).

    6. "Décodage des signes de communication qui ne sont pas vraiment identiques aux siens" (26).

    7. "elle tombe dans le piège de sa propre culture, seule référence possible" (26).

    8. "voit clairement l'abîme infranchissable qui se creuse et il y a quelque chose de tragique dans l'idée que l'image qu'elle se fait d'elle-même ne se superpose plus du tout à l'image d'elle que la classe lui renvoie" (27).

    9. "elle était passante transfuge dans une cité codée frappée d'interdiction, où la seule promenade côtoyait l'insolite et éveillait'la suspicion" (56).

    10. "Il y eut bien une contestation, mais, les élèves ne sachant pas pourquoi ils contestaient, la direction eut recours au procédé à la mode, remède à tous les maux, celui de la dynamique de groupe, à laquelle n'assistait aucun spécialiste" (75).

    11. "depuis les hauts lieux de l'autorité" and "une forme d'impérialisme du pouvoir" (32).

    12. "Roy" meaning king or highest authority.

    13. "sa *surdité* [est] une des raisons de ses difficultés. Sous le choc, [Maya] était restée sans voix" (5).

    14. *"Pourquoi attendre le printemps?"* (88).

15. "une Ancienne du 'Kébec'" (127).

16. The "three Claras" are not completely indistinguishable, as their names suggest. They are Clairette Légaré, Clarence Lindsay, and Clara Leibovitch.

17. "Fortes de leurs similitudes et de leur ancienneté," "s'octroyaient de droit de dévisager tout nouveau venu, de le scruter, de commenter ses comportement, de pointer du doigt sa différence, d'épier ses misères, de salir sa beauté si elle les poussait dans l'ombre, d'amoindrir ses qualités quand elles menaçaient de mettre à jour leurs lacunes, enfin, de bâtir sa réputation" (57).

18. "Clairette Légaré avait déjà affirmé qu'il sentait l'"egg roll", Clarence Lindsay avait décrété qu'elle n'aimait pas les Asiatiques et Clara Leibovitch, après qu'elle eut un peu hésité comme d'habitude, avait fini par rencheriri en déclarant qu'il parlait mal et qu'elle ne comprenait rien de ce qu'il disait" (54).

19. "Obviously, the three Claras don't perceive this as Madeleine does. From their standpoint they perceive things that make them lose their bearing and sharpen in them a sort of indefinable hatred, a hatred that could be said to be skin deep, transmittable and could also become contagious. In reality, they don't know exactly what in him [the young man] makes them so furious. And yet, this kind of fury is always justified by images deeply buried in our drawers of prejudices and in the bag of intolerance that we have inherited from History" (100).

20. "il y risquait moins de se faire dénoncer" (90).

21. "être immigrant[e], c'est vivre entre parenthèses" (79).

22. See pages 102-103.

23. "Et quoi encore, quoi encore, les urgences des hôpitaux engorgées, le métro où l'on se croit dans la tour de Babel, mon Dieu, mon Dieu" (103).

24. "Ile du Naufragé" (8).

25. "Ile Magique" (26).

26. "Entre les fleuves", title of the writer's second collection of poems and from which the last two quotations are taken.

27. Voilà que je reviens sur la place
de la douleur,
et me regarde face à moi-même.
Et regarde Montréal.
Et je vois double: l'Est et l'Ouest.
Je prends ma tête entre mes mains
Je crois voir Beyrouth.

Des lambeaux entre les deux.
Et l'horreur et l'exil,
Une guerre entre mes deux coeurs. (40)

28. "Je suis Arabe. Tiens, vous êtes Juive. Que c'est lourd, et le coeur, le coeur pèse, lorsque je chante, c'est le coeur de l'amour, c'est la terre antique qui aime, et la haine entre Agar et Sarah c'est de l'amour" (62).

29 "il n'existe aucun rapport de cause à effet entre l'origine socio-culturelle de l'auteur et la portée de son écriture. A cela il faut ajouter que le contexte intellectuel des années 80 est largement méfiant des certitudes identitaires" (393).

30. "la critique est soucieuse dans l'ensemble de souligner les *convergences* entre les écritures issues des communautés culturelles et les autres, de manière à reconnaître et à mettre en question la pertinence de la question de l'origine" (393).

31. It is notable that, in English Canada, authors such as Brand, Bannerji and Philip express themselves not only as writers of fiction but also as critical commentators of literary and social analyses. In Québec, however, a few exceptions aside (such as the contributors, mostly men, to *Vice Versa*), critics are associated with the dominant identity. Their reading of literary texts is thus conducted from their experience in the dominant culture; they do not live, on a daily basis, the consequences of belonging to a minority group. This basic difference has to be stressed. It may explain, at least in part, why many Québec critics or commentators of ethnic and racial minority writing tend to minimize the problematics of this writing.

32. "La spécificité culturelle de l'origine devient une matière à privilegiée à exploiter, oui, mais elle ne détermine en rien le caractère de l'écriture" (394).

33. Mais comment vous avouer que mon inspiration vient d'ailleurs, que je ne suis pas d'ici, même si j'aime un loup à Montréal, que ma langue vient d'ailleurs, que l'écriture est d'ailleurs, que mon rhythm à moi n'est pas celui de l'hiver, mais que ma passion pour vous me fait changer de langue, et je parle et je raconte, comme une femme arabe à une autre femme arabe ... *Les Métamorphoses d'Ishtar* (26).

34. "Réappropriation d'une québécité elle-même transculturelle". Leahy and Simon, p. 401, quoting Pierre Nepveu, 1989.

35. "Ainsi, c'est moins 'la littérature ethnique' comme telle qui doit être un champ privilégiée de recherche que les conceptions d'identités culturelles que véhicule le texte littéraire" (400).

36. "Vous me faites changer de langue, et ce que je disais en arabe je

le dis maintenant en français" (61).

37. "Qu'avez-vous fait de ma langue? Comment ai-je pu conserver ma voix? Au-delà de la mort, au-delà de la souffrance, vous avez une force!" (61).

38. "Qu'avait-on fait de son authenticité? Etre ou paraître? Sa vie? Elle n'était qu'un amas d'apparence [...] Paraître ou disparaître?" (*Le printemps peut attendre,* 70).

WORKS CITED

Allen, Lillian. *Women Do This Every Day.* Toronto: Women's Press, 1993.

Berry, J.W. and J.A. Laponce, eds *Ethnicity and Culture in Canada: The Research Landscape* Toronto: University of Toronto Press, 1994.

Bersianik, Louky. *The Euguélionne.* Montréal: Les Editions la Presse, 1976.

Brand, Dionne. *Bread Out of Stone.* Toronto: Coach House, 1994.

Brossard, Nicole. *L'Amer, ou le chapitre effrité.* Montréal: Quinze, 1977.

Camper, Carol, ed. *Miscegenation Blues: Voices of Mixed Race Women.* Toronto: Sister Vision, 1994.

Cooper, Afua. *Memories Have Tongue.* Toronto: Sister Vision Press, 1992.

Dahan, Andrée.*Le printemps peut attendre.* Montréal: Quinze, 1985.

Lalonde, Michele. *Speak White.* Montréal: l'Héxagone, 1974.

Latif Ghattas, Mona. *Le double conte de l'exil.* Montréal: Boréal, 1990.

Ltaif, Nadine. *Les Métamorphoses d'Ishtar.* Montréal: Guernica, 1987.

————. *Entre les fleuves.* Montréal: Guernica, 1991.

Morrell, Carol, ed. *Grammar of Dissent.* Fredericton: Goose Lane Editions, 1994.

Mukherjee, Arun, ed. *Sharing Our Experience.* Ottawa: Canadian Advisory Council on the Status of Women, 1993.

Philip, Nourbese. *Frontiers: Essays and Writings on Racism and Culture 1984-1992* .Toronto: Mercury Press, 1992.

Robin, Régine. *La Québecoite.* Montréal: Québec-Amérique, 1983.

Silvera, Makeda, ed. *The Other Woman: Women of Colour in Contemporary Canadian Literature.* Toronto: Sister Vision Press, 1995.

Théoret, France. *Bloody Mary.* Montréal: les Herbes rouges, 1977.

Verduyn, Christl. "La Voix féminine de l'altérité québécoise littéraire", *Mélanges de littérature québécoise et canadienne-française.* Y. Grisé et R. Major, eds. Ottawa: Editions de l'Université d'Ottawa, 1992, 379-390.

————. "Je: voi(e)s double(s): l'itinéraire littéraire de Nadine Ltaif," *Tessera.* 12 (Summer 1992), 98-105.

———— "Nouvelles voix/voies": *Québec Studies.* 14 (Spring/Summer 1992). 41-48.

———— "Memory Work/Migrant Writing: Mediating Me/Moi," *Intersexions: Issues of Race and Gender in Canadian Women's Writing.* C.S. Vevaina and B. Godard, eds. New Delhi: Creative Books, 1996, 244-254.

———— "Ecriture et migration au féminin au Québec: de mere en fille", *Ecriture migrante: Québec et France.* L. Lequin and M. Verthuy eds. Paris: l'Harmattan (forthcoming).

Williamson, Janice. *Sounding Differences: Conversation with*

Seventeen Canadian Women Writers. Toronto: University of Toronto Press, 1993.

Notes on Contributors

Jars Balan is a free-lance writer and independent scholar based in Edmonton. A specialist in the area of Ukrainian studies, he is the author of *Salt and Braided Bread: Ukrainian Life in Canada* (Oxford University Press, 1984), and the editor of two collections of Ukrainian Canadian literature: *Yarmarok: Ukrainian Writing in Canada Since the Second World War* (Canadian Institute of Ukrainian Studies Press, 1987), and *Echoes from Ukrainian Canada*, a special double issue of the Winnipeg journal *Prairie Fire* (Autumn 1992). He has edited a collection of essays entitled *Identifications: Ethnicity and the Writer in Canada* (Canadian Institute of Ukrainian Studies Press, 1982) and he has written numerous articles on Ukrainian Canadian literature. Recently, several of his works have appeared in Ukraine.

Dr. Karin E. Beeler is an Assistant Professor in the English Programme at the University of Northern British Columbia in Prince George, B.C., Canada. She has been teaching at UNBC since 1993 and specializes in Canadian literature, writing by women, and comparative literature. Recent publications include a comparative essay on Christa Wolf and Aritha van Herk in *Critique* and "Divided Loyalties in Eighteenth-Century Nova Scotia/Acadia: Nationalism and Cultural Affiliation in Thomas Raddall's *Roger Sudden* and A.E. Johann's *Ans dunkle Ufer*," *The Dollhouse Review*. She has co-organised a conference called *Inter-national Regions: Contemporary Writing in English Produced in Canada* (October 28-30, 1994).

Seamus Ceallaigh is of Gaelic origin and has completed a Ph.D. at the University of New Brunswick.

George Elliott Clarke received his doctoral degree in English from Queen's University at Kingston, Ontario, in 1993. His dissertation was a comparative study of English-Canadian and African-American poetry and criticism. He is currently an Assistant Professor of English and Canadian Studies at Duke University.

Roseanna Lewis Dufault is an Associate Professor at Ohio Northern University where she teaches French and Francophone Language, Literature, and Civilization. She has published two books, *Metaphors of Identity: The Treatment of Childhood in Selected Québécois Novels*

(New Jersey: Associated University Presses, 1991) and *Women by Women: The Treatment of Female Characters by Québec Women Writers* (Fairleigh Dickinson University Press, 1997). Her work appears in anthologies, such as *L'Autre lecture, critiques au féminin de textes québécois*, edited by Lori Saint-Martin, (Montréal: Editions XYZ, 1992), and to the journal *Québec Studies*. Dufault's research interests center around feminist issues and Québec's contemporary women writers.

Paul Hjartarson, an Associate Professor of English at the University of Alberta, focuses his teaching and research on early modern Canadian literature. His books include *A Stranger to My Time: Essays by and About Frederick Philip Grove* (1986) and *Baroness Elsa*, co-edited with D.O. Spettigue (1992).

Marie-Claire Huot is an Associate Professor at the University of Montreal, where she teaches new literary practices in the Department of Comparative Literature and Chinese contemporary culture in the East Asian Studies Center. She has published articles on Chinese cinema, contemporary fiction, and avant-garde art. In 1994 her book in French on new Chinese cultural practices, entitled *La petite révolution culturelle* was published. She is now writing a book in English on the same subject for Duke University Press, tentatively entitled *China's Other Bank: New Cultural Practices*.

Earl G. Ingersoll is Professor of English and Honors Director at the State University College at Brockport, New York, where he has taught since 1964. In addition to articles on British, Irish, and Canadian writers, he is the author of *Science and Technology in British Literature Since 1880* and the editor of *Margaret Atwood: Conversations*. He is secretary of the Margaret Atwood Society.

Bénédicte Mauguière is an Associate Professor at the University of Southwestern Louisiana. The author of *Traversée des idéologies et exploration des identités dans les écritures de femmes au Québec (1970-1980)*, she has also written numerous articles and papers on Québec literature and Francophone Women's literature for academic journals. She serves on several executive and editorial boards in Francophone and Canadian Studies.

Pierre Nepveu is a Professor in the Department of French Studies at the University of Montréal. Much of his research has focused on modern Québécois poetry, including an anthology prepared along with Laurent Mailhot (*La poésie québécoise, des origines à nos jours*, 1981 and 1986), poetry reviews published in literary journals such as *Lettres québécoises* and *Spirale*, and numerous articles (on Michel Beaulieu, Nicole Broussard, François Charron, and others.) Additionally, he has published four collections of poems, including *Episodes* (1977) and *Mahler*, and two novels: *L'Hiver de Mira Christophe* (1986) and *Des mondes peu habités* (1992). For several years his theoretical and critical work has been consecrated to the current state of Québécois literature (*L'Ecologie du réel*, 1988), especially focused on "transculturality," migrant writings, and the theme of "America." Pierre Nepveu also directs le Centre d'Etudes Québécoises (CETUQ), and is a member of the editorial board for the review *Spirale*.

Valérie Raoul is a Professor in the French Department and Director of the Women's Studies Center at the University of British Columbia (Vancouver) and former coordinator of the Women's Studies program. She has published two books on the role of the "journal intime" in the novel: *The French Fictional Journal, Fictional Narcissism/ Narcissistic Fiction* (a French version of which will soon be published through P.U.F.) and *Distinctly Narcissistic: Diary Fiction in Québec*. Her current research focuses on women's autobiographical writings, and their relations with narcissistic theory; she is preparing a study of several intimate journals written by women in France in the 19th century.

Henri Servin is Associate Professor of French at the University of Arizona. His research centers on the nineteenth-century literature of France, mainly Gustave Flaubert, as well as on the literature of Quebec. His publications include articles on Flaubert, Anne Hébert, Nicole Broussard and Marie-Claire Blais. He is currently working on particular themes represented in the poetry of Anne Hébert.

Eugenia Sojka has completed a Ph.D. at Memorial University of Newfoundland, and her specialisation is contemporary English Canadian and Anglo-Quebec women's writing and critical theory. Her two most recent publications are: "Can(n)on Firing: 'Fiction Theory' and the Texts of English Canadian and Anglo-Québec Women Writers" in

Critical Mass, and "Framing the Frame: A Suggestion about Critical Discourse for the Analysis of Canadian Feminist Language Oriented Writing," in *Free Exchange 1993*, University of Calgary Press.

Dr. Philip Spensley is Professor of Theatre at Concordia University in Montreal, a drama program which he founded. He was also co-founder of the drama program at the University of Guelph and has taught at Loyola of Montreal, the National Theatre School of Canada, and the Banff School of Fine Arts. He has helped develop a number of national and regional theatre organisations and has served as advisor to the Quebec Ministry of Education and the federal Department of Culture and Heritage. A professional actor, he played a lead role in *L'Affaire Tartuffe*, one of the plays discussed in his article. Among his awards are the Tyrone Guthrie Award (1969) from Stratford Festival and Wayne State University's Arts Achievement Award (1993). His research interests include Canadian theatre and contemporary issues.

Michel Thérien is a Professor and former director of the Education department at the University of Montreal. He specializes in the didactics of literature, with his research area in Francophone literature. He was also named Vice-Dean of Planning and Research for the School of Educational Sciences at the University of Montreal. Additionally, he is the director of a continuing education program, and is in charge of faculty publications and human resources.

Elizabeth Thompson is a writer living in Clinton, Ontario. She is the author of *The Pioneer Woman: A Canadian Character Type* (McGill-Queen's UP), as well as numerous articles on early Canadian literature. Dr. Thompson is the editor of a new critical edition of Susan Moodie's *Roughing It in the Bush* (Tecumseh Press).

Christl Verduyn is chair of Canadian Studies at Trent University. She has published *Margaret Laurence: An Appreciation* (1988), *Dear Marian, Dear Hugh: The MacLennan-Engel Correspondence* (1995), and *Lifelines: Marian Engel's Writings* (1995), which was awarded the Gabrielle Roy Prize for literary criticism. Recently she guest-edited a special issue of the *Journal of Canadian Studies* on Canadian literary pluralities called "Pulling Together/Tisser les pluralités littéraires au Canada."